Teaching Extensive Reading in Another Language

This comprehensive book by renowned scholars Paul Nation and Rob Waring accessibly covers all aspects of extensive reading in second and foreign language contexts. The book serves as a major update to the field on the topic, with current research findings on extensive reading as they relate to motivation, reading fluency, and vocabulary learning, among other topics.

Clear and straightforward, it includes case studies, strategies, and methods for implementing and assessing effective extensive reading in the classroom and provides resources and tools for preservice teachers of ESL/EFL and foreign languages.

Suitable for programs in TESOL and Applied Linguistics with courses in L2 reading, reading instruction, TESOL methods, and foreign language reading or teaching, it will appeal to students and preservice teachers as well as English language teaching professionals and EFL/ESL teachers.

Paul Nation is Professor Emeritus in Applied Linguistics at Victoria University of Wellington, New Zealand.

Rob Waring is Professor at Notre Dame Seishin University in Okayama, Japan.

ESL & Applied Linguistics Professional Series
Eli Hinkel, Series Editor

Teaching Essential Units of Language
Beyond Single-word Vocabulary
Edited by Eli Hinkel

What English Language Teachers Need to Know Volume I
Understanding Learning, 2nd Edition
Denise E. Murray and MaryAnn Christison

Pedagogies and Policies for Publishing Research in English
Local Initiatives Supporting International Scholars
James N. Corcoran, Karen Englander, and Laura-Mihaela Muresan

Teaching Chinese as a Second Language
The Way of the Learner
Jane Orton and Andrew Scrimgeour

Teaching Academic L2 Writing
Practical Techniques in Vocabulary and Grammar
Eli Hinkel

Quality in TESOL and Teacher Education
From a Results Culture Towards a Quality Culture
Juan de Dios Martínez Agudo

Language Curriculum Design, 2nd Edition
John Macalister and I.S.P. Nation

Teaching Extensive Reading in Another Language
I.S.P. Nation and Rob Waring

English Language Proficiency Testing in Asia
A New Paradigm Bridging Global and Local Contexts
Edited by Lily I-Wen Su, Cyril J. Weir, and Jessica R. W. Wu

English Morphology for the Language Teaching Profession
Laurie Bauer and I.S.P. Nation

For more information about this series, please visit: www.routledge.com/
ESL-Applied-Linguistics-Professional-Series/book-series/LEAESLALP

Teaching Extensive Reading in Another Language

I.S.P. Nation and Rob Waring

NEW YORK AND LONDON

First published 2020
by Routledge
52 Vanderbilt Avenue, New York, NY 10017

and by Routledge
2 Park Square, Milton Park, Abingdon, Oxon OX14 4RN

Routledge is an imprint of the Taylor & Francis Group, an informa business

© 2020 Taylor & Francis

The right of I.S.P. Nation and Rob Waring to be identified as authors of this work has been asserted by them in accordance with sections 77 and 78 of the Copyright, Designs and Patents Act 1988.

All rights reserved. No part of this book may be reprinted or reproduced or utilised in any form or by any electronic, mechanical, or other means, now known or hereafter invented, including photocopying and recording, or in any information storage or retrieval system, without permission in writing from the publishers.

Trademark notice: Product or corporate names may be trademarks or registered trademarks, and are used only for identification and explanation without intent to infringe.

Library of Congress Cataloging-in-Publication Data
Names: Nation, I. S. P., author. | Waring, Rob, author.
Title: Teaching extensive reading in another language / I.S.P. Nation and Rob Waring.
Description: New York, NY : Routledge, 2019. |
Series: ESL & applied linguistics professional series |
Includes bibliographical references and index.
Identifiers: LCCN 2019033597 (print) | LCCN 2019033598 (ebook) |
ISBN 9780367408268 (hardback) | ISBN 9780367408251 (paperback) |
ISBN 9780367809256 (ebook)
Subjects: LCSH: English language--Study and
teaching--Foreign speakers.
Classification: LCC PE1128.A2 .N3455 2019 (print) |
LCC PE1128.A2 (ebook) | DDC 428.0071--dc23
LC record available at https://lccn.loc.gov/2019033597
LC ebook record available at https://lccn.loc.gov/2019033598

ISBN: 978-0-367-40826-8 (hbk)
ISBN: 978-0-367-40825-1 (pbk)
ISBN: 978-0-367-80925-6 (ebk)

Typeset in Bembo
by Taylor & Francis Books

It is important to acknowledge the enormous influence of Stephen Krashen on the advocacy of extensive reading and on encouraging research on extensive reading. In the very early days of the comprehension approach (Gary & Gary, 1981; Nord, 1980; Winitz, 1981), he was a strong and uncompromising advocate for learning through comprehensible input (Krashen, 1985). His persuasive writing and engaging lectures provided many with the courage to try comprehension-based approaches, particularly extensive reading (Krashen, 2004). His strong and clear statements of the nature of learning through comprehensible input challenged researchers to test his claims, more often than not showing that what he was saying was supported by research. One of the great strengths of his scholarship is that he always connects research to practice. He is a researcher who supports and encourages other researchers. He is above all a researcher who speaks to teachers and learners, and his input is always comprehensible and interesting. He won't agree with all that is in this book, but he is clearly an inspiration behind it.

Contents

List of illustrations xi

1 Keeping Extensive Reading Simple 1

  An Example of an Extensive Reading Program 2
  What is Extensive Reading? 3
  Why Are Graded Readers Essential For Extensive Reading For
    Beginning and Intermediate Proficiency Learners? 5
  Extensive Reading and the Four Strands 6
  Planning an Extensive Reading Program 9
  Resources 16

2 What Are Graded Readers? 17

  Reading at the Right Level With Comprehension 19
  Large Quantities of Reading 23
  Reading With Enjoyment 23
  Criticisms of Graded Readers 24
  Do Graded Readers Contain Unnatural Language? 27
  What Does Using a Controlled Vocabulary Do? 28
  When Can Learners Move From Graded Readers to Unsimplified
    Text? 31
  Extensive Reading Without Graded Readers 32
  Conclusion 35

3 Case Studies of Extensive Reading Programs 36

  The SEG English Program in Tokyo, Japan 36
  The Book Flood Program in Fiji 38
  Park Language Academy in South Korea 39
  Kyoto Sangyo University 41
  Notre Dame Seishin University in Okayama, Japan 44

viii *Contents*

Extensive Reading in the Kathmandu Valley, Nepal 48
University of Information Technology, Vietnam National University
in Ho Chi Minh City 49
Sanata Dharma University in Yogyakarta, Indonesia 51

4 How Do You Set Up and Run an Extensive Reading Program?   54

How Do I Set Up an Extensive Reading Program? 54
How Do I Introduce the Learners to Extensive Reading? 57
How Can Learners Know Which Books Are at the Right Level For
Them? 58
How Do You Get Unmotivated Learners To Do the Reading? 58
What Should the Teacher Do During an Extensive Reading
Session? 59
How Can We Make Sure That the Learners Are Doing the
Extensive Reading? 60
How Should I Organize an Extensive Reading Library? 60
How Do I Set Up an Extensive Reading Program If My School Has
No Budget to Buy the Books? 61
How Much Time Should Learners Spend On Extensive
Reading? 62
Should an Extensive Reading Program Include a Speed Reading
Course? 62
How Much Should Learners Read? 63
Should Learners Look Up Unknown Words in a Dictionary as They
Read? 65
How Do I Measure if Learners Are Learning From the Extensive
Reading Program? 66
Should University Students Be Reading Graded Readers? 66
Commonly Asked Questions 67

5 How Vocabulary Is Learned From Extensive Reading   72

Learning Conditions and Extensive Reading 72
Enhancing Vocabulary Learning Through Extensive Reading 74
Using a Controlled Vocabulary 76

6 The Most Important Studies on Extensive Reading in a Foreign
Language   82

Learning Through a Book Flood (Elley & Mangubhai, 1981) 82
Word Frequency and the Richness of Vocabulary Learning
(Waring & Takaki, 2003) 85

*Extensive Reading and Enriching Vocabulary Knowledge
(Pigada & Schmitt, 2006) 87
How Much Extensive Reading Do Learners Need to Do?
(Nation, 2014) 89
Fluency, Graded Readers, and Extensive Reading (Beglar, Hunt, &
Kite, 2012) 91
Reading Fluency and Extensive and Intensive Reading (McLean &
Rouault, 2017) 93
How Much Vocabulary Can Be Learned Through Extensive
Reading? (Pellicer-Sánchez & Schmitt, 2010) 94
Balancing Ecological Validity and Control (Suk, 2017) 95*

7 Research Findings: Motivation and Pushing Learners to Read 97

*The Pleasure of Reading 98
The Reward of Success 98
The Satisfaction of Obvious Progress 99
The Virtuous Feeling of Doing Something of Value 99
The Power of Independence and Control 99
Factors Discouraging Extensive Reading 100
Pushing Learners to Read 101
A Coherent Approach to Motivating Learners to Read 103*

8 Research Findings: Does Extensive Reading Result in Reading Fluency and Comprehension Improvement? 104

*The Nature of Reading Fluency 104
Fluency Gains From Extensive Reading 104
Issues in Measuring Fluency 107
Extensive Reading and Comprehension 109
How Do You Measure Comprehension? 109
The Effects of Extensive Reading on Reading Comprehension 110
Extensive Reading and Language Proficiency 112
Extensive Reading and Writing 112*

9 Research on Vocabulary Learning From Extensive Reading 114

*Does Extensive Reading Result in Vocabulary Learning? 114
Vocabulary Learning in Single-Text Studies 116
Vocabulary Learning in an Extensive Reading Program 117
How Much Vocabulary Can Be Learned From Extensive
Reading? 119
Guessing From Context, Look-Up, and Deliberate Learning 121*

x   *Contents*

10   Developing Reading Fluency   123

A Reading Fluency Activity 123
The Nature and Limits of Reading Speed 123
The Nature of Fluency Development 126
The Nature of Fluency Development Activities 127
Increasing Oral Reading Speed 128
Increasing Careful Silent Reading Speed 130
Increasing Silent Expeditious Reading Speed 131
Frequently Asked Questions About Reading Speed 132

11   Designing Research Into Extensive Reading   136

A Critique of Some Specific Extensive Reading Studies 137
The Range of Questions That Have Been Investigated 138
Poorly Defining the Extensive Reading Construct 139
Issues in Studies Comparing Extensive Reading to Other Treatments 140
'Gains in Writing' Experiments 143
'Gains in Affect' Experiments 144
'Gains From Exposure' Experiments 144
Discussion 153

12   What Makes a Good Graded Reading Scheme?   156

Why Graded Readers At All? 156
What Makes a Graded Reader Series? 157
The Development Stage 163
Production, Manufacture, and Marketing Stages 171

13   A Way Forward   172

Being Clear About the Extensive Reading Message 172
Why Is Extensive Reading Not Well Accepted Yet? 174
The Future of Extensive Reading 176
A Research Agenda 177

References   183
Index   198

Illustrations

Figures

2.1	The Extensive Reading Foundation Grading Scale	22
2.2	Extensive Reading Foundation's Language Learner Literature Winner Award	25
2.3	Extensive Reading Foundation's Language Learner Literature Finalist Award	25
5.1	A Curve Plotting the Results of Cumulative Frequency-Ranked Count of a Text	78
8.1	Time Spent on Extensive Reading and Intensive Reading in a Well-Balanced Course	109

Tables

1.1	The Ranked Defining Features of Extensive Reading and Their Justification	4
1.2	The Criteria Typifying Each of the Four Strands with Example Activities	8
1.3	An Example One-Week Lesson Plan Covering the Four Strands for 4 x 50-Minute Classes Per Week	9
1.4	Minimum Amounts of Extensive Reading to do Each Week For Low Proficiency Learners	14
2.1	The Vocabulary Levels of Five Graded Reader Series	21
3.1	The *Kyoto Scale* of Extensive Reading Levels used on mreader.org	43
4.1	The Number of Words and Books Needed to be Read, and the Number of Hours It Will Take to Get to a Certain Level	64
4.2	The Number of Words Needed to Be Read to Get a Learner from One Proficiency Level to Another	65
5.1	Conditions Helping the Learning of Vocabulary	73
5.2	Corpus Sizes Needed to Gain an Average of at Least 12 Repetitions at Each of Nine 1,000 Word Levels Using a Corpus of Novels	79

xii *List of illustrations*

5.3 Density and Number of Unknown Words in a Typical Novel
     at Various Vocabulary Sizes (*The Devil's Company*, Liss, 2009)   80
6.1 Gains in the Fiji Book Flood Study   83
7.1 Enhancing the Various Motivations to Do Extensive Reading   100
12.1 A Proposed Graded Reader Scheme   159

Boxes

The Original   17
The *Oxford Bookworms* Level 4 Version   18

1 Keeping Extensive Reading Simple

This book might not be necessary because essentially extensive reading should be a straightforward simple activity – namely learners should read plenty of interesting books at the right level for them. Why write a book of several chapters that makes this simple activity seem more complicated?

One motivation for writing is that extensive reading is still not generally accepted by teachers and a book on the topic might help convince such teachers through the weight of evidence and example to make extensive reading part of their learners' program. Another motivation was that the existing books on extensive reading are not strongly research based. There is now a lot of research directly and indirectly about extensive reading and it would be useful to review this research critically to see what gaps there are in the research and its application, and what lessons for extensive reading can be learned from this research.

This first chapter then is a simple view of extensive reading answering the following questions.

What is extensive reading?
What are the principles that should guide an extensive reading program?
Why are graded readers essential for extensive reading for beginning and intermediate proficiency learners?
How do you set up and run an extensive reading program?

The remaining chapters of the book describe some extensive reading programs in very different situations, explain why extensive reading works, look at the research behind extensive reading, critically examine research on extensive reading, provide guidelines and suggestions for extensive reading research, and examine resources for extensive reading.

Let us look first at a case study of an extensive reading program drawn from personal experience.

2 *Keeping Extensive Reading Simple*

An Example of an Extensive Reading Program

This is an account of Paul Nation's first experience with extensive reading:

> The first extensive reading program that I ever set up was in a teachers' college in Indonesia in the early 1970s. I was familiar with much of the work of Michael West, knew about graded readers, and knew of the value of extensive reading. Our students were teacher-trainees in the first year of their coursework. Although they were all in the English Department, there was a very wide range of English proficiency. Many of the students were quite poor but had done well at secondary school.
>
> Our section of the teachers' college had a small library that was rarely used, with many of the books locked in glass-fronted cases. My colleague Gerry Meister and I searched the shelves of the library and found a surprising number of graded readers scattered through the shelves. They were from series such as the *New Method Supplementary Readers, Pleasant Books in Easy English, Collins English Readers*, and the *Longman Bridge Series*. We put them all together on a shelf in the library. I think we also bought a lot more graded readers.
>
> We realised that our students would need a dictionary to cope with the reading but they could not afford to buy one. So we made a small and primitive 1000 word bilingual dictionary and then a 2000 word dictionary based on West's *General Service List of English Words* (West, 1953). It consisted simply of English words with Indonesian translations. We made copies on our hand-cranked Gestetner machine. The librarians were told that the students would need to use the dictionary when they borrowed the graded readers. They were also told that they could sell the copies of the dictionary to the students for a very cheap price and keep the money themselves. The librarians had never worked so hard in their lives but they did so willingly. In the breaks between classes the students were rushing to the library to borrow the books.
>
> We gave each student a sheet of paper divided into twenty sections. In each section they wrote the name of the book they had read, its level, and a brief comment on it. They did the reading outside of class time and when they did writing in class time, they came up one by one to show their corrections to their previous writing and to show their extensive reading record sheet.
>
> It was during that time that Emmy Quinn and I wrote the 1000 word level speed reading book, *Speed Reading* (Quinn & Nation, 1974), now out of print but available free in an adapted form from Paul Nation's website. The general format was based on Edward Fry's *Reading Faster* (Fry, 1967) which had proved to be too difficult for most of our students. Fry's book was adapted from a Longman Bridge Series reader, *Mankind against the Killers* (the killers being various diseases), and was around the

Keeping Extensive Reading Simple   3

2000 word level. Our newly developed speed reading materials became part of our extensive reading program.

Some of the more proficient students quickly moved on to unsimplified reading, borrowing books from our personal libraries. Extensive reading was popular and I consider it had made a really important contribution to the students' English proficiency. When I visited the teachers' college many years later, I was pleased to find that many of the current staff members had been our students.

There was nothing at all complicated in what we did and it would be even easier to do today with bilingual dictionary apps and free electronic reader apps on smart phones, and freely available speed reading courses at numerous levels. If doing it again today, I would not change much except perhaps to start the program in class and I would measure the students' vocabulary size. There were no vocabulary tests available then. I would also probably be more diligent in pushing the more reluctant readers to read.

Did our program meet the requirements of an extensive reading program? What are these requirements?

What is Extensive Reading?

There are many forms of extensive reading but they all involve each learner independently and silently reading a lot of material which is at the right level for them.

The reading is independent because learners differ in proficiency, reading speed, and interests, and so ideally they need to read at their own level of text difficulty and at their own speed.

The reading is silent because it should eventually be done at a reasonable reading speed of around 200 words per minute (wpm) so that plenty of material can be read. The speed of speaking is around 100 to 150 wpm, so reading aloud will tend to restrict learners to reading at a slow speed.

Reading necessarily involves comprehension and so learners should be gaining comprehensible input and be focused on understanding what they read.

They should read lots of material because the amount of comprehensible input they get will directly determine how much vocabulary they learn, how well their reading fluency develops, and how much other aspects of language knowledge develop. The amount read per year should cover hundreds of thousands of words of text. If the learners are reading graded readers, this will involve at least tens or twenties of books per year, and in some cases many more.

The material should be at the right level for the learners so that only a small proportion of the words on a page are unknown (two words per hundred words or less) and so that the grammatical constructions are largely familiar.

It is good if the content of the books is interesting and motivating for the learners to read because this encourages them to comprehend and motivates

4 *Keeping Extensive Reading Simple*

them to read more. Table 1.1 outlines these features of extensive reading which have been ranked according to their importance for learning from extensive reading.

Reading with enjoyment has not been included as a defining feature of extensive reading, although it is obviously a very desirable feature because enjoyable reading motivates further reading and encourages comprehension. Many of the features described in Table 1.1, such as reading at the right level and reading a lot, help make reading enjoyable, and this in turn adds to learners' motivation to read. If a learner really wants to read something slightly above their level, the teacher should allow the learner to do so because motivation to read something may overcome all other factors. After all, the long-term goal is to build a reading habit.

Ranking the features is problematical because each feature relates strongly to the other features. However, the ranking is useful because it stresses what teachers and learners should be aiming for in an extensive reading program. Reading at the right level is the most important because if the text is too

Table 1.1 The Ranked Defining Features of Extensive Reading and Their Justification

Definition of extensive reading	Extensive reading involves each learner independently and silently reading lots of material which is at the right level for them.	
Feature of the definition of extensive reading	*Explanation*	*Justification*
Read at the right level	2% unknown words Largely familiar grammar	Moderately easy texts allow a lot of comprehensible reading and support the learning of unfamiliar items
Read with comprehension	Only a very small amount of dictionary use should be needed	Comprehension allows vocabulary learning and motivates reading
Read a lot	The minimum amount depends on proficiency levels but involves reading hundreds of thousands of words which would occupy upwards of 10 minutes reading per school day	The amount of comprehensible input directly affects the amount of language learning and reading skill development
Read independently	At any one time each learner is typically reading a different book from what others are reading	Each learner should read at the right level for them and should follow their interests
Read silently	Each learner is not reading the text aloud	Silent reading is usually much faster than reading aloud

difficult, then it is hard to read with comprehension, hard to read a lot, hard to read independently, and hard to read silently. A text which is too difficult will mean the students are reading in 'study' mode because they are focused on the language items rather than the content or the story. Comprehending what is read is clearly extremely important, but it is tempting to put 'read a lot' closer to the top of the ranking. Extensive reading programs should involve reading extensively, that is, reading a lot.

In the very early stages of reading while preparing students for independent self-selected reading, extensive reading preparation classes may involve the whole class reading the same book at the same time with the teacher guiding them through it. Very soon, however, the learners should move to more independent reading.

Extensive reading does not usually mean the whole class or each learner is working through a long difficult text. This is intensive reading and at best needs to be done strategically so that effort is not wasted on vocabulary that is not useful for the learners at their current level of proficiency. See Nation (2018) for a critique of such an intensive reading activity.

Extensive reading is not reading one or two books at the right level per school term. Extensive reading requires large amounts of comprehensible input.

But this is not to say that there is only one form of extensive reading. We could categorize extensive reading along a scale from the more controlled form to a freer version. At one end of the scale, the learners would use graded readers which have a tightly planned syllabus which scaffolds the learning, building on previous learning from level to level in an efficient non-random manner. This type of extensive reading is often required in a language course. At the other end, some practitioners suggest learners only read things they enjoy and should read only if they want to so they can get a 'reading habit'. While this is commendable, in practice this 'freer' version of extensive reading means that many learners will opt-out of the reading even if they know it will benefit them. Being able to choose anything to read also means they will be reading unstructured materials because book A is not connected to book B. At the early stages of extensive reading, the learners might benefit from having a structured approach restricting them to their 'level' in order to build foundation knowledge, and later they might have more freedom in what they read even if it is more challenging.

Why Are Graded Readers Essential For Extensive Reading For Beginning and Intermediate Proficiency Learners?

Let us look again at the definition of extensive reading: *Extensive reading involves each learner independently and silently reading lots of books which are at the right level for them.* The essential points in this definition are books at the right level and reading lots of books. Unsimplified texts written for adult native speakers of English require a vocabulary size of at least 5,000 words before they can be read with any ease and preferably a vocabulary size of

6 Keeping Extensive Reading Simple

around 9,000 words for 98% coverage of the running words in the text (Nation, 2006). Material written for young native speakers (Macalister, 1999; Webb & Macalister, 2013) is similarly difficult.

The vocabulary difficulty in unsimplified or uncontrolled text, such as materials written for native speakers of any age, comes from several related factors. First, there will be a large number of unknown words for a low and intermediate proficiency learner of English as a foreign language. Second, a large number of the unknown words will be far beyond the learner's current proficiency level. There are many more useful words to learn first. Third, the density of unknown words will be high. That is, on average there will be at least two or more unknown words in every single line of the text. Fourth, a very large proportion of the unknown words will occur only once in the text and will be unlikely to occur again soon in following texts (see Nation, 2019, in press, for a fuller discussion of these points). Fifth, unsimplified texts are written independently of each other, so the language items in book A are not likely to be in book B or C. The input, therefore, is randomly structured rather than building systematically on previous learning as graded readers do.

Graded readers avoid these difficulties by using only a relatively small, very useful vocabulary at a series of levels that can be roughly matched to the learner's vocabulary size and provide systematic scaffolding on the input as words and language items are written to appear often before previous memories are forgotten, allowing the language to be consolidated. More-over, graded readers provide excellent conditions for incidental vocabulary learning while providing the chance of successful enjoyable reading. We will look at graded readers in more detail in Chapter 2.

Extensive Reading and the Four Strands

Extensive reading is only part of a well-balanced course, and it is useful to see where it fits into the wider curriculum. One way of looking at what should be in a language course is to apply the principle of 'the four strands'. This principle says that a well-balanced language course provides opportunities for learning across four equal strands (Nation, 2007). These are the strands of *meaning-focused input, meaning-focused output, language-focused learning*, and *fluency development*.

Meaning-focused input involves listening and reading as naturally as pos-sible with a focus on the content of the material (e.g. a story), and roughly half the time in this strand should be given to listening and half to reading. Most of the reading in the meaning-focused input strand should be exten-sive reading. Ideally, the other half of the meaning-focused input strand should be extensive listening. Around two-thirds of extensive reading fits into the meaning-focused input strand. For low proficiency readers there is value in listening while reading, although the aim should be to read at faster than listening speed without listening support.

The second strand, meaning-focused output, involves speaking and writing. Although the strands are listed as separate items, in practice, listening and

Keeping Extensive Reading Simple 7

speaking are usually done together as one person's speaking is another person's listening. Meaning-focused speaking involves things such as conversation, discussion, giving a talk, and talking on the phone. Writing involves formal writing, writing emails and texts, taking notes, making a list, and writing stories. Reading aloud and reading a memorized dialogue might be more language-focused input that stresses accuracy and lacks the spontaneity of meaning-focused output. Output should only play a minor role in extensive reading, but it makes sense to link reading to speaking and writing as in oral and written book reports. This output should not take time away from extensive reading.

The third strand of a well-balanced course is the strand involving deliberate learning — language-focused learning. This involves intensive reading; doing exercises in a course book; the study of pronunciation, spelling, vocabulary, grammar, and discourse; and strategy training. This deliberate study of language should make up no more than one-quarter of the total course time. Unfortunately, in many courses it takes up much more time than that. Language-focused learning can support extensive reading through deliberate vocabulary learning using flash cards, through intensive reading, and through reading strategy practice such as guessing from context and note-taking. However, this language-focused learning in itself is not extensive reading.

The fourth strand is fluency development. This strand involves practicing to make the best use of what is already known in each of the four skills of listening, speaking, reading, and writing. Like each of the other strands, this should make up about one-quarter of the course time. The fluency development strand of a course involves developing listening fluency, speaking fluency, reading fluency, and writing fluency with such activities as speed reading. It is helpful to consider reading fluency as a part of the extensive reading program. Developing reading fluency through reading easy graded readers and through re-reading graded readers is clearly part of extensive reading and should make up around one-third of the reading in an extensive reading program. Doing a timed speed reading course with easy passages and questions should also be considered part of extensive reading because it contributes directly to the amount read, the degree of comprehension, and enjoyment.

The principle of the four strands is not a lesson plan or a sequence of learning. It is simply a principle for checking that, over a period of time of several weeks or months, the learners are getting a balance of opportunities for learning either in a particular class or in a series of classes making up a curriculum, including work outside class.

When first learning to apply the principle of the four strands, it is useful to think back over what has been happening in your classes over the previous month or so, and then to classify the various activities into the strands, noting roughly how much time was spent on each activity. Some activities like discussion activities may fit into two or more strands because they involve a bit of reading, some speaking, and some listening. In order to classify activities in this

8 *Keeping Extensive Reading Simple*

way, teachers need to understand the criteria that need to be met for each strand to exist. Table 1.2 presents these criteria.

Meaning-focused input covers both listening and reading (largely in the form of extensive reading), with reading making up half of this strand. An extensive reading program should contain an element of fluency development. In a well-balanced language course covering the four skills of listening, speaking, reading, and writing, reading fluency development should make up one-quarter of the fluency development strand and should be considered as part of an extensive reading program. Such fluency development would include doing a speed reading course (see Chapter 10), reading very easy graded readers, and quickly re-reading books that have been read before. An extensive reading program can also contain elements of meaning-focused output (talking about books and writing book reports) and language-focused learning (learning about extensive reading,

Table 1.2 The Criteria Typifying Each of the Four Strands with Example Activities

Strand	Criteria	Activities
Meaning-focused input	Texts that contain some but less than 2% unknown vocabulary and few unfamiliar grammatical features or the learners will be focused on the language itself rather than the meaning of the text A focus on comprehending with incidental language learning Large quantities of reading and listening Support for unknown features	Extensive reading Extensive listening Conversation activities
Meaning-focused output	Output that requires only a few unfamiliar language and content features A focus on communicating messages with incidental language learning Large quantities of speaking and writing Support for unknown features	Presenting a talk Conversation activities Writing emails
Language-focused learning	Deliberate intentional learning A focus on language features or strategies	Using word cards Doing course book exercises Learning how to use word parts Learning how to learn from a dictionary
Fluency development	Easy, familiar material with no unknown vocabulary or grammatical features Pressure to perform at a faster speed Quantity of practice across the four skills A focus on meaning rather than language features	Easy extensive reading 10 minute writing Speed reading Quick listening

Keeping Extensive Reading Simple 9

deliberately learning new words, and learning the strategies of guessing from context and dictionary use), but they should be very small so that most of the time in an extensive reading class is spent on extensive reading. Table 1.3 shows how extensive reading might fit into an English course involving four meetings a week. The items in italic make up the extensive reading program.

The time for extensive reading includes two-thirds meaning-focused input where learners read books with a few unknown words, and one-third fluency development where learners quickly read really easy graded readers with no unknown words to build reading speed. Reading speed courses bring learners' reading speed up to speeds closer to those of native speakers. The faster learners can read, the more they can read in the same time.

Note that if the activities in Table 1.3 are classified into the four strands, each strand would occupy roughly the same amount of time in the course (50 minutes for each strand).

The idea of the four strands separates different kinds of opportunities for learning. However, these opportunities are more effective if they are integrated in that they share content and follow on from each other. This integration increases the repetition of vocabulary and can deepen the quality of processing of the vocabulary.

Planning an Extensive Reading Program

As shown by the case study at the beginning of this chapter, it is not difficult to set up an extensive reading program. The main requirements are to have plenty of books or suitable reading materials on different topics at the right level and to encourage the learners to read them. This planning can be broken down into some simple steps.

Table 1.3 An Example One-Week Lesson Plan Covering the Four Strands for 4 x 50-Minute Classes Per Week

Lesson 1	*Lesson 2*	*Lesson 3*	*Lesson 4*
Speed reading (5min)	*Speed reading (5min)*	*Speed reading (5min)*	Dictation (15min)
Extensive reading (20min)	Intensive reading (35min)	*Extensive reading (20min)*	4/3/2 (10min)
Speaking & listening (25min)	10 minute writing (10min)	Speaking & listening (25min)	Writing (25min)
Homework			
Word cards (20min), *Extensive reading (20min)*, project work (20min), reading-while-listening (30min), writing (30min)			

10 *Keeping Extensive Reading Simple*

1 Make Learners Aware of the Value of Extensive Reading

Teachers should know the value of extensive reading and why it is a part of a language course. Learners should also know this. This knowledge can help make sure that extensive reading is done properly. If learners understand the value of extensive reading, they may do it more willingly and do more of it. A very useful guide to extensive reading is available as a free download in multiple languages from the Extensive Reading Foundation (ERF) website (www.erfoundation.org). The ERF also offers a Massive Open Online Course for teachers to learn about extensive reading and listening.

The research on extensive reading (see Chapters 6–9) shows that it has a wide range of effects on language proficiency. First of all, extensive reading helps learners become better at reading. Doing extensive reading improves both reading fluency and reading comprehension. When learners do extensive reading, their reading speed gets faster and their understanding of what they read gets stronger. Second, extensive reading improves language knowledge. When learners read texts at the right level, they learn new words and strengthen and enrich their knowledge of partly known words and phrases, and how these words interact with other words and the grammar. Learners also become familiar with groups of words that commonly occur together. They develop an understanding of previously unfamiliar grammatical features. This language knowledge helps with further reading, but it also can help in the other skills of listening, speaking, and writing. Third, learners gain enjoyment from reading and come to value the skill of reading. Fourth, they learn new things about the world through reading. This can obviously happen when they read factual material, but it also happens when learners read fiction because they gain insights into how others think, why they behave in certain ways, and what concerns them.

Learning through extensive reading is largely incidental, that is, the learners' attention is focused on the story not on items to learn. As a result, learning gains tend to be small. This is because students should already be reading a text they largely comprehend (with maybe only 2% unknown words) and so very few *new* words can be learned under these conditions. So, quantity of input is important so that the readers meet words, phrases, and grammatical features time and time again and build a network of knowledge relationships between them.

2 Find Your Learners' Present Vocabulary Level

Graded readers are books specially written or adapted for learners of a foreign language. This involves severely restricting the vocabulary that can occur to consolidate only that vocabulary, controlling the grammatical structures that can occur, controlling the plot, and matching the length of

Keeping Extensive Reading Simple 11

text to the vocabulary and grammar controls. The essential requirement for a book to be called a graded reader is that the vocabulary it contains should agree with the words on a pre-determined word list or syllabus. If the book is not written within a restricted vocabulary, it is not a graded reader.

Although there are now graded readers in Mandarin (http://mandarin companion.com/), Japanese (www.ask-books.com/tadoku/en/), and some other languages, by far most graded readers are written for learners of English as a foreign language. A graded reader written at the 400 word level should only contain words from a pre-determined list of 400 words, with a few additional words needed for that story which are typically pre-taught in the book, or are put in a glossary. All of the books at that level should be largely written within the same 400 word list in order to consolidate and strengthen the knowledge of them as a set. That means that a learner of English who only knows around 400 words should be able to read all of the books at this level and only meet a small number of unknown words. Unfortunately, publishers do not use the same lists, do not have the same sized levels in their series, and even worse often do not allow teachers, learners, or researchers to see their lists. In addition their strictness in following the lists is often inconsistent. Each book typically has topic words that are not in the lists but which are essential for the story. Nevertheless, graded readers are a tremendous resource for extensive reading, and are essential for extensive reading at the beginning and intermediate levels of language proficiency.

Graded reader series typically cover a range of levels beginning at around 300–500 words and going to around 2,000–2,500 words in length (see www.robwaring.org/er/scale/ERF_levels.htm for a very helpful analysis of graded reader series levels). The *Foundations Reading Library* by National Geographic Learning starts as low as the 75 word level, which means that anyone knowing around 75 words could read these books without meeting too many unknown words. This means that someone in their first few weeks of learning English could begin doing extensive reading.

The *Oxford Bookworms Series* published by Oxford University Press is a very well written and long-established series of graded readers. It has the following vocabulary levels:

See https://sites.google.com/site/erfgrlist/ (also linked on the ERF website) for more examples of series levels.

Anyone unfamiliar with graded readers should get hold of some, particularly at the lower levels, and read them, and should look at the websites for the *Oxford Bookworms Series*, the *Cambridge English Readers, Foundations Reading Library, Heinle Reading Library Illustrated Classics, Pearson Readers, Macmillan Readers*, and *Footprint Reading Library*.

Because graded readers are written within a controlled syllabus, many teachers consider it useful to know their learners' vocabulary sizes so that learners can be directed towards graded readers at the right level. Measuring learners' vocabulary knowledge is only a step towards working out their extensive

12 Keeping Extensive Reading Simple

reading level. It is likely that some of the words that they get correct on a vocabulary test of receptive knowledge are not known well enough to be immediately accessible when reading. Knowing learners' vocabulary size is useful, but must be checked against how comfortably learners actually read books at various levels.

The Vocabulary Size Test (see Paul Nation's website) is **not** a suitable measure for learners of English as a foreign language at beginner and intermediate levels, because there will be too many unknown words in the test. The most appropriate tests are the new Vocabulary Levels Tests, which test the 1,000, 2,000, 3,000, 4,000, and 5,000 levels. Not all the later levels (3,000–5,000) need to be used, especially with low proficiency learners. It is possible for very low proficiency learners just to use the 1,000 level. Although the Vocabulary Levels Tests use 1,000-word levels, a learner's vocabulary size can be calculated using the formula that comes with the test. For the Updated Vocabulary Levels Test (Webb, Sasao, & Ballance, 2017) this simply involves multiplying the score on the test by 33. The score on the New Vocabulary Levels Test (McLean & Kramer, 2015) should be multiplied by 42. Both tests are available from Paul Nation's website. For Japanese learners of English, the ERF Online Self-Placement test might be an alternative.

By far the best method is to put books in difficulty levels (perhaps color coded) and the learners go up and down the levels until they feel comfortable. These difficulty levels do not have to correspond to headwords, especially published headwords, as there is a lot of misdirected information in the published levels and actual reading level. The readers should be leveled by the student body for each other. Learners should be free to suggest a book be moved up or down a level depending on the book's content. Thus the learners are final judges of what levels books should be. After all, it is their library.

3 Provide Plenty of Interesting and Appropriate Reading Texts

The essence of extensive reading is reading a lot of interesting books at the right level. Fortunately for learners of English, there is a very large number of books to choose from (see https://sites.google.com/site/erfgrlist/). In addition, every year since 2004, the ERF has held the Language Learner Literature Awards to find the best graded readers. Anyone setting up an extensive reading library should look at the finalists and winners in the lists on the ERF website and consider buying those first. Before spending money on graded readers it is important to make sure that you know your learners' vocabulary sizes and reading levels so you can buy books at the right levels.

It is not a good idea to buy a lot of copies of one book. It is much better, in terms of providing choice and opportunities to read widely, to buy many different books. If the school does not have the money to buy books, see if it is possible for each learner to buy a different book and share that book with others. One solution is an online subscription service for graded readers that's available for a reasonable price (visit www.xreading.com). Alternatively, there

Keeping Extensive Reading Simple   13

are free extensive reading and listening materials available online at multiple levels of difficulty at several websites (e.g. www.er-central.com).

It is worth considering buying a mixture of fiction and non-fiction texts so that learners get experience in reading in a different genre. Some learners may be more attracted by non-fiction reading. As narrative text more closely resembles spoken language due to the dialogue it contains, it rarely covers many mid-frequency and technical words, so for this reason intermediate learners and above should have a heavier diet of non-fiction material to cover this vocabulary.

4 Get the Learners to Find Their Reading Level

When learners know their vocabulary size, they can start checking to see what level they should be reading. We cannot assume that learners who know 800 words should be reading books at the 800-word level. Once they have an idea of their vocabulary size, the learners should try reading a few pages of books at that level, the level just below it, or the level just above to see what level is right for them. A key acronym is READ:

> **R**ead something quickly and
> **E**njoyably with
> **A**dequate comprehension so you
> **D**o not need a dictionary.

On each page they read, there should only be a very small number of unknown words. There needs to be some unknown words because extensive reading should help learners increase their vocabulary knowledge, both depth and size, but there should only be a few unknown words so that they do not take a lot of attention away from the story.

5 Set, Encourage, and Monitor Large Quantities of Extensive Reading

Learners need to read a lot. The amount is most accurately expressed in running words (tokens), but teachers and learners tend to think of it in books or pages. That is, how many books or pages should be read, in a certain time? Nation and Wang (1999), using data gained from analyzing books in the *Oxford Bookworms Series*, suggested that learners should be reading around a book a week. Table 1.4 suggests minimum amounts expressed in running words based on the length of an average book at that level in the *Oxford Bookworms Series*, and time in minutes per school week based on a reading speed of 100 wpm. Note that the data given is a minimum and more is always better. For learners with larger vocabulary sizes see Nation (2014).

An average Level 1 *Oxford Bookworms* reader is 5,500 words long and draws on a vocabulary of 530 different words. Table 1.4 suggests that on average, reading one Level 1 *Oxford Bookworms* reader a week would take 55 minutes at

14 *Keeping Extensive Reading Simple*

Table 1.4 Minimum Amounts of Extensive Reading to do Each Week For Low Proficiency Learners

Word level	Running words per week	Books per week	Minutes per week @ 100 wpm
530 words	5,500	1	55
870 words	6,500	1	65
1,190 words	10,800	1	108
1,500 words	15,900	1	159

a speed of 100 wpm. That is around 11 minutes a day for a five-day week. At Level 2 (870 different words, 6,500 running words), learners would need to read around 65 minutes a week or 13 minutes per day in a five-day week. As learners' speed of reading increases to around 200 to 250 wpm, they will be able to read more in shorter time. So, at Level 4 of the *Oxford Bookworms Series*, where books are on average 15,900 words long, at a reading speed of 200 wpm, it would take 80 minutes to read a book. These figures suggest that learners should be doing extensive reading for at least an hour a week. Once again using data from the Nation and Wang (1999, Table 2) study, if learners read one *Oxford Bookworms* graded reader a week for 40 weeks of the year, reading seven books at each of the six levels in the series, they would read a total of 40 books consisting of around 600,000 running words.

Learners need to be strongly encouraged to do the necessary amount of reading. This can be done by at least initially running the extensive reading program in class time and carefully monitoring the reading and giving encouragement where necessary. Learners may be given quantity goals for their reading, such as a certain number of words per week. Other motivators include an explanation of the purpose of extensive reading, occasional oral book reports, short book reviews written on a slip in the book, and book displays. It may also be useful to get learners to briefly report to each other in small groups on their progress, problems, and successes in extensive reading.

6 Support and Supplement Extensive Reading with Fluency Development and Language-Focused Learning

Speed Reading and Easy Extensive Reading For Fluency

The most important and most effective way to support extensive reading is to provide learners with speed reading training. There are now speed reading courses in a controlled vocabulary at the 500 word level, 1,000 word level, 2,000 word level, 2,000 plus Academic Word List (570 word families) level (2,570 words), 3,000 word level, and 4,000 word level. They can be downloaded free from Paul Nation's, website (https://www.victoria.ac.nz/lals/about/staff/paul-nation). A speed reading course typically consists of 20

Keeping Extensive Reading Simple   15

passages within a very controlled vocabulary with each passage followed by ten comprehension questions. The passages in a course are all the same length and can be read in any order. Detailed advice on running a speed reading course can be found in Chapter 10. A speed reading course takes only a few minutes each time but has very marked effects on learners' reading speed. Most learners increase their speed by 50% and many double their speed. This is not too surprising as many learners of English as a foreign language have very slow reading speeds, well below 100 wpm. By increasing their reading speed, learners can read more, improve their comprehension, and gain more enjoyment from reading.

In addition to a speed reading course, about one out of every three books that a learner reads should be very easy with no unknown language items. These may be graded readers which are way below their current level or books they have read before. The goal should be to read them quickly so that the reading contributes to reading fluency development.

Adding Language-Focused Learning to Extensive Reading

Learning through extensive reading is largely incidental which results in small cumulative increases in knowledge. By adding a small amount of deliberate attention to vocabulary, either before, during, or after reading, vocabulary learning can be increased, making it easier for the learners to read and to move to a higher level of graded reader. Here are some simple ways to do this:

While reading, the learner can collect words while reading for later deliberate word study. Some dictionary look-up apps and some reading apps include this as a special feature.
Before each reading, the learner should skim the text to select five or six words to focus on. These words can be looked up before reading.
After reading, the learner can briefly reflect on the new vocabulary met while reading.

It is not a good idea to include lots of vocabulary exercises with extensive reading texts because these take time away from doing more extensive reading, and the exercises turn the reading into a language task rather than a reading task.

7 Help Learners Move Systematically Through the Graded Reader Levels

Learners should understand why they are doing extensive reading and how it helps them. In consultation with the teacher they should set goals of how many books they will read each month or how much time they will spend on extensive reading.

Getting the learners to sit a short, easy multiple-choice test after each book is easily done using the MReader resource at https://mreader.org/m readeradmin/s. The little research on the effects of sitting a test after each

16 *Keeping Extensive Reading Simple*

book suggests that such testing is not necessary (Robb, 2015; Robb & Kano, 2013), but it can be reassuring for the teacher and may help motivate some learners. The MReader resource is designed to take a minimum amount of time and to provide useful feedback for the teacher. Making the amount of extensive reading relate to the learners' grade for a course can have positive effects on the amount of reading done (Robb, 2013).

The single most important way that a teacher could improve their language program would be to include extensive reading as part of the program. Including extensive reading is reasonably easy to do, and it is likely to have strong and lasting effects on language proficiency.

Resources

The two best websites for extensive reading are:

The Extensive Reading Foundation (www.erfoundation.org)

> The Extensive Reading Foundation is a non-profit organization set up to further the interests of extensive reading. Its website has numerous practical resources (a large bibliography of research on extensive reading, a guide to extensive reading, lists of graded readers, links to useful sites such as MReader) and provides information on the extensive reading symposium usually held every two years, and the annual learner literature awards for the best graded readers.

Extensive Reading Central (www.er-central.com)

> This website has many free resources for students and teachers related to extensive reading. The site has thousands of free reading and listening activities for learners, each with quizzes which a teacher can track. There is also a dictionary look up function for each word which can be saved to a personal spaced-repetition learning area with four games. There is also a speed reading training area, and the TextHelper feature allows students to paste in tests, set their level, and get definitions or translations in several languages for words they do not know. The teachers' area of ER-Central hosts dozens of resources for teachers to learn about extensive reading. The Online Graded Text Editor feature allows graded reader authors to find out which words are out of level.

The freely available web-based journals *Reading in a Foreign Language* and the *Journal of Extensive Reading* contain numerous articles on extensive reading.

2   What Are Graded Readers?

Graded readers are books especially written for learners of English as a foreign language. They are different from other books in that they are written with strict vocabulary control and with consideration of other factors affecting comprehensibility, such as grammatical difficulty, sentence complexity, use of illustrations, and simplicity of plot. Graded readers are written as a series with multiple levels with each adding more difficult language, but also building upon the language of earlier levels systematically to provide reinforcement and consolidation.

Michael West can be considered the true originator of graded readers. He was the first to produce large quantities of readers and to develop strictly controlled and well trialled word lists. The first series of graded readers, the *New Method Supplementary Readers* published by Longmans, Green and Co. Ltd., were written to accompany his *New Method Readers*. The *New Method Readers* were not graded readers but systematically introduced new vocabulary and consisted of a series of seven books. There were *New Method Supplementary Readers* at seven levels to consolidate the vocabulary learning and give practice in reading. There is an excellent account of West's life at https://warwick.ac.uk/fac/soc/al/research/collections/elt_archive/halloffame/west/life/.

Here is an example of a piece from the original novel *Lord Jim* by Joseph Conrad and the corresponding piece from an *Oxford Bookworms* Level 4 graded reader based on that novel but written within a vocabulary of 1,400 headwords. A headword is a word and its closely related family members. The headword *finish* has the family members *finish, finished, finishing, finishes*. For more advanced learners of English, the words *unfinished* and *finisher* might also be included as members of the headword.

The Original

Originally he came from a parsonage. Many commanders of fine merchant-ships come from these abodes of piety and peace. Jim's father possessed such certain knowledge of the Unknowable as made for the righteousness of people in cottages without disturbing the ease of mind of those whom an unerring Providence enables to live in mansions. The little church on a hill had the mossy greyness of a rock seen through a

18   *What Are Graded Readers?*

> ragged screen of leaves. It had stood there for centuries, but the trees around probably remembered the laying of the first stone. Below, the red front of the rectory gleamed with a warm tint in the midst of grass-plots, flower-beds, and fir-trees, with an orchard at the back, a paved stable-yard to the left, and the sloping glass of greenhouses tacked along a wall of bricks. The living had belonged to the family for generations; but Jim was one of five sons, and when after a course of light holiday literature his vocation for the sea had declared itself, he was sent at once to a 'training-ship for officers of the mercantile marine.'

The *Oxford Bookworms* Level 4 Version

> Jim had spent his childhood in a comfortable, peaceful home in the southwest of England. His father was a vicar, a kind man who always did his duty, and who had no doubts about what was right or wrong. The family house was warm and welcoming, with plenty of room for Jim and his four older brothers to play in. Close to it, on a hill, was the small grey church, standing, like a rock, where it had stood for centuries. There had been vicars in Jim's family for a hundred years, but one of his brothers had already shown an interest in the Church, so his father had to find some other work for his youngest son. When Jim spent a whole summer reading sea stories, his father was delighted, and decided that Jim would join the merchant navy at once.

While the two pieces are recognizably the same part of the same story, they are very different. A learner of English as a foreign language with a vocabulary size of less than 1,500 words would be unable to make much sense of the original. Words such as *parsonage, abode, piety, righteousness,* and *unerring* would make comprehension difficult, and the third sentence beginning with *Jim's father possessed...*, while very witty, is a challenge even to a native speaker.

The *Oxford Bookworms* version is clearly and engagingly written. It is not written by Joseph Conrad but tells an interesting story in language that a foreign learner of English could easily follow. This is what graded readers do. They provide interesting and comprehensible reading for learners who at present are far from knowing enough English to read an unsimplified text.

In this chapter, we look at graded readers, examining what they are and their various forms, and considering their benefits and criticisms of them. We also look at extensive reading without graded readers and beyond graded readers, and at ways of lightening the load of reading unsimplified texts.

Because graded readers are essential for extensive reading programs for beginning and intermediate level learners of a foreign language, we will organize the first parts of this description and discussion of graded readers

What Are Graded Readers? 19

around the most important requirements of an extensive reading program – reading at the right level, reading with comprehension, reading a lot, and reading independently and silently.

Reading at the Right Level With Comprehension

Graded readers are books written for foreign language learners within a carefully controlled vocabulary and, for graded readers written within the most frequent 2,000 or 3,000 words of English, with some control over grammatical constructions and sentence length. This criterion of carefully controlled vocabulary and grammar is very important because it is the way that graded readers enable the most important requirements of extensive reading – reading at the right level, reading with comprehension, reading a lot, and reading independently and silently. Without careful vocabulary control, the large number of unknown words and the density of unknown words would turn reading into a very laborious activity. This criterion of controlled vocabulary and perhaps grammar is the single defining feature of a graded reader, distinguishing it from other books. It is thus worth looking in detail at what is involved in vocabulary control, so that this defining feature is clear. Many series of graded readers also give careful consideration to factors such as the simplicity of the plot, the number of characters, information density, the use of illustrations, and background knowledge.

The vocabulary control for a graded reader scheme should be based on lists of words for each level that have been made with reference to some kind of word frequency count. It should not consist of a list created from words used in the graded readers after they have been written. The earliest graded readers were based on an early version of Michael West's (1953) *A General Service List of English Words*, which contained around 2,000 words. The reason for the list being made independently from the books is so that the list consists of the most generally useful words for a learner of English (what West called "general service"). If the list was made from the books, there would be gaps in the list because certain useful words had not had a chance to occur in the books, and the list would contain topic words that were needed for particular stories but which are not as generally useful as other words not in the books. Good word lists cannot be made from frequency counts alone (Nation, 2016), because the needs of learners of English as a foreign language are not the same as those of native speakers, and the texts used in frequency counts often do not truly reflect the needs of learners of English as a foreign language.

Some reading schemes, especially those designed for native speakers, have a series of levels, but the levels are not based on word lists, see for example the lexile levels designed by MetaMetrics. They may be based on readability measures or intuitive approaches to what vocabulary to use. This is fine for native speakers, but the books in the scheme are not graded readers, and are likely to be difficult for learners of English as a foreign language, simply because young native speakers already know several thousand words when

20 *What Are Graded Readers?*

they begin to read. Any scheme for native speakers which was based on word lists would require lists way beyond the knowledge of beginning and intermediate learners of English as a foreign language. There is some evidence (e.g. Webb & Macalister, 2013) that materials written for first language children are not that different in frequency profile from that of adults, making them unsuitable for most EFL (English as a foreign language) learners. Graded readers, by contrast, control the language carefully to ensure a fluent reading experience that builds reading speed and enjoyment without the learner having to be troubled by too much unknown language. The quick way to check such schemes is to see if they provide a word count for each level of the scheme, and then to look at the easiest level books (Level 1 in the scheme) and see if the books contain words that would be beyond the stated word level or would not be known by low proficiency learners of English as a foreign language. The ERF website contains a list of publishers of graded readers (https://sites.google.com/site/erfgrlist/).

As much as possible, a graded reader should be written using only the words available at a particular level. Usually this is not possible because some topic-related words are essential for the story. For example, in a story about the elephant man, the word *elephant* is needed. These words are often pre-taught on pages before the main body text in the book, or are glossed in a section at the back of the reader. The best graded reading schemes will have a procedure to follow with such topic words. When writing these materials, the simplest procedure is to say that any word not in the list but which is used in a book must occur at least five times or more in the book. A slightly more elaborate procedure would be to say that words from the next highest level in the scheme can be used as long as they are repeated several times in the book. The point of such a procedure is first to make sure that the word outside the current level of the list is really necessary. If the word is not repeated, then it can probably be completely avoided. Second, the procedure makes sure that such words have a reasonable chance of being learned. This means that the effort that the learner puts into finding the meaning of the word will be repaid by a chance to learn it, even if it is unlikely to occur in other books at the same level. Third, the word might be illustrated, or made easier to understand by providing additional context, a process called 'adding redundancy'. It is careful vocabulary control that defines a graded reader and a graded reader series.

Table 2.1 shows the vocabulary levels of some of the well-known graded reading series. For a much more elaborate list see the ERF website.

The levels are cumulative, so in the *Oxford Bookworms* series, Level 2 adds 300 new words to Level 1 to make a total of 700 words. *Cambridge English Readers* also include a *Starter* level of 250 words. Notice the different levels in the various series, particularly the number of levels and the size of the steps from one level to another.

It is important to not mix up the advertised levels as set by the publisher when matching graded readers from different series. A Level 2 *Footprint* is written within 1,000 headwords, but the *Pearson Readers* Level 2 is written

What Are Graded Readers? 21

Table 2.1 The Vocabulary Levels of Five Graded Reader Series

Levels	Cambridge English Readers	Pearson Readers	Oxford Bookworms	Footprint National Geographic	Macmillan Readers
1	400	300	400	800	300
2	800	600	700	1,000	600
3	1,300	1,200	1000	1,300	1,100
4	1,900	1,700	1,400	1,600	1,400
5	2,800	2,300	1,800	1,900	1,600
6	3,800	3,000	2,500	2,200	2,200
7				2,600	
8				3,000	

within only 600. The differences are often more extreme at higher levels. For example, *Footprint* Level 6 has 2,200 headwords, and *Cambridge English Readers* has 3,800. Typically, when teachers are levelling the books in the library, they use a common levelling system like the ERF Graded Reading Scale (http://erfoundation.org/wordpress/graded-readers/erf-graded-reader-scale/).

Although publishers use different grading schemes, it is good for learners to read books from different schemes, as long as they are roughly at the right level for them. This is because there is a lot of overlap between the word lists from the different schemes and because although vocabulary is a major factor affecting reading difficulty for EFL learners, there are other important factors like background knowledge, reading skill, and motivation that can make reading a book easier. However, teachers must also not assume that the same words were used at the same level by all of the publishers. For example, a *Pearson Readers* 600 level book may not have the same word list at that level as a *Macmillan* 600 level word book. They will be roughly comparable, but are not based on the same syllabus, and this can affect readability and has implications for leveling books in a library, which we will come to later.

Because graded readers are written within a controlled vocabulary, some teachers might view them as not real books. In an attempt to deal with this misperception, Day and Bamford (1998) have suggested calling such books *Language Learner Literature*.

In this discussion we have largely focused on vocabulary. However, as Gillis-Furutaka (2015) shows, even graded readers present difficulties for readers who are reading at roughly the right word level. These difficulties include confusing plot structure, figurative and idiomatic language, cultural differences, pronoun reference, the absence of helpful illustrations and the presence of misleading illustrations, and the use of literary devices such as onomatopoeia. It takes much more than vocabulary control to make a good comprehensible graded reader. Bernhardt's (2005) compensatory model of reading suggests that vocabulary knowledge accounts for less than 30% of

Beginner				Elementary			Intermediate			Upper Intermediate			Advanced			Bridge			Near Native
Alphabet	Early	Mid	High	Early	Mid	High	Early	Mid	High	Early	Mid	High	Early	Mid	High	Early	Mid	High	
1 - 50	51 - 100	101 - 200	201 - 300	301 - 400	401 - 600	601 - 800	801 - 1000	1001 - 1250	1251 - 1500	1501 - 1800	1801 - 2100	2101 - 2400	2401 - 3000	3001 - 3600	3601 - 4500	4501 - 6000	6001 - 8000	8001 - 12000	12001- 18000 and above
Level 1	2	3	4	5	6	7	8	9	10	11	12	13	14	15	16	17	18	19	20

Figure 2.1 The Extensive Reading Foundation Grading Scale

Large Quantities of Reading

Learners of EFL are particularly fortunate in that there are about 5,000 graded readers at a variety of levels readily available for them to read from over 20 different publishers. (This information comes from https://sites.google.com/site/erfgrlist.) These books are typically priced at a level that makes them affordable for most learners. An imaginative initiative, the online reading virtual library *Xreading.com* (see Chapter 4) makes many graded readers from well-known publishers available in electronic form on the payment of a small monthly, or annual, subscription. Subscribers can read any titles and as many titles as they wish each month.

In a graded reading scheme, the length of the graded readers increases from one level to the next. At the beginning level, where the books are written within a vocabulary of a few hundred headwords, the books are rather short. For example, in Level 1 of the *Foundations Reading Library*, written within a vocabulary of 75 headwords, each book is around 500 to 600 words long. In the *Oxford Bookworms* series, the books at Level 1 (400 headwords) are between 5,000 and 6,000 words long. At Level 3 (1,000 headwords), they are between 9,000 and 12,000 words long, and at Level 6 (2,500 headwords) between 25,000 and 32,000 words long (around one-third of the length of the average novel). The aim for the learner is to start at the earliest level and become fluent at that level after reading several books at that level. The learner then moves up to the next level. Initially, the reading speed will drop as the number of unfamiliar words increases, but over time the learners pick up speed, and when they are reading fluently and comfortably, they move up to the next level.

Each series of graded readers provides substantial amounts of reading material, and when learners read many of the books at each level in a series, read at different levels in the series, and read from a range of series, there is no shortage of opportunity to read a lot, or in other words, to gain large amounts of enjoyable comprehensible input.

Reading With Enjoyment

Graded readers and graded reading schemes are designed to be attractive to learners and teachers. There are several ways in which they do this and some graded reader series have their own special way of ensuring that learners will want to read their books.

Graded readers deal with topics that are likely to attract readers. Most graded readers are fiction but there is now a growing number of non-fiction titles available. The National Geographic Learning *Footprint Reading Library*, for example, has a wide range of attractively illustrated

24   *What Are Graded Readers?*

readers including topics such as *The Lost City of Machu Picchu, Arctic Whale Danger,* and *Volcano Trek.* Oxford University Press has their *Factfiles* series that include topics such as *Animals in Danger, Brazil, London, Titanic,* and *John Lennon.* The *World History Readers* by Seed Learning is an example of how materials can be written for English learners, but can also be used by teachers from other disciplines who might want to recommend these titles to their learners.

The *Cambridge English Readers* series contains fiction titles but all of the books in the series are original titles. That is, they are not adaptations of books written for native speakers but are original stories written within a controlled vocabulary. Here are some of the titles, *Jojo's Story*★ (the asterisk indicates a prize winner of the ERF Language Learner Literature Award), *Ten Long Years, Dead Cold*★, *Berlin Express,* and *A Dangerous Sky*★.

One way of attracting readers is to publish familiar titles. In the *Oxford Bookworms* series these include *The Phantom of the Opera, Anne of Green Gables, 20,000 Leagues under the Sea*★, *The Merchant of Venice*★, and *The Great Gatsby.*

Pearson Readers include books that have also appeared as movies and the cover of each book is a very attractive scene from the movie. Their titles include *Gladiator, Titanic, Seven, 1984, Cinderella Man,* and *The Client.* Putting a scene from the movie on the cover is a very clever marketing idea because it makes the books seem like a regular unsimplified text for native speakers, and learners can look cool reading such books in public. For the same reason, some publishers indicate the vocabulary level of the book in small type or inside the book rather than display it obviously on the cover.

Some series are aimed at particular age groups, and some publishers have different series for different age levels.

Most graded readers are well written. There is strong competition in the graded reader market and this competition is increased through the ERF's Language Learner Literature Award where winners and finalists are entitled to put a logo on the cover of each book winning a prize (see Figure 2.2 and Figure 2.3).

We have now looked at how graded readers meet the requirements of an extensive reading program by providing material at the right level, by providing large quantities of reading material, and by providing interesting and attractive books that learners are likely to enjoy reading. Let us now look at the negative aspects of graded readers.

Criticisms of Graded Readers

Some teachers and researchers are uncomfortable using graded material because they feel that it is not 'authentic'. That is, they believe that because these materials have specially constructed material for learners, they are therefore not like the 'authentic' texts written for native speakers that the learners eventually will need to read. The implication is that only 'real' English is suitable, but this confuses the goal with the way to get there. When one starts to play the piano we do not start with *Rachmaninoff's Third,*

Figure 2.2 Extensive Reading Foundation's Language Learner Literature Winner Award

nor do native children start reading with Shakespeare, nor do we learn to drive in a Formula 1 car.

Another way to view authenticity is to see it not as a feature of the material itself but as existing in the relationship between the learner and the material. Authentic reading from this view involves reading in the way a proficient reader, such as a native speaker, would read (Widdowson, 1976) irrespective of their language knowledge. When learners of EFL read texts that are too difficult for them like *Lord Jim*, they do not have an authentic reading experience. The task becomes one of decoding words and phrases, and is not really reading in the traditional sense, because there are too many unknown words and other difficulties (Gillis-Furutaka, 2015). When they read a graded reader at the right level for them, they can have an authentic reading experience. They can comprehend the story, they can enjoy it, or they can be bored or irritated by it, and they can see the relevance or irrelevance of the book for their lives. This is an authentic reading experience and at the beginning and intermediate levels, graded readers are necessary for this authentic experience to occur. Without

Figure 2.3 Extensive Reading Foundation's Language Learner Literature Finalist Award

26   What Are Graded Readers?

graded readers at this level of proficiency, reading is a demanding, difficult chore with countless unknown non-repeated words.

Simplified texts are also criticized because the restriction on writers to use short, simple sentences can result in choppy and unnatural discourse (Yano, Long, & Ross, 1994; Honeyfield, 1977), and this may result in poor cohesive reference and an over-reliance on implicit rather than explicit conjunction relationships. These can make the texts difficult to comprehend. These criticisms may be true of poorly written simplifications, but there are many excellent simplifications which are a joy to read.

The winners of the annual ERF Learner Literature Awards are examples of the best of these. It is unfair and misleading to condemn simplifications as a whole because some are poorly done. Most graded reader series employ highly experienced editors like Jennifer Bassett, Rob Waring, and Philip Prowse, and have original books from very talented, experienced writers like Antoinette Moses, Sue Leather, Philip Prowse, and Alan Maley. It is not easy to get a graded reader published in a well-known series because the editors set very high standards. The use of a controlled vocabulary is a great challenge to writers but experienced teachers and writers respond well to this challenge, resulting in books that can truly be called language learner literature.

Graded readers are also criticized because they provide poor conditions for learning (Yano, Long, & Ross, 1994). These criticisms include the following. (1) Reading graded readers which are pitched lower than the learners' level can lower the quality of their output. (2) Removing difficult vocabulary denies learners access to what they need to learn. (3) Reading texts with little unknown vocabulary discourages the development of generalizable coping skills such as guessing from context and dictionary use. These are all criticisms of the ways in which graded readers are fitted into a language course, not of graded readers themselves. The use of graded readers needs to be managed through the matching of the level of graded readers to learners' proficiency levels and to the learning goals of the various strands of a course. Typically, in many courses learners would first meet new words or grammar in language-focused instruction such as in a textbook, but they need to see these forms again before they are forgotten and in a variety of contexts. Graded readers provide the practice that these forms need to become learned. Thus, the criticisms listed previously are really criticisms of poor syllabus design rather than criticisms of graded readers themselves.

Some graded readers and series of readers are criticized because their vocabulary control is not strict enough. Our expectations of vocabulary control in graded readers should not be set too high, because the main goal should be to write good stories. A series of graded readers may initially be written by level, not by book. So each of ten books, at say a level of 400 headwords, might be allowed around ten words beyond that level that are needed for the story. So, across ten books this is 100 words beyond the level at that particular level. Other beyond-list words might be allowed if they are illustrated, glossed, or dealt with in the text sufficiently. So in reality, if you analyze the ten books at the 400 headword level, you might find about 15% of the headwords are beyond that level.

In addition, not all of the 400 words will be used at that level and many of them might occur only once or twice across the level. It is highly unlikely that each of the 400 words would be repeated a minimum number of times needed for learning and learners would have to read many books beyond the level in order to meet the words enough times to learn them. The stories are not written to deliberately include all the words at a particular level, and it is good that this is not done, because writing to include certain words distorts the writing and makes it seem unnatural and awkward.

This flexibility in including words is one of the reasons why some publishers are reluctant to publish their word lists. They feel that they may be criticized because the expectation is that they will keep to only those 400 words but an analysis will show there are several words beyond the lists.

Another reason for reluctance in publishing lists is that these lists are not fixed. Some graded reader series have been going for over 25 years now and periodically they will need to update and revise their lists which can put older books out of step with the revised lists.

We still feel, however, that the benefits of publishing lists outweigh the disadvantages, especially now that lists can be published on the web and easily updated. These benefits include teachers being more aware of what vocabulary their learners need to know to read at a particular level, teachers and learners being able to find roughly equivalent levels across different series, and researchers being able to use tried and tested graded reader lists to check their own word lists. In addition, the availability of such lists would have the more general effect of underlining the value and importance of vocabulary control when preparing material for foreign language learners.

Do Graded Readers Contain Unnatural Language?

Extensive reading aims to provide learners with large amounts of comprehensible input. This input provides opportunities for meeting words, word groups, and grammatical features in typical and useful contexts. An essential requirement for learning a language is opportunities to meet the language in use. But, is the language of extensive reading representative of typical language use? Does writing within a controlled vocabulary result in unnatural language? Some studies have addressed this question. Claridge (2005) looked at Honeyfield's (1977) and Swaffar's (1985) criticisms of simplification and graded readers, and used these as criteria to compare two original unsimplified texts and two simplified versions. The criteria included word frequency distribution, authorial cues, discourse markers, collocations, and redundancy. She concluded that "the writing in well-written graded readers can be, for its audience, experienced as authentic and typical of 'normal' English" (p. 144).

28　*What Are Graded Readers?*

The mid-frequency readers, which are at the 4,000, 6,000, and 8,000 word levels for advanced learners, involve very little language control. Only the lower frequency words in the language are replaced by higher frequency words, and these replacements at the 4,000 word level average out at around three to four words per 300 word page. Over a whole novel of 100,000 words running, however, this results in the replacement of between 700 to 1,200 different words, which is a very large gain in vocabulary control and thus a substantial saving in wasted learning effort. The grammar of the mid-frequency readers is unchanged, and so except for the absence of the lower frequency words, they are very close to the originals (Nation, 2019 forthcoming).

Graded readers are books written within a controlled vocabulary and grammar and in this respect they differ from other books. However, they only use grammatical constructions and vocabulary that also occur in other writing. There is no special 'graded reader English'.

What Does Using a Controlled Vocabulary Do?

Controlling the vocabulary in a graded reader affects reading and vocabulary learning, and because of this affects the pleasure of reading.

Graded readers help to build the skill of reading by:

1　allowing large quantities of manageable reading at the right level for particular learners at any level of proficiency;
2　reducing the density of unfamiliar words making the reading less burdensome;
3　greatly reducing the number of unfamiliar words;
4　scaffolding vocabulary from one level into higher levels ensuring a constant flow of repetitions.

Graded readers improve vocabulary learning by:

1　allowing large quantities of manageable meetings with unknown and partly known words;
2　excluding a large number of words that are not useful at the learners' present level of proficiency;
3　providing words that are **all** worth learning now;
4　reducing the density of unfamiliar words and thus supporting guessing from context.

The major effect of using a controlled vocabulary is that it excludes words that are not worth learning now because there are more useful words to learn. This is a major effect because in uncontrolled text, the longer the text, the greater the number of unknown words. So, in a text like a novel, there are likely to be well over a thousand unknown words, and most of these will occur only once and will be way beyond the learners' current vocabulary size (see Nation, 2019 for a study of the mid-frequency readers which provides evidence for these points).

There is a negative aspect to vocabulary control, namely that a controlled text is likely to be less precise than one written without vocabulary control. This occurs because more general high frequency words like *walk* are used instead of more specific words like *stroll, strut*, or *amble*. What is lost in specificity, however, is gained in comprehensibility. If the reader does not know the low frequency word, then comprehension as well as specificity is lost. It is this aspect that makes writing a graded reader a challenge. How can you write an interesting, exciting book using only a very limited number of different words? One answer is to illustrate the books well to help tell the story. Another can be found in the lists of winners and shortlisted titles in the annual ERF Language Learner Literature Award. It is possible to write very good books just as it is possible to write not so good books. This is true of writing within a limited vocabulary and writing uncontrolled text for native speakers.

It has been said that writing graded readers is like trying to tell an interesting story on the back of a stamp. Colin Mortimer used to compare EFL materials writers writing within a limited vocabulary to Shakespeare writing for the Elizabethan stage. The Elizabethan stage did not allow flashbacks, elaborate scenery, or voice-overs, but within those limitations Shakespeare wrote masterpieces. The EFL materials writer and the writer of graded readers also work within a tough set of limitations, but within those limitations they can also strive to create masterpieces.

Graded readers are an extremely valuable resource for learners of a foreign language, particularly those at the beginning and intermediate levels of language proficiency. They allow learners to learn from meaning-focused input and they support and add to fluency development. They also allow learners to do authentic reading and to experience the joy of reading engaging well-written books and the joy of experiencing success in using a foreign language. As we will see in later chapters in this book, their use is well supported by research and by the enjoyable experience of learners.

Beyond Graded Readers

As Table 2.1 showed, graded readers end at around the 3,000 to 4,000 word levels. Unfortunately a vocabulary size of 3,000 to 4,000 words is still not enough to cover most of the words met in unsimplified texts like novels, newspapers, or movies. Nation (2006) suggests that vocabulary sizes around 6,000 to 9,000 words are needed to gain 98% coverage of the running words (tokens) in an uncontrolled text.

In the past, a series to bridge the gap between graded readers and unsimplified text, appropriately called the *Bridge Series*, was published by Longman, Green, and Co. The Bridge Series contained 32 titles including fiction works, such as *Animal Farm, Lucky Jim, Persuasion, The Red*

30 *What Are Graded Readers?*

Badge of Courage, and *Great Expectations*, and non-fiction works, including *The Mysterious Universe, Changing Horizons*, and *Mankind against the Killers*. Although the series is now out of print, the number of printings for some of the books shows that they, at least, sold well. The following is a note describing the series that appeared in the introduction to *Animal Farm*. The note is included here largely for historical interest to show what level of vocabulary control was used because it is now difficult to find copies of the *Bridge Series* books.

> The *Bridge Series* is intended for students of English as a second or foreign language who have progressed beyond the elementary graded readers and the *Longman Simplified English Series* but are not yet sufficiently advanced to read works of literature in their original form.
>
> The books in the *Bridge Series* are moderately simplified in vocabulary and often slightly reduced in length, but with little change in syntax. The purpose of the texts is to give practice in understanding fairly advanced sentence patterns and to help in the appreciation of English style. We hope that they will prove enjoyable to read for their own sake and that they will at the same time help students to reach the final objective of reading original works of literature in English with full understanding and appreciation.
>
> *Technical Note*
>
> In the *Bridge Series* words outside the commonest 7000 (in Thorndike and Lorge: *A Teacher's Handbook of 30,000 Words*. Columbia University, 1944) have usually been replaced by commoner and more generally useful words. Words used which are outside the first 3,000 of the list are explained in a glossary and are so distributed throughout the book that they do not occur at a greater density than 25 per running 1,000 words.
>
> (from the introduction to Orwell, 1945)

The *Bridge Series* involves a reasonable amount of glossing (the glossary is in the form of a list with definitions at the back of the book) and a small amount of adaptation.

The mid-frequency readers are also an attempt to fill the gap between the end of graded readers and unsimplified text (Nation & Anthony, 2013). The mid-frequency readers are freely available from Paul Nation's website. They consist of fiction and non-fiction texts that are out of copyright or in creative commons. Each text exists in three adapted versions. One version is at the 4,000 word level where learners are assumed to know the most frequent 4,000 words of English according to the BNC/COCA lists on Paul Nation's website, and the target words which make up less than 2% of the running words are at the 5,000 and 6,000 word levels. Most words beyond those levels, except for repeated topic words, have been replaced by words below the 6,000 level. Another version is at the 6,000 word level with target words from the seventh and eighth 1,000 levels, and the most difficult version is at the 8,000 word level with target words from the ninth and

What Are Graded Readers? 31

tenth 1,000 levels. There is no abridgement of the original text and there is no change to the grammar except for occasional small changes resulting from the vocabulary control. The main effect of the adaptation is the absence of several hundred low frequency words that occur only once or twice in the original text.

The mid-frequency readers include the following titles with the eventual aim being to have around 40 titles which would then be enough to gain sufficient input to have a chance of learning the most frequent 9,000 words of English (Nation, 2014): *The Art of War, More William, Glimpses of Unfamiliar Japan, Alice's Adventures in Wonderland, Narrative of the Life of Frederick Douglass an American Slave, Free Culture, Wuthering Heights, The Adventures of Sherlock Holmes, The Garden Party and Other Stories, Jane Eyre, A Modest Proposal, A Christmas Carol,* and *Metamorphosis.*

We can justify using mid-frequency readers on the basis of a substantially reduced vocabulary load, but they may prove to be unnecessary (Uden, Schmitt, & Schmitt, 2014). This is because some learners are willing to put up with a heavy vocabulary load just for the joy and feeling of achievement in reading an unsimplified text.

When Can Learners Move From Graded Readers to Unsimplified Text?

Uden, Schmitt, and Schmitt (2014) looked at the gap between the end of graded readers and unsimplified text. Graded readers end at around the 3,000 word level, but a vocabulary of around 8,000 words is needed to get 98% coverage of unsimplified text.

The Uden, Schmitt, and Schmitt (2014) study looked at four learners of English involved in extensive reading with vocabulary sizes ranging from 4,700 words to 6,000 words. The comprehensive and innovative tests measured comprehension, fluency, and reading ease/pleasure of two Level 6 graded readers from the *Cambridge English Readers* series and two unsimplified novels. Reading fluency was measured on short excerpts from the books.

The study also involved vocabulary tests made for each book based on the vocabulary found in the books. These tests indicated that the learners involved had around 99% coverage for the *Cambridge English Readers* books and 95–96% coverage for the unsimplified novels.

The comprehension score was lower for the unsimplified novels but was still at an acceptable level. Reading rate also decreased slightly with the move to unsimplified novels. The reading rates ranged from 136–219 words per minute. Individuals tended to read within the same rate band for different books, which agrees with Carver's (1976) research with native speakers. The ease/pleasure scores dropped for unsimplified texts, but were still positive. Uden, Schmitt, and Schmitt are suitably cautious in their conclusions:

32 *What Are Graded Readers?*

> While we believe that mid-frequency graded readers ... are also useful, we feel that encouraging motivated readers to move to unsimplified novels after the highest graded reader levels can be pedagogically sound advice, especially if learners ... choose easier unsimplified texts, which they feel comfortable with.
>
> (Uden, Schmitt, & Schmitt, 2014, p. 20)

This is good advice.

It needs to be noted that the learners had substantial vocabulary size scores of around 5,500 words for one learner and 6,600 words for the other three when they began reading the unsimplified texts, and the accuracy of these scores was supported by the tests of words occurring in the books. For vocabulary growth, these learners seem to have been way beyond the *Cambridge English Readers* Level 6 books which are written at the 3,800 word level, although such texts would be useful for enriching known words and developing fluency and comprehension.

The major motivation for developing the mid-frequency readers is that unsimplified texts contain large numbers of words that occur only once and which are way beyond learners' current vocabulary needs. These large numbers can be over 1,000 unknown words in a typical 100,000 word novel. The relatively small amount of adaptation that occurs in a mid-frequency graded reader greatly reduces misdirected learning effort.

However, the Uden, Schmitt, and Schmitt study shows that learners can move successfully from the highest levels of graded readers to unsimplified texts with some increase in difficulty if they have a large enough vocabulary size, and well-motivated learners may be able to tolerate the large number of unknown words occurring only once without substantial loss of reading pleasure.

Two additional interesting findings of the Uden, Schmitt, and Schmitt study are first that the learners enjoyed their reading and were reading a lot without any outside pressure to do so. Second, learners sat the Vocabulary Size Test when they began reading Levels 5 and 6 readers and after they had read around 20 readers and before they began reading the unsimplified novels. There was a substantial vocabulary size increase of around 600 to 800 words for three of the learners over this five-month period. Not all of this can be attributed to the reading, but it surely helped.

For learners wanting to make the jump, it is advisable to read narrowly in one area, especially one in which they are interested, to become familiar with its vocabulary and expressions, a method called *narrow reading*. When the learners have become familiar with that area, they can move onto others. This controlled input method will prevent them being too overwhelmed with unknown language which they will not often meet again if they read too widely.

Extensive Reading Without Graded Readers

Extensive reading at low and intermediate levels of proficiency typically requires large numbers of graded readers. While such readers are available in

What Are Graded Readers? 33

English, for learners of other languages they either do not exist or are very few indeed. How can learners of languages other than English do the large quantities of comprehensible reading that are important for language learning?

1   Learners can deliberately learn a lot of relevant words quickly. Using word cards or flash-cards apps can help do this.
2   Learners should know about the nature of vocabulary and vocabulary learning (metacognitive knowledge) and use this knowledge to be strategic in dealing with vocabulary while reading. That is, they should be aware that half of the different words in a text will occur only once, and they should be aware of the importance of repetition and deliberate attention for learning vocabulary.
3   Learners should choose 'easy' books – for example, children's books such as those used to teach reading. These will still be difficult but will be much more manageable than texts for adults.
4   They should choose books where they have a lot of background knowledge or read an L1 version first. For example, they should read in a subject area they have studied, or read a novel they have already read in their first language.
5   Learners should do narrow reading – stick within the same topic area. For example, they should read recipe books, or follow a continuing story in the newspaper.
6   Learners should read electronically with easy look-up such as with Kindle.
7   Learners should re-read the texts they have read before.
8   Learners should combine incidental and deliberate learning.
9   Learners should get someone to adapt a text using software such as the *Online Graded Text Editor* or the *AntWordProfiler* application.

Hitosugi and Day (2004) introduced extensive reading into a low-level course for learning Japanese. Because of a lack of graded readers in Japanese, children's books were used. This issue was discussed with the students (university students) so that they were not put off by the inappropriate cognitive level of the books. The books did not require knowledge of *kanji* (the ideographic writing system of Japanese) but could be read with knowledge of the syllabic writing systems (*hiragana* and the related *furigana*, and *katakana*). The books were ranked into six difficulty levels according to a variety of criteria such as length, supportive illustrations, writing systems, and content difficulty. The books were tagged for difficulty level to guide the students. A challenging target of 40 books was set to get full credit for the extensive reading section of the course. Reading was done outside class but some extensive reading-related activities were done in class time. One effect of the in-class activities was to motivate the out-of-class reading. Most students read a large number of books, averaging 32 books per student. The students in the extensive reading classes made substantial gains in reading

34   *What Are Graded Readers?*

compared with those in the non-extensive reading groups, and had much more positive attitudes to learning Japanese.

Sequencing Unsimplified Texts

Unsimplified texts differ in their readability levels. They also differ in the amount of low frequency vocabulary that they contain. Several researchers have looked at the idea of using analyses of text coverage using word lists and frequency profiling programs, such as the *Online Graded Text Editor* (www. er-central.com/OGTE), *AntWordProfiler* (www.laurenceanthony.net/softwa re/antwordprofiler/), or *Vocabprofile* (www.lextutor.ca), to create a sequence from those containing a relatively small number of unknown words to those containing a lot (Ghadirian, 2002; Huang & Liou, 2007; McQuillan, 2016). Learners could then begin their reading of unsimplified text with those that have the smallest amount of unknown vocabulary, eventually moving to texts with a heavier vocabulary load. Ghadirian's (2002) goal was to identify the higher frequency words of English and then look at how the sequencing of unsimplified text could be arranged to help learn these higher frequency words. Ghadirian used short news texts (300 to 1,500 words long) from the Voice of America. He found that such sequencing was feasible, but his study also showed that there was a need for well-designed word lists to provide a consistent basis for sequencing.

McQuillan (2016) describes the sequence of material as going from graded reading to light reading to challenging text and sees it as a complementary alternative to graded reading > mid-frequency reading > challenging text. McQuillan found that it was possible to find plenty of texts that gave learners 98% coverage of the text at vocabulary sizes at each of the 1,000 word family levels from the 4,000 word level upwards. Many of these books were from various series of books that provided the opportunity for narrow reading, thus increasing the likelihood of considerably reduced vocabulary load in terms of the total number of different words met. These series were largely, but not completely, books written for young readers. There is a caution, however, which is noted in McQuillan's (2016) study (p. 75, footnote 4), namely that while the careful selection of texts can provide favorable text coverage for known words and thus reduce the density of unknown words, it does not remove the problem of the large number of words occurring only once which are outside the learners' knowledge. McQuillan notes that continued reading of a particular series can reduce the proportion of these unknown one-timers, but the number still remains in the hundreds. The major effect of simplification (Nation, 2019 forthcoming) is to get rid of these unknown one-timers and thus make reading less burdensome. As Uden, Schmitt, & Schmitt (2014) note, learners may be prepared to do this extra guessing or look-up work to read the books that interest them.

Using Narrow Reading to Control Vocabulary Load

Narrow reading involves reading in the same topic or subject area. By staying within a limited topic area, the total number of different words met is greatly reduced. Studies by Sutarsyah, Nation, and Kennedy (1994) and Quero (2015) suggest that narrow reading may involve only half of the number of different words needed to read a diverse collection of texts of a similar length.

Gardner (2008) explored the meaning of 'narrow reading' by looking at the effect of thematic tightness, author, and register (narrative vs expository) on word repetition. Related thematic content had the strongest effect on the repetition of content words especially in expository texts. Related narrative affected repetition of proper names such as the names of people and places. Theme/topic-based expository reading has the greatest effect on vocabulary repetition, and probably on the number of different words, though this remains to be investigated. Gardner's unit of counting was word types and this meant that exactly the same form of a word had to occur for it to be counted as a repetition. In narrative texts, familiarity with the characters increases reading fluency (Chang & Millett, 2017).

Hwang and Nation (1989) and Schmitt and Carter (2000) found that narrow reading provided a small number of opportunities to learn through increased repetition of topic-related words. Kang (2015) found that the increased repetition provided by three related texts resulted in better knowledge of the target words. Unfortunately, there was no test of vocabulary knowledge of the words that occurred in the unrelated texts. Teachers (Hawker & McPherson, 1990) and learners (Chang & Millett, 2017; Cho, Ahn, & Krashen, 2005) see the advantages of narrow reading.

Conclusion

For beginning and intermediate learners of English, graded readers should be the heart of any extensive reading program. They allow the essential requirements of an extensive reading program to be met – reading at the right level, reading with good comprehension, reading a lot, reading independently, reading silently, and reading with enjoyment. The advantage of a controlled vocabulary is that there are no unrepeated words outside the level that learners are reading at, and so every word met is worth learning. However, narrow reading does not overcome the problem of the large number of low frequency words occurring only once in the text. Even though the overall vocabulary load is reduced, there will still be a substantial number of unrepeated words way outside the learners' current level. As Gardner's (2008) research shows, the advantages of narrow reading will be greatest in expository text, where topic-related vocabulary (technical vocabulary) occurs. Even unrepeated technical vocabulary is worth learning by someone specializing in that technical area.

In the next chapter we look at several examples of extensive reading programs.

3 Case Studies of Extensive Reading Programs

This chapter looks at a wide range of examples of successful extensive reading programs with the purposes of showing what extensive reading programs are like and providing one kind of evidence for the value of such programs. This evidence from case studies is largely in the form of the enjoyment learners get from the reading, and the large amounts of reading that they do. The case studies also highlight the huge variety of extensive reading programs, some very large catering to thousands of learners, and some small and local. Some have generous funding while others survive on the generosity of others. Despite this, several things are common to all of them. All of these programs have a dedicated resourceful teacher or teaching team committed to extensive reading and willing to adapt the program as necessary. Vital to the success of these programs is learner training, orientation, and follow-up to keep the learners on task and motivated.

These case studies do not follow a set format. Some were written in consultation with those involved in the programs and others were written solely by the authors of this book. This has resulted in a mixture of styles in this chapter but we hope that the uniqueness of each program and the responses to the challenges each program faced comes through clearly.

The SEG English Program in Tokyo, Japan

SEG is a *juku*, or tutorial (cram) school, in Tokyo, Japan, for 7th to 12th graders (learners around 12 to 18 years old) who would like to learn English or math in addition to their ordinary school lessons. Most classes are 160 minutes long and are held from 5pm to 8pm, with learners coming once a week for 31 weeks of the year and in addition usually attending up to 19 seasonal intensive lessons during school breaks, making a total of 50 classes per year.

Half of each English lesson, well over one hour, is extensive reading (and/or listening) largely conducted by Japanese teachers, and the other half is grammar, oral communication, and writing mainly conducted by native speakers of English. A few learners choose to spend the full 160 minutes on extensive reading.

Case Studies of Extensive Reading Programs   37

Class sizes are small at around 12 learners per class. Each classroom has many shelves of books to read, including graded readers and books written for native speakers averaging 10,000–20,000 books per classroom. The books written for native speakers include popular novels and magazines. One-eighth of the English program income used to be spent on books, but nowadays one-20th is spent on books. During the extensive reading class, each learner simply sits quietly reading a book of their preference. The teacher sometimes selects books for learners even when the learners are high level. During the class, the teacher is sitting quietly at the front of the class reading, or doing some administrative work.

During the session, we observed that the learners read largely without consulting dictionaries and were reading at a reasonable reading speed of 150 words per minute or faster. Several of the learners were reading unsimplified novels. At the end of the extensive reading session that we observed, for our benefit the teacher asked the class if they enjoyed doing the extensive reading. They all answered yes. Then he asked, "Would you do this reading at home?" Most replied that they would not, largely because there were too many other things to do. After class when we talked to some of the learners on their way home, we found they spoke English well and were being honest when they had said they enjoyed the extensive reading.

What is striking about this program is that parents were paying a substantial amount of money for their children to attend these classes where for around half of the time the teacher did not teach and the learners sat quietly reading. The fee is around 260,000–300,000 Japanese yen (US$2,500–$3,000) for 50 classes. The reason why the parents were willing to pay was because the learners who attended the school did very well in the entrance exams for Japanese universities and thus the student numbers have increased. The growth in numbers of learners attending the school to learn English went from 46 in 2004 to 1,026 in 2011 to 1,618 in 2018.

Akio Furukawa, the owner of the school, attributes the success of his program to (1) the choice of plenty of books at each level that are easy to read, and (2) the large amount of reading that the learners do. The reading is done each week mainly because the learners do it in class time. Only around one-third of the learners also read at home. The learners begin reading very easy graded readers. The *Oxford Reading Tree*, for example, is popular because it starts with very short stories, around 50 words long, but other short simple readers are also popular with the low proficiency 7th grade learners.

Akio Furukawa keeps careful records of how much his learners read. The advanced 7th graders read well over 10,000 words a month in the first six months, and the learners in grades 8 to 12 read at least 300,000 words a year, with the top learners reading well over a million words a year and some reading over four million words a year. Each week each learner in grade 7 borrows on average around ten books (which tend to be short and image heavy) from the school and each learner in grades 8 to 12 borrows three books (which tend to be thicker and have more text per page). This

38 *Case Studies of Extensive Reading Programs*

means the more advanced a learner becomes, the more volume of text they read. The learners write down the titles of the books or packs on the sheet in the classroom. The learners are not tested on the books they read.

The school keeps parents well informed of the progress their children are making. Twice a year the learners sit the standardized ACE test (Assessment of Communicative English) or TOEFL ITP test (for higher graders), which is also used in High Schools throughout Japan. The use of these tests allows individual progress to be measured and also allows comparison between learners at SEG and learners not at SEG. Parents can easily know the total amount of words that their children have read and what books they have read by looking at the reading log notebooks that their children have. The reading log is a printed, commercially available book in which students write their reading record.

The SEG school is clearly a commercial success, and much of this success can be attributed to the extensive reading program. The program gives high priority to getting the learners to do large amounts of enjoyable comprehensible reading at a level which is comfortable for them. It is also worth noting that extensive reading is not seen as the only component in an effective English program. Half of the class time is spent in small classes interacting with a native-speaking teacher.

Setting up the extensive reading program at SEG was a very brave step. Would parents pay for their children to attend an English program where for half of the time the teacher does not teach? Would learners be willing to go to such a school? Common-sense says no, but the success of the school shows that a well-run extensive reading program has marked effects on both proficiency and motivation. As a result of its success, other schools using the SEG model are planned in Korea, Taiwan, China, and elsewhere. The SEG program shows that extensive reading results in significant proficiency gains, and if learners and parents are made aware of these gains, they are very willing to support such programs.

The Book Flood Program in Fiji

The Book Flood extensive reading program is looked at in Chapter 6 of this book as a piece of experimental research. It is also included here as a case study because it was such an effective program that required minimal teacher training, a relatively modest set of resources, and no extra class-time beyond the usual English program. It worked with primary school level learners who largely came from very poor families. The results of the program were so positive that the Book Flood was seen as a model that could be easily and effectively applied throughout the world wherever English was taught 'in difficult circumstances', and there are numerous examples of its successful use in such situations (see Elley, 2000; Elley, 2001).

The teacher training component of the Book Flood involved a three-day workshop, aimed at familiarizing teachers with the shared book approach. This approach involves the teacher reading a story to the learners and capturing their interest by engaging with them about the story during the reading. The activity works well with 'blown-up books' which are very large copies of books, at least four times the size of a regular book. The size of the blown-up book makes the pictures and text easy for the whole class to see. Teachers can make their own blown-up books but there are commercial copies of some books available in the blown-up form, or they can display them via an overhead projector.

The shared book activity in many ways is like a parent reading to a child, where the reading is shared between the parent and the child. Typical steps involve first looking at the cover of the book and reading the title and then asking the children what the story is likely to be about. They may also be asked what they already know about the topic. Then as the story is read, the children are invited to comment on what has just happened in the story and what might happen next. Unfamiliar words and expressions can also be discussed. During the course of a school year, the class may come back to the same stories several times, often because they request them. The reading might be followed up by role play, word study, and writing.

Shared reading is a way of showing learners how to read and that reading is fun. It is, however, only part of a reading program and in the Book Flood experiment learners spent around half an hour each day doing silent reading. The Book Flood was not additional to their EFL program but replaced around three-quarters of it. The teachers in the silent reading treatment did not receive any training.

Each class in the Book Flood study had a box of around 250 high-interest books that was kept in the classroom so that the books were easily accessible. Some of the books were displayed so that they could be easily seen and might attract the learners. Each learner chose what books they would read and were not tested on their reading of each book and did not have to write reports on their reading. They simply did the reading.

The important features of a Book Flood are the easy availability of interesting books, the raising of children's interest in reading, and the sustained allocation of time to do uninterrupted silent reading.

Although Book Floods have been used with great success in well-off parts of the world such as Brunei and Singapore, they are particularly attractive and effective where resources and opportunities for teacher-training are limited. The Book Flood studies show that teachers do not need substantial re-training to run an extensive reading program. They just need to make sure that there are books at the right level to read and time to do the reading.

Park Language Academy in South Korea

Dakto-bak Yongeo-scul (Dr. Park's English School) is run by Jeongsuk Park who has operated the school for five years in Jinju, Gyeongnam province, South Korea. The school is known as a *hakwon* (a private after-school institute), or a cram school, which caters to students whose parents pay for them to attend weekday and/or weekend classes. Unlike other *hakwons*, its

40 *Case Studies of Extensive Reading Programs*

focus is extensive reading. The students are typically younger learners in small classes who often receive one-on-one instruction. Seventy percent of the students are elementary school children, 30% are middle school students from 7th to 9th graders.

The school has approximately 10,000 English books, of which 70% are leveled books for English-speaking native children and the rest are graded readers for non-native English learners by the major publishers. As well as the extensive reading component of the school, students also receive intensive reading and grammar instruction by the Korean teachers. Speaking and writing are instructed by a native teacher. The core element of the school is reading: 60% is extensive reading, 20% is intensive reading using an online reading program, and the remaining 20% is grammar and writing.

Typically, students read the books recommended by Korean teachers in class. The teachers check each student on their understanding of what is read to ensure understanding and choose books for class and take-home. The students are encouraged to use the CDs accompanying the books.

The school believes that books should be read with more than 80% understanding. So, the teachers carefully examine their students reading to see if students read with good understanding or if they pretend to read but without much understanding of what is being read. If the students show reluctance or boredom, the teachers interview them to gather information in order to provide them with more suitable books. Internal research has found that students do not improve their reading ability when they are reading the books of a much higher level than their own level.

One female student, for example, was not improving her reading so the teachers intervened. It was found she was reading books which were far too difficult for her and expecting her ability to increase. After a few times of teacher intervention, she was able to read well and became a fluent reader. After three months, her EPER (Edinburgh Project on Extensive Reading) scale score increased by one level, from H to G (0 to 32 in raw score).

For intensive reading, the school uses an online reading program, *Little Fox* (www.littlefox.com). Students are required to repeatedly read the online stories as homework. In class, students do activities such as making a story-map, reciting, and doing a presentation of the stories read online at home. This intensive reading of the online program helps students acquire the English vocabulary and structures quickly by reading repeatedly, which helps them to learn to read better without much time spent on explicit grammar teaching.

For evaluation, students are given the EPER paper test which is available from the ERF, to ascertain if they are ready to move up a level. On average, it takes elementary students 8.3 months to move up a level on the EPER scale, with middle-schoolers taking 6.2 months. In addition, the TOEIC Bridge is given to the students who read more than one million words. One 8th grader got a perfect score (180/180) on the TOEIC Bridge after studying for five years at the school. The average score of the students at the school is much higher than the national average. A 'reading survey' is also given to the students

Case Studies of Extensive Reading Programs 41

to gauge their reactions to the reading program. The survey shows very positive feedback on the overall reading program, which means that the school program is well accepted by students as well as their parents.

Dr. Park's English School is an excellent example of how a dedicated and resourceful teacher can create an oasis of extensive reading in a country largely focused on intensive reading and test preparation. Its success as a forerunner extensive reading school has led it to be a model for many copy-cat extensive and pleasure reading schools that have emerged in recent years in South Korea to varying degrees of success.

Kyoto Sangyo University

Kyoto Sangyo University (KSU) based in Kyoto, Japan, has run an extensive reading program since 1985 and has gone through three distinct stages. Initially, when the program first started in the 1990s, the KSU program only used SRA reading sets for lower ability students and native level materials for the higher students. The books were transported to classes on library carts and included *The Hardy Boys, Nancy Drew*, and more modern series such as *The Baby Sitters Club*, the *Great Brain* as well as works by popular authors such as Judy Blume, Eve Bunting, and selected materials from the American Library Association.

These materials were used under the assumption that these books were not only similar to the literature books the students were already studying, but were considered manageable, as the KSU students tended to be above average for university students in the region. Moreover, the administrators believed that native-speaker materials were more motivating and that some of the graded readers published at the time were more difficult than the native-speaker materials due to a lack of redundancy. Over the past 20 years or so the quality of the graded readers has improved in that they now follow many of the conventions of native materials albeit with a reduced vocabulary (see Claridge, 2012 for one example). Over time, KSU added graded readers to accommodate students of varying abilities, and now students predominantly read graded readers and the SRA materials are no longer used.

The volume of reading was calculated using a 'page-weighted' formula depending on the average number of words per page. If a typical book has 200 words per page, the reading would be multiplied by 1.0, but if it had 300 words per page, the factor would be 1.5. Initially, students were expected to read 100 pages per week or 1,000 pages per semester. However, it was found that students tended to cram the reading towards the end of the semester. At this time, KSU also expanded the reading to far more of the student body which made organizing the program more work.

With a change in the curriculum, there was no longer a suitable class for use of the SRA kits, so in their second phase, the KSU extensive reading program switched to a pure outside reading requirement, adopting the Accelerated Reader software, which was intended for use by native-speaking children.

42 Case Studies of Extensive Reading Programs

However, numerous problems made it far from ideal. All students were shown the same set of ten questions, leading to rampant cheating. There was no access control by book level. There were no quizzes on graded readers except for a maximum of 100 'teacher-made quizzes' which was severely limiting, and it became necessary to monitor the students while they took the quizzes during the lunch hour. These issues led the extensive reading program organizer, Tom Robb, to create the online quiz system now called *MReader* (https://mreader. org), upgraded from the original *Moodlereader* version in 2012, to help manage and streamline the extensive reading program. This system became so successful that MReader is now used by over 100,000 students all over the world and is sponsored by the ERF and most of the graded reader publishers.

Currently, the main KSU collection has about 12,000 books in a special extensive reading section of the library, of which about 50% are standard graded readers including sets of up to 20 copies of popular titles for use as a class set. In addition to the main library, currently there are another 3,000 books in the 'Global Commons' Free Access Center, which is located on Level 1 of the same building where most language instruction takes place. It caters not only to English, but also to the other nine languages that the students can major in. The Global Commons also stores approximately 30 'class sets' of 25–30 titles each that are in baskets that teachers can simply pick up and take to class. There is also a section called 'Books for Fun' which has higher level reading material that is popular with young readers, but these lack MReader quizzes. Students can borrow up to three books at a time, and more during vacation periods.

These books in both locations are stored by levels corresponding to the MReader leveling system. The MReader system (also known as the *Kyoto Scale*) is loosely based on reported headword counts, but further adjusted by close inspection of the text series, with reference to the *Yomiyasusa Levels* (www.seg.co.jp/sss/YL/) created by Akio Furukawa of SEG. The Kyoto Scale divides all books into ten levels of increasing difficulty. Table 3.1 shows a very rough correspondence between the Kyoto levels and other language level criteria (mreader.org, 2018) and is used to roughly determine initial reading levels for the students. The site recommends that their initial reading level be a little below their actual current ability to ensure a confident start to reading extensively (https://mreader.org/mreaderadmin/s/html/Kyoto_Scale.html).

Currently, students are required to read a specific minimum of words for their first four semesters (two years): 80,000, 120,000, 140,000, and 160,000 in each semester with their word counts tracked by MReader. Students failing to reach the minimum will fail that semester's reading course, which must be repeated the following year. None of the previously read books in that semester counts towards the repeated class; they start from scratch. On average, students read approximately 620,000 words, with some over 1,500,000 words.

First year students have five 90-minute classes per week, two content based, two communicative, and one reading class with most extensive reading done outside of class time. They also have a writing class, a

Table 3.1 The *Kyoto Scale* of Extensive Reading Levels used on mreader.org

Kyoto	TOEIC	TOEFL	CEFR	ERF Scale	Lexile	Yomiyasusa Level	XReading
Starter	200	300		BE	50–200	0.4–0.6	1
Level 1	250	350	A1	BM	100–300	0.7–0.9	2
Level 2	280	365	A1	BH	175–400	1.0–1.1	3
Level 3	320	380	A1	EE	250–500	1.2–1.5	4
Level 4	380	400	A2	EM	325–600	1.6–2.5	5
Level 5	450	430	A2	EH	400–700	2.6–3.1	6
Level 6	500	450	B1	IE	475–800	3.2–3.7	7
Level 7	650	550	B1	IM, IH, UE	600–900	3.8–4.4	8,9,10
Level 8	850	600	B2	UM, UH, AE	700–1,000	4.5–5.4	11,12,13
Level 9	950	677	C1	AM, AH+	900+	5.5–6.5	14+

44 *Case Studies of Extensive Reading Programs*

computer literacy class, and two more classes focusing on study skills and introductions to areas of specialization within the English Department. Second year students have five 90-minute classes per week with the same structure plus elective courses delivered in either English or Japanese. Third year students have one smaller *enshu* seminar class of 90 minutes, plus electives and the fourth years have an optional *enshu* class, plus electives. In addition, there is a program with a lower requirement for those majoring in other languages, plus special courses for those who would like to do more Extensive Reading for credit. There is also a three-week theme-based study tour with a choice of five locations around the world between first and second year and a special English program where the students receive a certificate if they take 68 credit hours of English-only courses. There is also a range of over 20 'Special English Courses' open to any language major who meets the entrance requirements on many specialized topics.

Much of the extensive reading is done outside of class, with their 90-minute 'Reading' course devoted to intensive reading, skills building activities, and other aspects, although some extensive reading is done in class in the first term to prepare them to read independently outside of class. They are given a reading speed test at the beginning of their first and second years, as well as the TOEFL Paper-Based Test at the beginning of their first year and at the end of the first and second years.

The KSU program is an excellent example of how a large university can set up and manage a huge extensive reading program successfully across dozens of classes and years and for thousands of students. In order to achieve this, it had to re-invent its extensive reading program several times. This led it to create the powerful extensive reading management software MReader which relieves teachers of some of the barriers to starting an extensive reading program including knowing how to level the graded readers, recording and validating what has been read, and tracking reading volumes among other things. If it hadn't been for the efforts of the KSU program coordinator and team to create MReader and open it to any teacher worldwide, many extensive reading programs would have had to set up their own systems, meaning some of them may not have been able to start. For this reason alone, the extensive reading community has a lot to thank the KSU program and its team for. It is worth looking at the research coming from the program (Robb, 2002; Robb, 2013, Robb, 2015; Robb & Kano, 2013).

Notre Dame Seishin University in Okayama, Japan

Notre Dame Seishin University's (NDSU) extensive reading program started in 1994. It is an example of a program that started small and grew, because of its demonstrated success, until it became a firmly established part of the university. It is also a program where the extensive reading is well integrated with other parts of the English program, across the four skills of listening, speaking, reading, and writing.

Case Studies of Extensive Reading Programs   45

The initial stock of titles for the NDSU program was purchased from the British Council in Kyoto which did not need some 200 used graded readers. These books were carried to class each week in book bags to be used in a stand-alone extensive reading elective class which ran for several years and functioned as a pilot program to assess its effectiveness. The 90-minute class opened with learners reading any title they wanted, returning books they had read, and filling in reading record logs. All this would take 45 minutes or so. After the silent reading, students discussed their reading and shared their favorite titles. The next 30 minutes involved the class listening to a graded reader CD which usually had to be one or two levels easier than their current reading level so they could listen fluently. After every major element in the story, the students discussed what was happening and what would happen next. At the end of the story the class would do several follow-up activities focusing on the stories. One story would typically take two to three weeks to finish. The final 15 minutes of the class was spent on developing reading skills using *Reading Power* (Mikulecky & Jeffries, 1994). Students were also encouraged to read for homework. This class was very popular among the students who were mostly non-English majors especially when they saw their TOEFL scores increase. The typical student would read between 25–40 graded readers each semester, or around 100,000 words.

Due to the success of the pilot extensive reading class, the university allocated a dedicated Reading Room and added thousands of books over the next three years to expand the reading to all first year students. The library followed the initial eight level system used in the book bag pilot program which involved putting books into levels with a similar headword count based on the Extensive Reading Foundation Graded Reader Scale. The lowest level has books up to 300 headwords and includes *Foundations Reading Library* Levels 1–6, *Cambridge Starters, Oxford Bookworms Starters*, and so on. A small piece of brown tape was stuck to the top of the spine of the book so students could identify they were 'brown level'. The rest of the books were similarly categorized into the remaining seven levels and were allocated different colored tape: yellow, blue, green, and so on. The books were placed on shelves grouped by color making it easy for the students to find the books and return them. Books with CDs were put together in clear plastic packets and formed part of the extensive listening component. The library is decorated with several posters promoting books from the publishers, some tables and chairs and a sofa and several computers with audio tracks from the graded readers installed on the iTunes software. The Reading Room is always open and no librarian is present allowing for easy access and check out. Most students returned their books to the 'bag drop' but every year about 10% of the 3,000 or so books were lost. It was found that replacing the lost books was cheaper than paying someone to be a librarian. The Reading Room was used for several years by all first and second year students in the university, totaling 1,200 or so students per year.

46 *Case Studies of Extensive Reading Programs*

In 2015, the university library worked in conjunction with the English Education Center to create a Language Learning Corner in the university library. The Language Learning Corner contains a graded reader collection, primarily English, but also with Chinese, French, and German books, that is administered using the library's check-out system. A space was made available immediately inside the main library entrance for these books so students could find them easily. All books were given barcodes following the university borrowing system and the stock management is administered using the student library identification card. Additional shelving and book carousels were purchased to allow more books to be seen by the cover rather than the spine. In 2016, an additional reading area was made in the university's new self-access room. Altogether, the university now has about 4,000 graded readers, including 330 e-book titles, and an additional 400–500 first language high-interest teen and young adult materials. These are in addition to the thousands of native-speaker novels which were bought for the study of English Literature many years ago after the closure of a US library, but they are rarely looked at, let alone checked out, even by the teaching staff.

Students are required to read differing amounts depending on which classes they are in and their major. The English non-majors are required to read a minimum of 50,000 words and/or 10–15 books each 16-week semester depending on each book's length. They average around 63,000 words of reading with some reading well over 100,000 words. The English Department teachers all require different reading amounts, some two books a month and others two per week or more. The current targets for two of the five first year teachers are a minimum of 100,000 words per semester for a bare pass, 120,000 for a C grade, 150,000 for B, 180,000 for A, and 200,000 or more for A plus. In some cases, the students are restricted from reading the easiest levels or the top levels (books beyond 11,000 words) unless they get special permission, to prevent them from reading difficult long books with 20,000 or 30,000 words that they struggle to understand. The English majors are also required to read two *Footprint Reading Library* books per month as part of the English Reading class taught by the Japanese staff. The words for these books do not count to their total. Students are also required to read between 5–8 books during the summer vacation.

Initially, the students reacted negatively to this amount of reading but once they understood that they could not learn English without meeting millions of words and that their course book was not building depth of knowledge, they accepted they needed to read. The first 15 minutes of some English classes is given over to free-reading to emphasize its importance.

The reading is checked and assessed in two ways. The first validation comes from the use of the MReader quiz system which allocates a word count only if the student passes the test. The volume of reading and the need to pass the quizzes soon led to students trying to get around the system. Typical strategies involved taking quizzes for books of movies that they had watched, or looking up summaries of famous stories like *Frankenstein, Jane Eyre*, etc. on websites and

Case Studies of Extensive Reading Programs 47

taking the quiz without actually reading the books. These two types of books, books of movies and famous stories, are banned for English majors. A further method they used was to team up in groups of three to five with each member reading one book and then take the quiz for each other. Fortunately, MReader has a 'cheating' function that can show which students are reading the same titles and whether they take the tests within a few minutes of each other. MReader is set to allow quizzes to be taken at set minimum time intervals to prevent students from swapping their mobile phones to take a quiz for a friend. Once the students knew that the teachers were monitoring this, and they had been found out, in large part they stopped doing it. Students found doing this consistently have their word counts cut by 40,000 words. There were also a few reports of the use of internet-based groups such as LINE or Twitter in which students ask, or pay, other students to take MReader quizzes for them. As the stakes are lower in the non-English major classes, less cheating is noticed.

The second check that the reading is done comes from the post-reading activities such as oral reports, written book reports, poster presentations, character and plot analyses and profiles, making quizzes for other students, making graphic organizers explaining the story, re-writing the stories with different characters, endings, or settings, or writing a letter to a character from the story and so on. The activities are designed so that the students must read the book in order to do the activities. The types of follow-up activities used depend on whether the reading is part of the main oral communication class or the writing class. It was found that assessing the follow-up activities rather than the reading itself leads to more reading being done and more on-task focus. In some classes, the graded reading, and its follow-up, is allocated 35% of their grade to emphasize its importance.

The end-of-semester questionnaires show that the students understand the importance of the reading and listening but find it difficult to remember to do it given their busy schedules and other classes. Nevertheless, once a reading culture has been established, the students do the reading more willingly and some students do far more than is required.

Overall the extensive reading program is successful, but it needs more co-operation between the teachers in the English Department to integrate it at the department level rather than allowing each teacher to decide the volume of reading and the grade allocated to it by class. Other plans for the extensive reading program are to increase the amount of shelf space for showing the covers of the books; upgrade the Reading Room; integrate the reading program with the third year English majors' classes; and introduce a wider range of materials including newspapers, magazines, and so on.

The NDSU extensive reading program is quite typical of many extensive reading programs in universities in Asia. It has evolved over time starting as a single class using book bags and expanding to a department and then being integrated into the university library and across all departments. One of its many strengths is the deliberate integration of extensive reading with other work on the other language skills.

48   *Case Studies of Extensive Reading Programs*

Extensive Reading in the Kathmandu Valley, Nepal

In Spring 2014, a university sponsored volunteer initiative by Ann Mayeda started the Extensive Reading Program in Nepal (NEP). Over 2,000 books and graded readers were donated or solicited from publishers, booksellers, and libraries and distributed to four schools in the Kathmandu Valley in Nepal. An 'Extensive Reading Kit' was also distributed which included reading record log worksheets, book report forms, and a guide to extensive reading which allowed the reading program to start with minimal effort. On a second trip, a further 700 books were purchased including some locally published materials such as Nepal-specific folk tales and stories which reflected the Nepali context.

A similar project called Namaste Library Project (NLP) was set up by Vicky Allen at the Namaste Community Foundation, a children's home, in Pokhara, Nepal in 2013. Donations of money and books were received from publishers and individuals there, as well as from the ERF. In all, over 300 books were bought but many of them were not sufficiently low level. The learners assisted in the labeling and leveling of the books and contributed to the design of the check-out system. Other volunteers helped paint the library and find suitable furniture. Three desktop computer systems were purchased with the help of the ERF so the students could check their understanding of the books using the MReader quiz system. Initially, many of the students would not read easier books, preferring difficult regular classics, but once these students understood they were processing words and not their meanings and were failing the quizzes, they realized they needed to read something at their level. The students were greatly excited when the icon of books they had read appeared on their desktop which led to a rivalry to collect icons as fast as possible. Within the first four weeks, the students had read 360,000 words and passed 213 quizzes.

Considerable time had to be spent on getting the students to read silently in both the NEP and NLP programs. Nepali children typically read or whisper aloud when reading and this is probably due to the way they are taught to read in their first language and a belief that the ability to read aloud means they understand it. A lot of time had to be devoted to training them to read silently. It soon also became evident that learners also needed a lot of time to become familiar with these types of books which they had never seen before, and had to be trained to not just look at the pictures. The program coordinators for both programs stressed the importance of these types of training and such training is relevant in other regions where students are unfamiliar with these materials.

Teachers from each school were trained about extensive reading, its importance and purpose, and the place of reading in the broader curriculum. However, the teacher training also was a challenge for some teachers who were used to the more traditional ways of teaching reading and took time to understand that their role was more as facilitators, role models, and guides than as stand-at-

Case Studies of Extensive Reading Programs   49

the-front teachers. It became clear that the training should be with the actual classroom teachers responsible for the learning, rather than any teacher at the school. In two of the NEP schools, the actual class teachers did not attend the workshops and the training was less effective than it should have been. This lack of communication led to a difficult start.

Some months after the NEP program started, the volunteers returned to the schools to interview the teachers. They found that the reading had not only had a facilitating effect on the learners but also on the teachers who were enjoying the books as much as the learners. One teacher admitted being initially skeptical but was converted when he saw the benefits the learners were getting from the reading and became convinced of the necessity of extensive reading as part of an overall balanced curriculum. The teachers and administrators were very keen to find evidence of language improvement and attitudinal changes in order to be convinced that they needed to change their curriculum to accommodate the reading.

These two programs highlight the importance of not only the universality of the benefits of extensive reading but also the need to be aware of the possible missteps one can make by not fully understanding the local context when introducing extensive reading programs, especially from the outside. There needs to be an understanding of the local teaching and learning methods, the local mindset and attitudes to language learning as well as the local cultural setting in which the extensive reading program will be embedded. Sufficient learner and teacher training needs to take place over several visits; suitable materials must be found and data should be gathered on the effectiveness of the program to provide evidence to the administrators and parents of the need for the program to continue. There is a great danger that single visits may not lead to long-term programs being sustainable, especially programs with inadequate book borrowing systems, insufficiently trained teachers and students, and a lack of integration of the reading into the curriculum.

University of Information Technology, Vietnam National University in Ho Chi Minh City

This program was started by Vuong Ho of the University of Information Technology (UIT), Vietnam National University in 2015. It is embedded in a specific teaching context and has had to respond to teacher and learner expectations that challenged its development. It is a good example of how an extensive reading program can be set up in spite of initial difficulties. It is also a good example of how other well-established programs in other countries can support the establishment of a new program.

Most Vietnamese teachers employ the Grammar-Translation Method, which exclusively emphasizes the rote learning of the language's grammar rules and word-for-word translation, so that they can focus their students on grammar-oriented exams. With little exposure to English-speaking environments outside the classroom, Vietnamese students have few opportunities

50   *Case Studies of Extensive Reading Programs*

to truly practice English to improve their language proficiency. Because the UIT English curriculum has to strictly follow the Department of English's programs, it has been impossible to integrate extensive reading into the official curriculum, and this makes this program entirely voluntary despite being set in an educational institution.

The situation is even more challenging for Information and Communication Technology students at UIT due to the lack of time allotted to the English program. The program comprises 180 periods each lasting 45 minutes. Despite this, they are still required to gain a TOEIC score of at least 450 on the listening and reading sections to meet graduation requirements.

Due to the lack of resources to build an extensive reading program library and to make language teaching and learning more effective at UIT, at the beginning of 2016, Vuong Ho conducted a joint extensive reading program with the Nagoya Institute of Technology (NIT), Toyota College in Aichi Prefecture, Japan which already had an established extensive reading program. The joint program involved (1) NIT lending a large number of graded readers from their library for two years to UIT to start the extensive reading program; (2) teacher visits to both schools to conduct extensive reading research and present their findings; and (3) the setting up of extracurricular activities for learners to practice English reading beyond the classroom involving NIT students visiting UIT.

The extensive reading program started with 42 first-year students from elementary to pre-intermediate English levels agreeing to join the extensive reading program for two consecutive academic school years. After two years, the extensive reading club was able to build its own extensive reading library with more than 1,000 graded readers donated and sponsored from overseas organizations, including the Tadoku (Extensive Reading) group from NIT, Toyota College, Akio Furukawa's library from SEG, and the Extensive Reading Foundation.

The books are kept in the 'English Zone' and this room is locked with the keys held by the teacher and a responsible student and is open once or twice a week at set times depending on the students' schedules. The books are kept in a locked bookcase. Each book has a label with word counts and a difficulty level (based on the SEG system which is commonly used by Japanese teachers) for easy reference. Some learners in the extensive reading program monitor the borrowing of the books and a Google sheet is used to record the borrowing process.

The learners are encouraged to read at least one graded reader per week outside the classroom, with continuous encouragement and reminders from the teacher. They choose their books according to either the level of difficulty or their own interests. The students record their reading in their journals, and they meet the teacher at least once a week to borrow books and to receive some feedback or suggestions. The students should read at least 50,000 words in each of the two semesters (and the non-compulsory summer program), and

Case Studies of Extensive Reading Programs   51

they are expected to read a total of 150,000 to 300,000 words per year. At the end of each semester, a TOEIC-based reading comprehension test is conducted to evaluate the learners' reading levels. It is expected that the learners will keep on with their reading and read at least one million words during their four-year college life, so that extensive reading can more positively affect TOEIC scores and their English proficiency.

To meet these goals, the learners need encouragement from the teacher to keep their reading progress on track. There are extensive reading meetings weekly or fortnightly for extensive reading members to discuss their reading progress and do some extensive reading activities, such as book talk, book discussion, or role play. As well as this, some big extensive reading events are held every semester to keep the learners enthusiastic. These include theme-based reading events for *Detective Week*, Halloween, and Christmas, extensive reading seminars for learners and teachers. Learners are also divided into smaller groups so that they can monitor their friends' reading progress together.

The success of the program is striking in that the learners are taking part in the extensive reading program voluntarily, not for credit. The group has expanded from the initial 42 voluntary students to over 100 students within two years. Internal research shows positive attitudes towards reading in English and the program has developed the learners' reading autonomy. This can be seen from the increasing number of books they borrowed, and the move to read higher difficulty level books over time. This program is an example of how a single resourceful and motivated teacher can achieve good results in spite of the surrounding environmental and financial constraints facing the program at the beginning.

Sanata Dharma University in Yogyakarta, Indonesia

The following case study describes the introduction of extensive reading and the setting up of an extensive reading association. It marks the beginning of what could be an important initiative for this university and the schools it serves within Indonesia with the aim of being a model for other parts of Indonesia.

Sanata Dharma University (SDU) is a leading teacher training institution in Indonesia. In 2016 under its English Language Education Study Program (ELESP), Yuseva Ariyani Iswandari (the Chair), Lhaksmita Anandari, and Ouda Teda Ena of the university formed the Indonesian Extensive Reading Association (IERA; http://iera-extensivereading.id/). It was formally affiliated with the ERF in 2016. The main purpose of the establishment of IERA is to introduce the concept of English extensive reading to English teachers and students at schools.

The extensive reading collection at SDU serves two purposes: first, to provide reading materials for the SDU students; and second, to display extensive reading materials for school partners under the ELESP teaching practicum. Recently the extensive reading collection has also been used to introduce extensive reading in the teacher professional education program.

52 Case Studies of Extensive Reading Programs

The collection and the extensive reading classes are made available at certain times for outsiders to see. As a result of this outreach program, several schools in the area have started their own extensive reading programs, some with graded readers and others digitally using www.er-central.com or the reading materials on www.lextutor.ca. The program receives about 5 million Indonesian rupiah per year (US$330), not for books, but for maintaining the library and setting up extensive reading programs at those schools.

The books are kept in the 'IERA Reading Corner' which contains some 800 books, 750 of which are donated graded readers from private collections, book lotteries, and other donations, plus 50 more Asian Story leveled readers – 450 of these books were donated by Mark Alberding with help from the ERF. The Regional English Language Office of the US State Department has also stated its intention to support this program. The library was purposefully called a 'reading corner' to prevent the university library commandeering the collection which would prevent the books being used in the outreach program. It would have also meant that the books were available for general use and the lack of titles would have prevented the books from being used in specific classes. The room has display shelves, carpets, tables and chairs and a sofa to make reading comfortable. The room is open only on Mondays, Wednesdays, and Thursdays from 9am to 4pm and is run by an assistant to the teaching staff. Students can borrow any books they like but must register their time in the room and record what they read and for how long. Currently, these data are collected on paper but hopefully will be digitalized soon.

The books are labeled by their headword counts and categorized and displayed by level by publisher rather than by a uniform leveling system across all publishers. In the near future and as the library grows, the coordinator plans to put the books by level. The aim is to make the extensive reading program seem achievable, fun, and motivating and to develop a positive attitude to reading. The program coordinator decided not to organize the books by level at this stage in the development of the program because the students are in an EFL setting. She wants the students to be able to choose the book they like regardless of level so they can get interested in reading.

The reading is assigned to seven classes (typically 25–30 students each) in their first or second years of the undergraduate program. They visit the room and work with their reading and vocabulary teachers and return to the classroom to read about one book per week, more for the teacher training students. The reading is validated by using the online forum ExseLSa, in-class discussions, and by submitting a reading record sheet. Students are not assessed using MReader at this stage but may be in the future. The students were motivated by writing a letter and making a Skype call to Michael Lacey Freeman to discuss his award-winning book 'Egghead'. The students report a very positive reaction to the program. Most of the students, and even the teachers on the professional program, had never seen books like graded readers and were using the library for their own education.

Case Studies of Extensive Reading Programs 53

This program shows how resourceful and motivated teachers can not only create their own extensive reading program, but also use it as an 'ER lighthouse' to spread extensive reading across the region. Their work for IERA also has had an effect nationally with the staff setting up 'ER Roadshow' tours of Indonesia which has led not only to heightened interest in IERA itself, but to an increase in membership of their Facebook page.

These case studies reflect a wide variety of circumstances and challenges and the responses show how local conditions need to be carefully considered when introducing and designing an extensive reading program. However, the case studies also show that setting up a program usually requires someone to make a brave step to try something that may not work but which is well supported by research and examples in other countries.

4 How Do You Set Up and Run an Extensive Reading Program?

How Do I Set Up an Extensive Reading Program?

The three most important things to give attention to when setting up an extensive reading program are that (1) there are plenty of texts at the right level for the learners, (2) the learners are given the time and firm encouragement to do plenty of reading, and (3) there are two strands to the extensive reading program – the meaning-focused input strand where learners read texts which are at the right level for them with a few words just beyond their present knowledge, and the fluency development strand where the learners read texts which are very easy, but they read them as quickly as possible with a focus on increasing their reading speed.

While the benefits of extensive reading are straightforward, implementing a program can present a number of challenges. The first challenge is financial. To start a program, a relatively large number of books is needed. If a school has 100 students, a library of 100 books will be insufficient because that will not give learners enough choices, especially if the learners are reading at different levels. At minimum the number of books should be several times the number of learners with a good mix of levels and genres. However, this should not deter teachers from setting up a library with a smaller number of titles. In practical terms, if a reading program has 20 learners reading from a set of 30 books at that level, and each learner borrows one book, each learner has 11 books to choose from. Once a library of graded readers is built, it has to be managed. As reading is typically done outside of class, learners will be taking books home. While theft of books is unlikely, graded readers, which are relatively small, are easily lost or forgotten, and because they change hands often, they are more likely to be damaged. Often learners who have over-run the return date are embarrassed to hand books back to a teacher, so many libraries have a 'book-drop box' for students to return their books without the fear of being scolded. Building a library and having someone available to manage it can come at considerable cost. In fact, some libraries have found it cheaper to accept book losses rather than pay someone to manage the library itself.

For academic programs where assigning grades to learners is expected, such as universities and high schools, tracking students' reading progress is

Setting Up an Extensive Reading Program 55

necessary. If learners feel that their effort is not assessed, or at least acknowledged, the reading will only be done by the most motivated students. However, in a typical extensive reading program, where learners are all reading different books, each at their own pace, tracking can be difficult, especially for large classes.

Other challenges are guiding learners to books that are appropriate for their reading ability, and giving learners access to the audio narrations. Most publishers make professionally narrated audio to accompany their graded readers. This is great for linking the spoken word with the text, or practicing extensive listening. However, the audio often comes on a CD, and most learners today do not have CD players. To solve this, some schools install the audio tracks onto a computer so students can listen to them at any time.

Fortunately, there are some digital solutions created specifically to overcome these challenges. One is MReader which is a learner management system with online quizzes for over 7,000 graded readers and other books language learners typically read. Teachers can set their classes up on MReader, and then, after reading a book, learners can login and take a quiz for that book. If they pass the quiz, they get the word credit for that book. A major benefit of MReader is that it is free; however, it provides only quizzes, not the books themselves.

Another option is Xreading (www.xreading.com) which is a website created specifically to help schools implement extensive reading programs. It gives learners unlimited access to a digital library of over 1,000 graded readers from major publishers that they can read on their computer or mobile device. Besides the books, it has audio narrations of the stories at various speeds, quizzes, ratings, and background information. Additionally, Xreading allows teachers to track their learners' reading progress, including the books and number of words they have read, their reading time, and reading speed.

Xreading is not free. It is a commercial site that requires subscriptions, either paid for by the schools, or the learners themselves, however, the cost is low. The highest cost for a subscription is US$5.00 per month, but very large discounts are available depending on the country, class size, and length of subscription. For example, in Japan the cost per student is approximately US $2.00 per month (with a six-month subscription), while in Vietnam the monthly cost is closer to US$0.50 cents per student. For the duration of their subscription, learners can read as many books as they wish.

Most major publishers of graded readers, such as Cambridge University Press, National Geographic Learning, Pearson, Macmillan, E-Future, Seed Learning, Helbling, and Compass Publishing, plus many smaller publishers, have made their graded readers available on the site, and new titles are regularly being added. Xreading also hosts titles by individual or independent authors. The titles include a lot of the prize-winning graded readers from the ERF Language Learner Literature Awards. The mid-frequency readers are also available through Xreading.

56   *Setting Up an Extensive Reading Program*

One of the most important features of Xreading is that it allows simultaneous access to the books. In other words, all learners in a school can read the same book at the same time. This means that every book has the potential to be a class reader. This also means that Xreading doesn't have just 1,000 books, but rather 1,000 books per student.

There are short quizzes available for each book that learners can take online, or teachers can print and administer in class. Quizzes can help determine if a student has genuinely read the book, and they give learners a sense of accomplishment. Additionally, almost every book has an audio accompaniment, so learners can read and listen or just listen to a book. The audio speed can be adjusted to suit the learner's reading speed. There are also book ratings and reviews to help in the selection of books.

The reading can be done on a personal computer, tablet, or cell-phone that is connected to the internet. One drawback to reading on Xreading is it requires internet access; however, an app which will allow offline reading is being developed. There are a few other limitations to Xreading. Currently Xreading is for use at institutions and not for independent learners. Learners have to be part of a class, although there is no minimum size for a class or institution, so a teacher who gives private lessons to a few learners can still use it. Due to licensing restrictions from the publishers, not all books are available in all countries.

There are enormous advantages in having an electronic library of graded readers for extensive reading. First, a school does not have to set up an extensive reading library. The electronic library is already there, with books at a complete range of levels from beginning to advanced. The website uses the ERF set of levels to deal with the varying sets of levels used by publishers. Second, the learners' borrowing and reading is monitored and their comprehension can be quickly tested. The teachers or the learners do not have to do any record-keeping. The learner management scheme provides feedback on the books read and their level, the number of words read, reading speed, and comprehension scores. Third, the learners have access to an electronic word look-up dictionary as they read, so they can read independently. Xreading is also considering providing speed reading courses, such as the material by Sonia Millet hosted on Paul Nation's website.

As it is, Xreading takes away the cost, time, availability, and management issues that might prevent teachers from running an extensive reading program. Teachers just need to decide to make extensive reading part of their course.

Clearly, the easiest way to set up an extensive reading program is to use an extensive reading subscription site like Xreading which provides the material and organizes most things for you. However, to see more clearly what is involved, let us look at setting up a program which uses hard-copy books.

Very simply, the steps involved are these:

1   Get plenty of books at the right levels for the learners.

Setting Up an Extensive Reading Program 57

2 Set aside a regular time for silent reading, about 15 to 20 minutes at first, but later extensive reading including reading fluency practice should make up close to a quarter of the total in-class and out-of-class learning time and should mostly be done out of class
3 Get the learners to choose the book they want to read.
4 Let them get on with the reading without interruption.
5 Each time they finish reading a book, get them to fill in a brief report form or sit a short test on the book so you can log their progress and monitor it, and then let them choose a new book to read.
6 Encourage them to do plenty of reading.
7 Gradually help learners see the value of extensive reading and help them develop strategies to maintain their reading and to learn from their reading.

You need to have plenty of books at the right level for your learners. That is, you need some books which contain a small amount of unknown vocabulary for them, and you need some books that are very easy for them to read and which contain little or no unknown vocabulary. Ideally, however, there should be plenty of extensive reading books available at the right levels.

For teachers looking to set up an extensive reading library we recommend downloading the free guide to extensive reading from the ERF website. It is available in multiple languages.

How Do I Introduce the Learners to Extensive Reading?

When learners are new to extensive reading, it is very useful to set aside a regular time for such reading. It is important to briefly prepare learners for this reading by explaining that:

- it is a time for silent reading,
- the main aim of the reading is to understand and enjoy the book they are reading,
- they should choose a book which is at the right level for them; if a book is too difficult, it should be changed for one which is less difficult,
- there are two types of extensive reading – reading where there are a few unknown words, and reading for fluency – and learners should do both kinds of reading at various times during the extensive reading program,
- the reading is not assessed but the learners must keep a record of what they have read,
- it is important to do large quantities of reading and the best learner is the learner who reads the most,
- learners can look up words in dictionaries while they read, but if they can guess the meaning of the word then they should just carry on without looking up the word.

58 *Setting Up an Extensive Reading Program*

At various times it is useful to hold class discussions about the goals and issues in extensive reading, so that learners can see the value in it and commit themselves to doing it properly. Getting learners to understand the steps, reasons, values, and effects of doing extensive reading can be a good way of keeping them motivated to do the reading.

The next step is to get the learners doing extensive reading regularly. First, they choose a book which seems to be at the right level for them and which looks interesting. Then they sit down and quietly read the book. They can look up unknown words in their dictionaries if they wish (bilingual dictionaries and electronic dictionaries are very satisfactory resources for learners), but if they find that they are looking up more than two or three words on the page, they have probably chosen a book which is too difficult for them and should exchange it for another more suitable one. At the end of the reading time, they place a bookmark in the book to mark where they are up to, and continue to read the book for homework if they are allowed to take it home, or read it in the next extensive reading session in class. When they complete a book, they quickly fill in their report form for it, and choose another book to read.

An extensive reading session is as simple as that – the learners get on with the job of reading.

How Can Learners Know Which Books Are at the Right Level For Them?

The easiest way to see if a book is at the right level is for a learner to choose a book and if it seems easy to read and there are only a small number of unknown words (no more than two or three words per page) and they understand almost everything, then that is a suitable book. Research has shown that learners can make good judgments about this (Wan-a-rom, 2010).

It is useful if teachers know the vocabulary sizes of their learners, and learners should also know their current vocabulary size. This can be found by sitting the first few levels of the Updated Vocabulary Levels Test developed by Webb, Sasao, and Ballance (2017), or the New Vocabulary Levels Test (McLean & Kramer, 2015). Both tests are available from Paul Nation's website at www.victoria.ac.nz/lals/staff/paul-nation.aspx. The learners' vocabulary size can then be roughly matched to the graded reader levels.

For fluency development, the learners should choose very easy books containing no or few unknown words. Re-reading books that they have read before is also good for fluency development.

How Do You Get Unmotivated Learners To Do the Reading?

The research on this issue is reviewed in Chapter 7. There needs to be a combination of factors all encouraging learners to read. First, the learners have to realize that there are books that they are capable of reading. This involves matching each learner with the right books. Second, they need to experience that reading can become enjoyable. Third, they need to see that their reading improves as they do more reading and that reading helps their language knowledge in a variety of ways. These all involve learners doing the reading, at first under close supervision and monitoring. This reading should be accompanied by the teacher helping the learners understand how to do extensive reading and the benefits of extensive reading, and guiding them to read the most appropriate materials.

If the learners are not motivated, extensive reading should be done in class time and should count towards some kind of assessment. The assessment can be based on tests on the books done through MReader or Xreading.

There are several teachers who have faced this problem of unmotivated readers, who have solved it, and who have written about their success. In our experience, most of the resistance to extensive reading comes from a poorly stocked, unbalanced, or inappropriate library collection. The most obvious solution is to ensure the learners are reading something interesting so teachers can ask learners which books to buy by taking them to the bookstore or showing them publishers' catalogs. Learners can be encouraged to put smiley faces ☺ or ☹) inside the front cover of the books to indicate their feeling to other learners, and as feedback for the teacher.

The more learner involvement in the library there is, the greater their sense of attachment to it. If they are also assigned jobs such as making book displays, giving book reports, making posters for the library, or turning the book into a class play, these jobs can have a great effect on learner engagement and relieve the boredom of filling in forms or reports. There are many more ideas in the ERF Guide to Extensive Reading.

What Should the Teacher Do During an Extensive Reading Session?

Some teachers consider that they should also read quietly during an extensive reading session to act as a model for the learners. One advantage of doing this is that learners can see that if they talk or misbehave during the extensive reading session, they are interrupting the teacher's reading in the same way that they are interrupting their classmates' reading. This may encourage them to get on with their own reading. However, this should only be done once the learners' needs are taken care of, such as advising them about their reading or directing them in their tasks.

Every so often, the teacher should look at learners' report sheets, or talk quietly with the learners individually to see that they are reading enough and that they are reading at the right level. The teacher should also check to see that each learner is doing some reading for fluency development (by reading very easy books quickly) and some reading for normal language development (by reading books which contain some unknown words). This checking can be done during the extensive reading session, although the disadvantage of this is

60 *Setting Up an Extensive Reading Program*

that it does interrupt some learners' reading so the teacher should whisper or sit near the learner.

The teacher can also use this time to quietly observe the learners and see who is reading well and who is not. It is highly likely that giving some individual counselling and attention to those who are not reading will result in a stronger commitment to the extensive reading program. Teachers can look for learners who turn pages slowly, or look in their dictionary too often, or who look disinterested in their book and go and talk to them.

How Can We Make Sure That the Learners Are Doing the Extensive Reading?

Teachers need some way of the learners keeping a record of what they have read and their brief reaction to it, so that the learners can see how much they have read and the teacher can monitor the amount of reading that they did. A simple way to do this is to have a table like the following on a sheet of paper.

Title of the book	Series & Level	Purpose	Date begun	Date finished	Comment on the book	Interest

In the column headed 'Purpose' the learner can indicate whether the book was read for fluency development or for normal reading. In the column headed 'Interest', the learner can give the book a ranking from one to five in terms of how interesting the book was for them. This gives the teacher some idea about which are the popular books and other learners can look at their friends' rankings to see what books they might want to read next (see the www.er-central website for other worksheets).

The learners can also log on to a website that provides tests for each graded reader and keeps a record for the class that the teacher can access (http://moodlereader.org/index.html/).

How Should I Organize an Extensive Reading Library?

It is important that an extensive reading program includes texts at a variety of vocabulary levels.

Although publishers use different grading schemes and different lists, it is best if an extensive reading program does not limit itself to one series of readers but chooses the best from a variety of series. The matching of learners' vocabulary levels to graded readers is a very inexact process and always will be so. Any one graded reader only uses some of the words available at a particular level in the

Setting Up an Extensive Reading Program 61

scheme, and so having graded readers from different schemes is not a big issue when it comes to finding suitable texts for learners.

The books in an extensive reading library should be clearly labeled so that learners are aware of the level of each book. Although publishers put this information somewhere in the book or on the back cover, it is not always easy to find. Moreover, as not all publishers follow the same scheme, it is best if institutions use their own leveling system. One solution is to label the books with colored stickers with each color representing a different level, or with a number on the sticker to indicate a standard set of levels. Most libraries have six–eight levels. The ERF provides an overall set of graded reader levels that shows how one series compares to another along a standard scale on its website at www.erfoundation.org and these levels can be used as a basis for colored or numbered stickers.

Each class may have its own extensive reading library but this is probably a wasteful use of resources, and it may be enough to have a library on a trolley which can be wheeled from class to class, or an easily accessible central library where the learners can go to borrow books. Alternatively, some teachers use a small suitcase to carry the books around and keep them locked up. The advantage of using a central library which has a formal book borrowing system is that the teacher then does not have to keep track of the books.

Whatever kind of library is used, it is important that the books are easily accessible and attractively displayed. Learners may need a lot of encouragement to begin doing extensive reading seriously, and the accessibility and display of books is one part of providing this encouragement. Learners can work in groups to make displays about the best books as determined by the class. They can also show the Language Literature Award winners, or a horror series, a travel display, and so on. Getting learners involved in building these displays and presenting on them to the class not only requires the learners to get to know their library better, but creates a closer personal attachment to it.

How Do I Set Up an Extensive Reading Program If My School Has No Budget to Buy the Books?

The first thing to do is to see what graded readers are already available within the school. By looking carefully within the school library, it may be possible to find some graded readers that the school already own. Indeed, the librarians themselves may not be aware of these books in their stock, especially if they were bought years ago and by different staff. If the school has no graded readers and no money to buy them, then one alternative is to ask each learner to buy a graded reader and to make sure that each learner buys a different title. Teachers can recommend they each select a book from a publisher's catalogue at the appropriate level, or by taking them to a bookstore. In this way learners can read the book that they have bought and then lend it to their classmates and maybe later donate it to the school

62   *Setting Up an Extensive Reading Program*

library. To help the learners and teachers make a decision, some publishers make the first chapter of a graded reader freely available on the web.

It is also possible to do fund raising activities in order to raise money for graded readers such as sponsored reading marathons, selling cookies at the school festival, or doing chores in the neighborhood to earn money to buy books. Classes can compete to raise the most. Teachers should ask the school principal, the city education board, or the state board which often have grants for these types of projects. Sometimes generous companies will donate money or resources. This is likely to be more successful if teachers co-operate in the fund raising and in the subsequent use of the graded readers. It is best, of course, to get a recurring budget for books rather than a one-time lump of money because books get lost and pages come out. However, when funds become available, it is best not to spend it all at once so that more of the books in demand can be added to tune the library to the learners' needs. It is likely teachers will not know this until after the library has been running for a while.

Xreading is a subscription scheme for reading electronic graded readers and this could be used instead of hard-copy readers. Each learner needs to pay a small fee for access to a very large number of graded readers at a wide range of levels.

How Much Time Should Learners Spend On Extensive Reading?

Ideally just under one-quarter of the total course time (including class time and homework time) should be spent on extensive reading. This includes extensive reading for fluency development.

Spending just under one-quarter of the course time on extensive reading may seem like a lot but this is actually more of an under-estimate of the time needed than an over-estimate. Some researchers have suggested that almost all of the course time should be spent on extensive reading or extensive listening. There is good evidence, however, that important learning occurs through meaning-focused output and language-focused learning, and thus that these should also be part of a well-balanced course.

While the time spent on extensive reading may initially be class time, over a period of time, extensive reading can become more of an out-of-class activity.

Should an Extensive Reading Program Include a Speed Reading Course?

It is very useful if an extensive reading course is accompanied by a speed reading course. The purpose of this is to increase the learners' reading speed so that they can read more fluently and thus read more within the same time. A speed reading course involves passages followed by comprehension questions. Free speed reading courses at various levels from the 500 head-word level written by Sonia Millett can be found on Paul Nation's website (www.victoria.ac.nz/lals/about/staff/paul-nation). The books in the *Reading for Speed and Fluency* series (Nation, 2018) are published speed reading courses at the 500, 1,000, 1,500, and 2,000 word levels. Speed reading courses should only involve vocabulary that the learners already know because their aim is fluency development not language learning.

How Much Should Learners Read?

Research by Nation and Wang (1999) on the *Oxford Bookworms* series suggested that learners should be reading one graded reader a week in order to get enough repetitions of the new words at a level in order to be sure that vocabulary learning occurs. So, when we say that learners should do large quantities of extensive reading, we mean that they should be reading at least one book a week. Books differ in their length and in the Nation and Wang study, the books at the easiest level were around 5,000 words long. If the learners are reading really short books, then at the beginning level they should be reading around 5,000 words a week. A list of the lengths of thousands of graded readers is available on the ERF website.

This sounds like a lot of reading and it is, but it must be remembered that such reading only involves a small number of unknown words (around two to three unknown words per hundred running words of text) and thus can be read quite quickly. If learners read at the very slow speed of 100 words per minute (wpm), it would take 50 minutes to read 5,000 words.

Research by Waring (2013) shows that even adding one or two graded readers per week to an existing course greatly increases the amount of vocabulary learners meet, and increases the number of repetitions of many of the words which leads to higher rates of vocabulary learning.

Table 4.1 shows the amount of reading a learner has to do to in order to reach a specific proficiency level if the learner meets all of the words at that level 20 times. For example, an absolute beginner wanting to learn the 300 words at the beginner level would need to read 52,157 words in order to meet those 300 words at least 20 times. As Table 4.1 shows, at a slow reading speed of 90 words per minute this would take a total of 9.7 hours (52,157 divided by 90, and then divided by 60 to change minutes into hours). An absolute beginner wanting to reach the upper intermediate level will need to read 653,595 words to meet all the 2,400 most frequent words 20 times to get to that level.

Table 4.1 just considers how much an absolute beginner would need to read. Table 4.2 uses the same data to see how many words would have to be read to go from any one level to another. For example, a beginner who already knows 300 words would need to read 85,660 words of graded readers to meet the additional 500 words at least 20 times to get to the 800 word elementary level. Once they had got to the elementary level, they would need to read another 169,308 words to learn the additional words at the intermediate level.

An absolute beginner knows little or no English. As shown in Table 4.1, a beginner is assumed to know around 300 words. To meet the 500 additional words needed to get from the beginner level to the intermediate level

Table 4.1 The Number of Words and Books Needed to be Read, and the Number of Hours It Will Take to Get to a Certain Level

	Beginner	Elementary	Intermediate	Upper intermediate	Lower advanced	Upper advanced
To meet all these words 20 times …	300	800	1,500	2,400	3,800	4,500
… learners need to meet this number of words.	52,157	137,817	307,125	653,594	1,545,595	2,222,222
If learners read this number of words per minute …	90	130	150	150	150	150
…it will take them a total of … hours.	9.7	17.7	34.1	72.6	171.7	246.9

Setting Up an Extensive Reading Program 65

Table 4.2 The Number of Words Needed to Be Read to Get a Learner from One Proficiency Level to Another

Absolute Beginner to Beginner	Beginner to Elementary	Elementary to Intermediate	Intermediate to Upper Intermediate	Upper Intermediate to Lower Advanced	Lower Advanced to Upper Advanced
52,157	85,660	169,308	346,469	892,000	676,628

(800 words), a beginner would need to read around another 169,308 words. Table 4.2 just looks at the amount of words to be read. This can be converted into time required by choosing a reading speed and dividing the number of words by the reading speed. For example, to read the 85,660 words needed to go from the beginner to elementary level at 90 wpm would take 952 minutes or almost 16 hours.

The point of Tables 4.1 and 4.2 is not to provide definitive amounts of reading and time, but is to show that learners need to read a lot to increase their vocabulary size, but the amount of reading required and the time needed to do it is feasible.

It should be noted that these data show how many words need to be met based on the assumption that 20 meetings is sufficient for immediate recognition. Research shows that the uptake rate from reading varies considerably with some estimates that as high as 30 repetitions are needed or even higher depending on the word. If this is so, the data will under-estimate the task at hand. Similarly, the reading speeds are only indicative, and the reader should only look at these tables as a guide as there will be considerable individual variation. On the plus side, once a learner has read a certain volume of text to reach a certain level, they will have had significant exposure to many words above that level (up to 19 times) and this partial knowledge is not accounted for here but will serve the learners well as they increase their level. The tables also assume that the only language input is through reading. Clearly extensive reading needs to be only part of a language course and the other parts of the course will provide many opportunities to meet and use the target words.

The data from these tables support the idea that learners should read for 15–20 minutes a day. If an absolute beginner wants to get to the lower advanced level of 3,800 different words, she needs to read about 1.5 million words. Reading 20 minutes a day at a speed of 150 wpm, five days a week, 40 weeks a year will take her close to three years. Two minutes a day will take 25 years. Teachers and curriculum designers should bear this in mind when planning how much reading needs to be done.

Teachers are not advised to sit their learners down and just get them to read for these amounts of times. This reading should be part of an overall balanced curriculum.

Should Learners Look Up Unknown Words in a Dictionary as They Read?

It is often strongly recommended that dictionaries should not be used during extensive reading and when trying to read fluently. The main motivations for this piece of advice are the following:

1   If learners look up a lot of words, it means that they are reading a text which is not at the right level for them to read smoothly and quickly and their brain is in a 'study' mode, not one focusing on the meaning of the text itself. Using a dictionary may encourage reading of text which is in fact unsuitable for extensive reading for that learner.
2   Using a dictionary discourages guessing the meaning of unknown words from context. Guessing from context is a very important vocabulary coping strategy that needs a lot of real-time practice.
3   Using a dictionary slows down reading and so less is read. One estimate suggests that students reading and looking up two words in every 100 in a dictionary read at about 15–20 wpm. This is because their attention goes back and forth from the books to the dictionary.
4   Not all words are equally important. Some words will be met again soon and others probably not for months. Many students are not good at selecting the most appropriate words to look up in a dictionary and adopt a 'dictionary reflex' where they immediately look up anything they do not know. This wastes valuable learning time as they should be focused on optimizing their learning and should only focus on words they will likely need again soon.

However, as long as learners do not need to look up many words, looking words up in a dictionary is good because it increases the chance of words being learned through certain access to the meaning and deliberate attention, and may contribute to improved comprehension. The best advice is to only use a dictionary during extensive reading when they really need to use it, and make sure that the dictionary is not used very often. Some teachers suggest learners only choose one word for every two pages to look up.

How Do I Measure if Learners Are Learning From the Extensive Reading Program?

Probably, the best measure for determining the success of an extensive reading program is observing how much the learners read and whether they read with enjoyment. If it is necessary to give learners a grade for extensive reading, it could be based on the number of books, pages, or words that the learners have read. The learners can be required to take an online test to show they have read and understood each book. Alternatively, a reading comprehension test could be given using the same kind of material that was used for extensive reading.

However, in high-stakes situations where the learner's grades are determined at least in part by the volume read, it is almost certain some students will try to cheat the system (see Chapter 3) and in these circumstances it may be best to grade students on the tasks after extensive reading such as their reports, oral presentations, and so on. If so, it is essential the post-reading task is set up so that it can only be done after having read the book. A simple summary report, for example, might be lifted from a publisher's website, so a summary may not be a useful test. See the ER Central website for further ideas on assessing extensive reading (www.er-central.com/).

Should University Students Be Reading Graded Readers?

Graded readers typically cover the 3,000 most frequent and common words in English. Learners studying at university through the medium of English need a much larger vocabulary than this, ideally more than 8,000 words, but learners can succeed at university with vocabulary sizes as low as 5,000 words, although they will struggle with their reading. It is thus important to test learners' vocabulary size using the Updated Vocabulary Levels Test or New Vocabulary Levels Test (www.victoria.ac.nz/lals/about/staff/paul-na tion) to see how many words they know before starting extensive reading.

If the learners know more than 3,000 words, graded readers will only be useful for fluency development, and it would be much more useful for learners to read extensively in their subject areas. The technical vocabulary of their subject areas will cover a large proportion of the running words in their subject matter texts (Chung & Nation, 2003), and this vocabulary is important for them.

If the learners know fewer than 3,000 words, then reading graded readers is a very effective way of helping gain control of the very important high frequency words of English, as well as helping develop reading fluency.

One major problem facing many university courses is that the students need to read in a certain academic field such as dentistry, medicine, engineering, and science. However, very few graded readers are available on these topics – especially non-fiction materials. The vocabulary in fiction tends to be more like spoken vocabulary partly because it often contains dialogue, but also because the mid-frequency technical vocabulary is rarely used. It is therefore essential that learners who have mastered, say, 1,500 to 2,000 basic words should start to read in their topic area as well as continuing to read graded readers. One way around this problem is for the teacher to require the learners to print out or photocopy a text on a certain topic, maybe from a webpage, magazine, journal, or suchlike in their discipline. This text will contain lots of words they do not know, but a high percentage of technical vocabulary they need for their field. The learner then reads the text with a dictionary and annotates the print-out by writing the definitions or translations on the paper. The learner brings the paper to class and explains what it is about to a second learner who has also done this. They then swap the papers and read them. The second reader now will have an easier time reading it because of all the work the first learner did. The second reader can

68　*Setting Up an Extensive Reading Program*

now also annotate the text with words she or he does not know. If the whole class does this every week and shares these texts, the class will soon have a library of hundreds of student selected, student interest materials graded by the students with very little work done by the teacher.

Commonly Asked Questions

We have looked at extensive reading and graded readers, and how to run and set up an extensive reading program. We will now look at the goals and values of having an extensive reading program, and some frequently asked questions.

How Can I Convince Other Teachers That It Is Good to Do Extensive Reading?

First, make sure that they really know what extensive reading is, particularly that it involves reading a lot at the right level.

Next, mention some of the books and research about extensive reading to show them that this is a well-researched area. Chapter 6 looks at the most important studies on extensive reading. It is worth mentioning some of these studies, and the books by Day and Bamford (1998, 2004). If there is a local or national extensive reading group, it is worth letting the teachers know about this. The ERF holds international conferences on extensive reading every two years and attending these is a fantastic way to exchange ideas and make contacts. Encouraging senior teachers to attend these talks can make them more aware of what is needed when setting up and running a library.

Next, talk about the goals of extensive reading and why it is important to have a range of opportunities for learning across the four strands of meaning-focused input, meaning-focused output, language-focused learning, and fluency development.

Get the teachers to experience extensive reading. Cho (2014) showed that getting teachers to experience extensive reading themselves over a two-week period had a strong and lasting effect on their willingness to make extensive reading part of their teaching program.

Finally, talk about how easy it is to organize and run an extensive reading program, especially one involving reading online.

What Are the Goals of Extensive Reading?

When learners do extensive reading, they learn a lot of things without realizing that the learning is going on. This is because they are focused on enjoying the book that they are reading. This kind of learning is called 'incidental learning', because from the readers' viewpoint, this learning is not the main purpose of the reading. The main purpose is to understand and enjoy what is being read.

Setting Up an Extensive Reading Program   69

The goals of a language program can be classified under the headings of language, ideas, skills, and text. The first letters of these four words make up another word, LIST, which is a useful way to remember this list of goals:

Language goals include the learning of spelling, vocabulary, and grammar.
Ideas goals include learning new ideas through reading, such as learning new facts about the world or experiencing interesting stories.
Skill goals include the four skills of listening, speaking, reading, and writing, and in a reading course these goals are particularly focused on the skill of learning to read with good comprehension and with fluency. As learners become more fluent in their reading, then they can more easily apply critical skills and application skills to what they are reading.
Text goals include becoming familiar with the text or discourse of the language that they are meeting. That is, learning how different written texts and conversations are organized and the conventions that exist in such texts. Essays and instructions, for example, are not structured the same way as poems or magazine articles.

It is clear from the research that teachers can expect more than just improvement in reading from an extensive reading program. They can expect that learners will grow in their knowledge of the language, develop good reading skills, come to enjoy reading, and also show an improvement in other skills besides reading.

How Much of the Course Time Should Be Devoted to Extensive Reading?

A well-balanced language course spends an equal amount of time on each of the four strands of meaning-focused input, meaning-focused output, language-focused learning, and fluency development (Nation, 2007). Meaning-focused input involves learning from listening and reading where the learners' main attention is focused on the message. That is, their focus is on comprehending what they listen to or read.

Meaning-focused input should make up one-quarter of the time on a course. Around half of this time should be spent on reading (the other half is spent on listening) and most of this reading should be extensive reading. The language-focused learning strand, typically occurring in course books, should build the learners' knowledge of text structure, guessing skills, and their ability to decode ideas from a text. The fluency development strand should make up one-quarter of the time on a course, and this time should be shared between listening fluency development, speaking fluency development, reading fluency development, and writing fluency development. Most, but not all, of the reading fluency development time should be spent doing extensive reading of very easy books where there are no unknown language items and where the topic is to some degree familiar to the learners. There should also be a small language-focused learning aspect to extensive reading where learners learn about the goals of extensive

70 *Setting Up an Extensive Reading Program*

reading, about the importance of reading a lot, about the importance of reading at the right level, and about the importance of noting down any new words which are met on word cards or in a flash-card program so that they can be deliberately studied later. In total, adding these three strands together means that just under one-quarter of the total course time (which includes time for doing homework) should be spent on extensive reading for meaning-focused input and for fluency development.

Why Are Teachers Reluctant to Set Up Extensive Reading Programs?

In spite of the large amount of research and writing on the benefits of extensive reading, there are not as many extensive reading programs in schools as there should be. Why is there this lack of extensive reading programs?

One answer may be that teachers do not know of the research on the benefits of extensive reading. Another answer is that extensive reading does not involve teaching, and so when learners do extensive reading, teachers feel that they are not doing their job. That is, they feel they are not teaching in front of the class. They may think "How can I be earning my salary when I am just sitting here reading as the learners quietly get on with their reading?" These teachers seem to think that learning stops when they stop teaching. Learners may also have the expectation that the teacher should be teaching. This is related to the belief that learning only occurs as a result of teaching. This is clearly a false belief because there is a lot of evidence to show first that plenty of learning happens within extensive reading without direct teaching, and second that direct teaching is not particularly effective in encouraging learning.

In a well-balanced language course, three-quarters of the time should be spent on message-focused activities that do not involve the teacher in direct language teaching. These include extensive reading, extensive listening, writing, and conversation and group work activities like ranking activities, problem-solving activities, and retelling activities.

The remaining one-quarter of the time should be spent on language-focused learning which includes learning from word cards (a very effective and efficient learning procedure), individual learning activities involving prepared exercises and computer-based learning, and direct teaching as in intensive reading and the teaching of vocabulary, spelling, pronunciation, and grammar. Overall, direct teaching should make up less than one 16th of the time in a language course (Nation, 2007). Teachers need to realize that individual and group work activities are sources of learning even though they do not involve direct teaching.

Macalister (2010a) found that teachers also said that they did not have enough time in their program for extensive reading and that providing this time would require substantial curriculum and assessment change. Time is not necessarily a big issue for extensive reading. It is probably most effective to introduce extensive reading as a classroom activity using only a small amount of class time (a few minutes a day for two or three days a week), with the aim of increasing this time

Setting Up an Extensive Reading Program   71

either in class or using out-of-class time. If the reading is done electronically, the amount of time needed and the intrusion into other activities is made much less.

Teachers also need to consider that some of the activities that they spend a lot of time on in class might not be resulting in much learning. The replacement of these activities by extensive reading, as was done in the Elley and Mangubhai book flood study (see Chapters 3 and 6), could result in much more learning.

Should Learners Have to Sit a Test For Each Book They Read?

The reasons for sitting a test on each book such as those in MReader are to make sure that learners do the reading they are supposed to do, to motivate the learners to do the reading, to give the learners feedback on their comprehension so that they can feel happy about their progress, and to provide data for research, and to convince others that the reading is being done and comprehended. Research by Stoeckel, Reagan, and Hann (2012) suggests that the effects of such tests on motivation are minimal. However, a teacher should consider all the reasons just mentioned, and if there are at least one or two of them that are relevant to their particular group of learners, then they should get them to sit the tests. Otherwise, just let them get on with the reading.

However, there are a substantial number of teachers who believe that no assessment is needed. The main argument for this is that the reading should be pleasurable and by adding a test it makes it feel like yet another school test, so learners begin to see extensive reading only as a school subject, not as a tool for a life-long reading habit. An extreme form of this is to allow learners not to do extensive reading if they do not want to, based on the notion of respect for learner choice. A major issue with this position is that given the option of not reading, naturally many learners will opt-out often because they are busy with other things. But this will mean they will miss out on meeting the massive volume of text that is necessary to consolidate their language so their ability can grow.

How Can I Learn More About Setting Up an Extensive Reading Program?

Download and read the Guide to Extensive Reading from the ERF website.

As the case studies in Chapter 3 show, it is not difficult to set up an extensive reading program. Even a very minimal program that can later be developed is a good start. As we shall see in the following chapters of this book, there is plenty of research to show that an extensive reading program brings a lot of useful benefits for both learners and teachers, and many teachers are now setting up such programs.

5 How Vocabulary Is Learned From Extensive Reading

Learning Conditions and Extensive Reading

Vocabulary learning is only one of the goals of extensive reading, but vocabulary learning makes use of conditions that also apply to other aspects of language knowledge. Vocabulary learning from extensive reading occurs as a result of repeated meetings with words, word families, and lexical phrases in context, and as a result of the quality of these meetings.

Vocabulary learning can broadly be split into two stages. The first is the form meaning stage which is an initial stage where the learner matches a word's meaning to its spelling or pronunciation. Initial learning of vocabulary in text can come from guessing from context, from glossary or dictionary look-up, or from a teacher or friend. This initial learning is typically only the first small step in the cumulative learning of the word. Later meetings will strengthen and enrich this learning as long as these meetings are close enough in time for the memory of the previous meetings to be recalled.

The second stage of vocabulary learning involves learners meeting the secondary meaning senses of a word, its nuances of use, its collocations and colligations, how to use the word in context, and its pragmatic values such as whether the word is typically spoken or written, polite, casual or neutral, or a general or academic word, and so on. Much of this secondary level of word knowledge cannot be learnt intentionally but has to be learnt incrementally from massive exposure. Each exposure adds a little bit more of the sense of how a word lives with its neighbors which enables learners to feel comfortable with it, thus making it available for use in speaking and writing. If learners only learn at the initial stage of word learning, they will know many words, but not deeply. A program of systematic massive exposure to text through extensive reading and extensive listening provides the environment for this sense of language to grow.

Let us look first at the general conditions needed for vocabulary learning to occur and then see how these conditions relate to vocabulary learning from extensive reading.

In Table 5.1 the conditions for learning are more effective as you move down the table and across the table from left to right. So, repeated speaking

How Vocabulary Is Learned 73

Table 5.1 Conditions Helping the Learning of Vocabulary

Conditions	Incidental receptive	Incidental productive	Deliberate receptive	Deliberate productive
Noticing	The first meeting in input	The first use in output	Dictionary look-up Guessing from context	Asking for a word
Verbatim retrieval	Repeated listening and reading	Repeated speaking and writing	Word card learning: form to meaning	Word card learning: meaning to form
Varied retrieval	Extensive listening and reading Negotiation	Extensive speaking and writing Negotiation	Vocabulary exercises	Vocabulary exercises
Elaboration	Following instructions Watching movies Reading comics	Memorable or object-related spoken or written communication	Keyword technique Word part analysis Dictionary strategy	Picture labeling

and writing are likely to be more effective than repeated listening and reading. Also, extensive speaking and writing are likely to be more effective than repeated speaking and writing. That is, the vertical and horizontal progressions in the table indicate deeper levels of processing. In Table 5.1 the diagonal relationships are not clear. That is, we cannot say for example if repeated speaking and writing is shallower or deeper than extensive listening and reading. In other words, we do not know if the receptive/productive distinction is in step with the vertical elaborated processing distinction.

After the condition of Noticing, the subsequent vertical levels involve retrieval of some sort. The finding that spaced retrieval strengthens learning is one of the most robust findings in memory research and it has direct implications for vocabulary learning (Barcroft, 2007; Nakata, 2011). Research on generative use (Joe, 1998) has shown that varied retrieval (the word is met again in a different form or in a different context) results in stronger learning than verbatim retrieval (the word is met again in the same form and in the same context) (see Webb & Nation, 2017 for a discussion of this). Research on word part learning (Wei, 2015), the keyword technique (Pressley, 1977), and speculation about the appropriateness of the form-meaning relationship (Deconinck, Boers, & Eyckmans, 2017) has shown that elaboration through analysis improves retention. D'Agostino, O'Neill, and Paivio (1977) suggest that some of this better retention can be explained by dual coding where the word is stored with both linguistic and visual links.

Deliberate learning typically results in faster and stronger learning than incidental learning (Min, 2008; Mondria, 2003; Wesche & Paribakht, 2010). This

74 How Vocabulary Is Learned

is because of the focused and sustained attention given during intentional learning (Barcroft, 2004). This attention, however, works best when the repetitions are spaced rather than massed. This applies to spacing both within a learning session and between learning sessions (Nakata, 2015; Nakata, 2017).

There is a wide range of activities in Table 5.1, but only a small number of these involve extensive reading. The first meeting with an unknown word in extensive reading most likely will involve receptive noticing. Noticing can also occur when a previously met word is met again but there is no successful retrieval of meaning. Occasional dictionary use should be allowed in extensive reading because dictionary look-up has positive effects on vocabulary learning through noticing (Knight, 1994; Hulstijn, Hollander, & Greidanus, 1996; Laufer & Hill, 2000; Peters, 2007) and on comprehension. If learners are reading texts at the right level for them, then dictionary look-up, either electronic or hard-copy, is unlikely to interrupt reading too much, but it should be kept to a minimum. When reading extensively, learners should only need to use their dictionary to facilitate and enhance comprehension of the book being read and they should get back to the reading as soon as possible.

The vast majority of repeated meetings with words in extensive reading involve varied use. That is, words typically occur in different contexts and occasionally in different inflected and derived forms. These varied meetings set up excellent conditions for vocabulary learning through retrieval. In an extensive reading program, most vocabulary learning should occur through (1) deliberate noticing through guessing from context, and (2) varied repeated retrieval.

Enhancing Vocabulary Learning Through Extensive Reading

Teachers and, as a result, publishers are tempted to add questions, activities, and bilingual glossaries in the margins of graded readers. In effect, this turns graded reading into a language course rather than seeing it as one kind of important meaning-focused input. The negative effect of this is that the conditions for learning from meaning-focused input (material at the right level for the learner, a small amount of unfamiliar and partly familiar language, a focus on understanding the message, and quantity of input) may get lost. Time spent on answering questions and doing activities takes away from reading, and interferes with the pleasure that can come from successful reading. Bilingual glossaries in the margin take away the opportunity for retrieval. While it is good for the repetition of vocabulary and for deepening the quality of meetings with words to link extensive reading with other activities and strands, it is more important that extensive reading should involve large quantities of enjoyable reading at the right level. Other activities should not get in the way of this.

That said, there are learners who prefer the support of glossaries and prefer to take quizzes or post-reading questions because they like 'knowing' they got something right. However, too much of this will not lead the learners into reading for its own sake, because it makes them dependent on

How Vocabulary Is Learned   75

these activities. Clearly there is a balance to be made between these two positions which a teacher must navigate carefully and thoughtfully.

A major theme in this book is that it is best to keep extensive reading simple, just involving a reader and a text at roughly the right level. Any additional supports and activities (1) should be truly supportive for learning and reading, and (2) should take very little time away from reading. Here are the most useful supports and activities that meet these two criteria. They are presented in order of importance with the most important first. They are dictionary or glossary look-up, putting unfamiliar words onto word cards or into a flash-card program, and doing word card learning before reading a text.

Dictionary or Glossary Look-Up

Looking up the meanings of words increases learner satisfaction when reading, increases vocabulary learning, and can have positive effects on comprehension (Abraham, 2008). With a good electronic reading app such as Kindle, or online reading websites such as ER-Central.com, look-up can be very speedy. This involves simply touching the word in the electronic text. Some apps and websites allow the word just looked up to be quickly added to a list for later flash-card learning.

Learners appreciate being able to look up the meanings of unknown words (Cheng & Good, 2009; Lenders, 2008; Ko, 2005). This fits with common-sense because word knowledge is essential for comprehension. Look-up has a stronger effect on vocabulary learning than on comprehension, but has positive effects on both (see Nation 2013a Chapter 5 for a review of glossing research).

The main concern should be making look-up as easy as possible while still maintaining a deep quality of processing. The use of hard-copy dictionaries seems to discourage look-up, and the use of highlighted hyperlink glosses encourages too much look-up (Hulstijn, Hollander, & Greidanus, 1996). Electronic reading on a tablet or electronic reader brings the advantages of quick look-up and storage for later word study. However, some research suggests that fewer words are remembered looking up words on devices rather than paper dictionaries as they involve fewer attentional resources when looking up words.

Putting Unfamiliar Words Onto Word Cards

Incidental vocabulary learning from extensive reading requires many meetings with words to gain word knowledge that will last. One way of speeding up vocabulary learning and making it more secure is to add deliberate learning. The simplest way to do this is for the learners to make word cards or to enter words into a flash-card app while they read. A website like ER-Central allows learners to save any word they look up for later learning. The major advantage of doing this during extensive reading of graded readers is that every word met in a graded reader is worth learning because

76 *How Vocabulary Is Learned*

most words are likely to be high frequency words especially at lower levels. See Nation (2013a, Chapter 9) for a review of research on learning from word cards.

Doing Word Card Learning Before Reading a Text

Before reading a text, a learner can quickly look through it for any unfamiliar words, put them on word cards, and then deliberately learn them. Then when reading the text, the reading should be a bit easier and the meetings with the words should strengthen and enrich knowledge of them.

Using a Controlled Vocabulary

Dealing with vocabulary in a text for vocabulary learning or for comprehension is essentially a battle against Zipf's Law. So, let us look at Zipf's Law and its implications for vocabulary learning and comprehension, and then see how its negative effects are reduced by using a controlled vocabulary.

Zipf's Law was named after George Kingsley Zipf who was one of the earliest psycholinguists. His best known books include *The Psycho-Biology of Language* (Zipf, 1935) and *Human Behavior and the Principle of Least Effort* (Zipf, 1949). Zipf had noticed, as others had, that if you list the words in a text according to their frequency, the frequencies drop very quickly and drop in a predictable way. The formula he used to describe this is now called Zipf's Law and states that rank times frequency equals a constant figure. 'Equals a constant figure' means 'always gives the same answer'. Let us look at an example using a text on reading fluency. Here are the most frequent ten words in English.

Word	Rank	Freq	Rank x Freq
the	1	69	69
of	2	35	70
and	3	23	69
reading	4	17	68
A	5	14	70
on	6	12	72
to	7	10	70
is	8	9	72
in	9	8	72
words	10	7	70

Not all texts fit as nicely as this and we have adjusted some figures to make the pattern clearer, but the pattern is always roughly the same. If we apply the formula of Zipf's Law (Rank x Frequency = a Constant) to the first row, we can see 1 (the rank) times 69 (the frequency of the most frequent word, *the*, in the 1,000 word text I used) equals 69. If we apply the formula to row two, we get roughly the same answer (2 x 35 = 70), and roughly the same answer applies to all the following rows.

Note how quickly the frequencies drop in column 3. By the time you are halfway down the full list of 367 different words in the text, each word has a frequency of 1. In other words, half of the different words in a text occur only once, and that is usually true even if the text is very long. Here is an example using the last ten words in the frequency list from the same fluency text.

Word	Rank	Freq
ways	349	1
we	350	1
week	351	1
weeks	352	1
Weir	353	1
were	354	1
whole	355	1
with	356	1
written	357	1
you	358	1

Because this text is only 1,000 words long, some of the one-timers are high frequency words in English.

The frequency figures drop quickly at the beginning of the list because the second word is half the frequency of the first (most frequent) word, the third word is one-third of the frequency of the first word, the fourth word is one-quarter of the frequency of the first word, and so on.

If we draw a graph for all the data from a frequency count like this using cumulative coverage of a text, we always get the same shaped curve (see Figure 5.1). As long as our text is not too short, we get the same results no matter what kind of text we count and no matter what language we count. Sorell (2012) has a very clear and useful description of Zipf's Law and its background. See Nation (2013a, pp. 32–35) for a further discussion of Zipf's Law and vocabulary.

Here are the practical implications drawn from Zipf's Law:

1   A small amount of vocabulary will make up a very large proportion of the words in a text or a collection of texts. These are the words worth learning first. Typically we draw a line between these words and the rest at around the 2,000 or 3,000 word level. In Figure 5.1, this is the point where the curve starts to level off. These words are called the high frequency words and they are the words that are typically covered by

78 How Vocabulary Is Learned

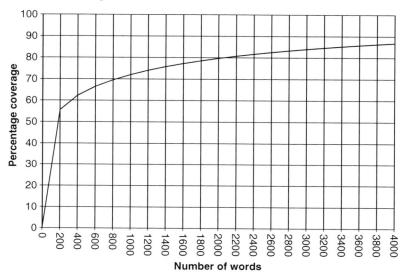

Figure 5.1 A Curve Plotting the Results of Cumulative Frequency-Ranked Count of a Text

graded reading schemes. Because these words occur so often, there is plenty of opportunity to meet them when reading. Depending on the type of text, these 3,000 words cover around 70% to 90% of the running words in a text.

2 The rest of the different words in a text make up a large number of different words and cover only a small proportion of the running words in a text. Typically these words come from a wide range of frequency levels. These words from the third 1,000 different words on used to be called the low frequency words. However, now they are divided into two groups (Schmitt & Schmitt, 2014) – the mid-frequency words (the fourth 1,000 to the ninth 1,000 inclusive), and the low frequency words (from the tenth 1,000 on). The 6,000 mid-frequency words have been distinguished as a separate group because along with the high frequency words they include most of the vocabulary needed to read unsimplified text. They are also a reasonably stable group of words and include most of the words that young native speakers of English know by the time they enter secondary school. Lists of these words (the BNC/COCA lists) can be found on Paul Nation's website. Because the mid-frequency words do not occur so frequently (in the British National Corpus they make up around 9% of the running words), large amounts of input are needed to meet these words in order to have a reasonable chance of learning them incidentally. Table 5.2 (from Nation, 2014) shows how much reading per year would be

How Vocabulary Is Learned 79

needed to have a chance of meeting the words at each 1,000 word level at least 12 times.

Table 5.2 shows that for the first level of mid-frequency words (the fourth 1,000 word families), learners would need to read around 500,000 running words in that year to get enough repetitions to learn many of these words. This is around five or six average length novels. Each year after this, the amount of reading needed to be done increases by roughly another 500,000 words a year. So, to learn the fifth 1,000 word families, learners would need to read around one million running words in that year (around ten novels). These are manageable amounts of reading, but would require persistent effort (McQuillan, 2016). Large amounts of input are needed to learn words incidentally through reading.

In text written for native speakers, there are lots of low frequency words. For example, in the average novel, around 100,000 running words long, there will be around 2,000 different words beyond the 3,000 word level. Around half of those words will occur only once (Nation, 2018). So that means that a learner who knows around 3,000 words will need to guess and perhaps look up around 2,000 words, and around 1,000 of those look-ups will be words not met again in that novel or even in the next four or five novels. This is a very large amount of largely wasted effort. The way to avoid such wasted effort is to read material that excludes those words by replacing most of them with known words. That vocabulary-controlled material is called graded readers, or for words beyond the 4,000 word level, mid-frequency readers. Uden, Schmitt, and Schmitt (2014) present evidence to argue that learners can largely cope with the move to unsimplified text when they finish reading graded readers at the 3,800 word level (Level 6 of *Cambridge English Readers*). However, they do not consider the large amount of wasted effort involved dealing with very low frequency words that occur only once in a novel. Using vocabulary-controlled material greatly reduces

Table 5.2 Corpus Sizes Needed to Gain an Average of at Least 12 Repetitions at Each of Nine 1,000 Word Levels Using a Corpus of Novels

1,000 word list level	Corpus size to get an average of at least 12 repetitions at this 1,000 word level (repetitions)	Number of novels
2nd 1,000 families	171,411 (13.4)	2
3rd 1,000 families	300,219 (12.6)	3
4th 1,000 families	534,697 (12.6)	6
5th 1,000 families	1,061,382 (13.7)	9
6th 1,000 families	1,450,068 (13.1)	13
7th 1,000 families	2,035,809 (13.7)	16
8th 1,000 families	2,427,807 (14.1)	20
9th 1,000 families	2,956,908 (12.0)	25

80   *How Vocabulary Is Learned*

the vocabulary burden of reading and allows attention to be focused on words that are the next most useful words to learn.

Related to the number of unknown words and the low frequency of those words is the density of unknown words. An ideal density for reading is around one or two unknown words per 100 running words. This would mean between three to six look-ups per page of a book. This is still quite a lot. Table 5.3 (from Nation, 2018) shows the density and number of unknown words in a modern novel.

Table 5.3 shows that learners would need to know around 6,000 or 7,000 words for the density and number of unknown words to become easily manageable when reading an unsimplified modern novel.

Zipf's Law describes the distribution of vocabulary in a text. It shows that there are really useful words to learn first when beginning to learn a language. It shows that we can organize vocabulary into stages that provide the best return for each stage of learning. It also shows that there is great value in using vocabulary-controlled material in teaching materials and in reading materials, because such material makes sure that learners are not over-burdened with large numbers of unknown words that are not repeated and that are not worth learning at learners' present level of proficiency. Vocabulary-controlled reading material also ensures that there is a low density of unknown words so that learners can guess from context and do not have to frequently look up unknown words.

The use of vocabulary-controlled materials for extensive reading is a major way of dealing with the negative aspects of Zipf's Law. The use of vocabulary-controlled material ensures that learners can get comprehensible input at every level of language proficiency so that they do not have to wait for several years until they know several thousand words before they can experience the joy of reading with relative ease in a foreign language.

Table 5.3 Density and Number of Unknown Words in a Typical Novel at Various Vocabulary Sizes★ (*The Devil's Company,* Liss, 2009)

Vocabulary size	Unknown word density	Number of unknown words
1,000 word families	14.20%	3,177
2,000	8.12%	2,421
3,000	5.18%	1,831
4,000	3.61%	1,403
5,000	2.90%	1,117
6,000	2.34%	850
7,000	1.93%	678
8,000	1.56%	515
9,000	1.34%	384

★Proper nouns, marginal words, transparent compounds, and abbreviations are counted in known words.

How Vocabulary Is Learned 81

There are other complementary ways of dealing with Zipf's Law, largely through the deliberate learning of vocabulary, and these are an important part of a well-balanced language course.

In the next chapter, we look at the most important research studies relating to extensive reading, and from Chapter 7 on we look even more widely at the research on extensive reading.

6 The Most Important Studies on Extensive Reading in a Foreign Language

This chapter focuses on the most important studies on extensive reading. Its aim is to critically evaluate the strongest evidence for extensive reading to see if there is a convincing empirical research base for advocating extensive reading in a foreign language. The studies reviewed here are the ones most suitable to be used as evidence when advocating extensive reading.

The selection of the studies depended on a variety of factors and although there are clearly subjective elements in the choice of studies, most researchers will largely agree with the choice. A justification for the choice of each study is given when each one is introduced.

This chapter focuses on experimental research and corpus-based research. In Chapter 3, there are case studies of effective extensive reading programs which give weight to anecdotal common-sense evidence as well as experimental data.

The order of the studies in this chapter reflects the strength of the research-based support they provide for advocating extensive reading. The first study reviewed is thus the most important and in several ways that study is like the tip of an iceberg in that it was the first of several studies in different countries using very much the same methodology under the oversight of Warwick Elley. They all achieved similar striking results.

Learning Through a Book Flood (Elley & Mangubhai, 1981)

Elley and Mangubhai (1981, 1983) conducted a 'Book Flood' study in 1980 with 9-to 11-year-old primary school learners of EFL in classes 4 and 5 in Fiji. This study is deservedly regarded as the classic study of L2 learning from extensive reading because it is one of the earliest published experimental studies of extensive reading, and also because of its quasi-experimental design with control groups, its reasonably large size involving 24 school classes (16 experimental and eight control) and over 600 learners, the length of its application over an eight-month period of time involving 20 to 30 minutes of reading per school day, its non–additive nature (it was not an add-on but replaced regular teacher-fronted classes), and its strong ecological validity (the experiment involved normal rural schools with their usual teachers experiencing all the usual ups and downs of the school year). The study was inspired by a Book

The Most Important Studies   83

Flood in the island of Niue by Peter De'Ath in the late 1970s. In a move reminiscent of Michael West in Bengal many years earlier, De'Ath wrote his own books, the Fiafia Readers, to suit the learners involved.

In the Fiji Book Flood, all the learners were pre-tested with the same 35-item reading comprehension pre-test. There were no other pre-tests. The same test was used as a post-test for class 4 learners but a different reading comprehension post-test was used with class 5. In addition, class 5 learners had three other post-tests – listening comprehension, English structures, and composition. Class 4 learners also had three post-tests in addition to the reading comprehension test. These were all different from the class 5 post-tests and were English structures, word recognition, and oral sentence repetition. Only half of the class 4 learners were given the word recognition and oral repetition tests.

The use of the same reading comprehension pre-test for classes 4 and 5 made it possible to calculate the typical amount of progress in reading comprehension without the Book Flood that is made in one year for the experimental groups combined before the intervention (14.87 out of 35 for class 4, 17.85 for class 5 – a gain of 2.98). Because class 4 used the same test as a post-test, it is possible to measure the progress class 4 made in the eight months of the Book Flood (pre-test 14.87, post-test 20.11, a gain of 5.24). So, the extra raw score gain because of the Book Flood intervention is 5.24 minus 2.98 which equals 2.26, meaning that the Book Flood group made close to twice as much gain as would be expected from the usual classes (see Table 6.1).

In the 1981 report, Elley and Mangubhai reported both raw scores and gain scores. In the 1983 report, they reported only residual gain scores, presumably because they considered these gave a more accurate result. Whatever way it is calculated, the Book Flood groups did better than the control groups, by roughly the same proportion. The results were statistically significant. Are they pedagogically significant? Is an extra improvement of just over two points out of 35 enough to get excited about? It clearly is, because that extra improvement would represent many months of work in a classroom without a Book Flood. In addition, that improvement shown by the reading comprehension results for class 4 was accompanied by better scores for the Book Flood groups over the control groups on a variety of measures.

Elley and Mangubhai stress that the class 4/class 5 comparison is over a 12-month period while the pre-test/post-test comparison is over an eight-month

Table 6.1 Gains in the Fiji Book Flood Study

Class 4 pre-test	Class 5 pre-test	Difference
14.87	17.85	2.98
Class 4 pre-test	Class 4 post-test	Difference
14.87	20.11	5.24
		5.24–2.98 = 2.26 gain

84 *The Most Important Studies*

period − "we can conclude that both book groups made approximately 14 months growth in 8 months" (Elley & Mangubhai, 1981, p. 15). It needs to be noted that the eight-month period does not include a long vacation while the 12-month period includes a six-week Southern hemisphere summer break. Nonetheless, even excluding the six-week vacation, it still gives a substantial extra amount of school time (more than two months) to the class 4/class 5 comparison over the pre-test/post-test comparison.

A striking feature of the results is the robustness of the Book Flood intervention. The experimental groups always out-performed the control groups. Where two teachers did not follow the prescribed treatment, the results reflected what they did rather than what they were supposed to do. The positive effects of the Book Flood treatment were still maintained a year later.

The Elley and Mangubhai study provides strong support for extensive reading and to some degree also for extensive listening through the shared book approach. Elley and Mangubhai consider that the main causative factors were "related to greater and repeated exposure to print in high-interest contexts, in conditions where pupils were striving for meaning and receiving support to achieve it regularly" (Elley & Mangubhai, 1983, p. 66).

There are numerous weaknesses in the study. Different tests were used for classes 4 and 5 making comparison impossible. The only true pre-/post-test measure was the reading comprehension test for class 4. Only some of the class 4 learners sat two of the post-tests. It would have been good to have a vocabulary size measure, but none were available at that time. The control over the time spent on reading is stated as being "Book Flood schools replaced 20–30 minutes of Tate reading activities each day with Shared Book or Silent Reading activities" (Elley & Mangubhai, 1983, p. 57). This margin of time difference (20 to 30) is quite large and may have reduced the effectiveness of the Book Flood to some degree. The strengths of the study were its large size, and the robustness and consistency of the results.

How could the Book Flood study be improved? The biggest improvement would be to have the same pre- and post-tests for both class 4 and class 5, so that each post-test was also a pre-test, and have all classes sit exactly the same pre- and post-tests. Because vocabulary size measures are now available, it would be very useful to include one of these in a long-term reading intervention, because extensive reading is likely to have a marked effect on vocabulary growth and vocabulary size underlies effective language use.

Although the books used in the Book Flood study were not graded readers, this exclusion was not based on a rejection of graded readers. They were just not readily available for purchase at the time (Warwick Elley, 2017, personal communication). The shared book approach ensured that there would be some support for learners with unknown vocabulary and structures. Moreover, the books were short, so the number of unknown words was not too burdensome. Perhaps the overwhelming factor in the choice of books was their attractiveness to the learners, with high interest ensuring the likelihood of sustained reading.

The Most Important Studies   85

What can we take from the Elley and Mangubhai Book Flood study?

1   With minimal training, teachers can run an effective extensive reading program, even with young learners.
2   Extensive reading results in greater improvements in reading comprehension, listening comprehension, English structures, word recognition, and repetition of oral sentences than more form-focused teaching.
3   The gains from extensive reading persist a year later.
4   Shared reading is as effective as silent reading.
5   The improvements in reading comprehension are substantial.

The Book Flood study has been repeated in many different places largely with Warwick Elley's close involvement. These places include Singapore, Brunei, Sri Lanka, South Africa, the Solomon Islands, and Vanuatu. These include both developing and developed countries, and learners from a range of age levels. A 2001 issue of the *International Journal of Educational Research* guest-edited by Elley (2001) contains accounts of these experiments. In all cases the Book Flood groups achieved much better results in reading comprehension improvement and in most cases a range of other measures than the control groups, with results very similar to the Fiji Book Flood study. What is striking about these replications is the consistency and robustness of the results under a very wide variety of circumstances, many of them apparently unfavorable to educational innovation. For a relatively small financial cost to buy high-interest books and a very small amount of teacher-training, striking results can be achieved.

Word Frequency and the Richness of Vocabulary Learning (Waring & Takaki, 2003)

The Waring and Takaki (2003) study focused on vocabulary learning from the reading of one graded reader, roughly an hour of reading. It was a very carefully controlled study. Waring (2001) critically reviewed previous research and was determined not to repeat the weaknesses he found in the previous vocabulary learning and extensive reading research design. It is also noteworthy because it is one of the few pieces of extensive reading research which has been replicated (Brown, Waring, & Donkaewbua, 2008). It is also one of the early studies to use several tests of the same words so that strength of knowledge of vocabulary could be calculated. This study has been reviewed in Nation and Webb (2011, pp. 99–103) from a research design perspective.

Waring and Takaki (2003) replaced 25 words of various frequency levels in a graded reader with nonsense words that looked like English words. After reading, the university level learners were tested on each of the 25 words using a word form recognition test (Circle the words you met in the story), a multiple-choice test (Choose the L2 meaning), and a translation test (Translate these words into the L1). Because nonsense words were used, no pre-test was necessary. The same three tests were administered three times – an immediate post-test, a one-

86 *The Most Important Studies*

week delayed post-test, and a three-month delayed post-test. In their discussion of the results, Waring and Takaki gave emphasis to the delayed post-test results and the translation test because they considered that this test best represented the knowledge required for reading. While they had their reasons for this emphasis, this focus unnecessarily plays down the results of their study. For example, on the immediate post-tests, the learners scored 15.3 out of 25 for word recognition, 10.6 for multiple-choice, and 4.6 for the much more difficult translation. This meant that for an hour of reading, almost five words (4.6) had been learned well enough for the learners to supply a meaning for the word with no context clues, another six (10.6 minus 4.6) were well on the way to being known receptively, and another five were partly familiar (15.3 minus 10.6). These three gains of different strengths are a very good incidental vocabulary learning outcome for an hour's reading, particularly since during the intervention the words had to be guessed from context with no dictionary look-up. The delayed post-test results were lower but there were no opportunities to meet any of the words again. It is reasonable in an extensive reading program using graded readers to expect words to recur if a lot of reading is being done. Even the one-week delayed post-test results of 11.1, 7.9, and 1.9 are still a very valuable vocabulary learning outcome for an hour of reading.

What can we take from the Waring and Takaki study?

1   From reading a graded reader, learners learn a reasonable number of words to various degrees of knowledge through guessing from context.
2   This learning needs to be strengthened by further reading within a few days because forgetting will reduce this learning.
3   Repetition of the words helps learning and so extensive reading needs to involve regular opportunities to meet the same words again, possibly through further reading or re-reading.

The learning in the study depended on guessing from context. If the learners were able to look up meanings, learning would have been much greater, but that would have added another variable to the study.

The Waring and Takaki study contrasts strongly with the Elley and Mangubhai study. The Waring and Takaki study is short, intensive, and very carefully controlled. We can say with a high degree of assurance that the learning occurred from the extensive reading and how much learning occurred from the study. It is, however, only a brief snapshot of what would occur in an extensive reading program. The Elley and Mangubhai study more realistically represents what happens in an extensive reading program and because of this we are necessarily less confident about the causes of learning. How much contact was there with English outside classes? How much learning was the result of teacher input and support? How much was from the actual reading? The use of a control group helps answer some of these questions but much remains uncertain. Teachers would be impressed by the results of the Elley and Mangubhai study and academics would be impressed by the results of the

The Most Important Studies   87

Waring and Takaki study. That is of course partly why both kinds of studies are needed. We need research that looks at extensive reading in normal situations, and we need research that focuses on important aspects of extensive reading excluding other factors.

The Waring and Takaki study just used one graded reader. The Brown, Waring, and Donkaewbua (2008) study used three different graded readers and one of those books, *The Elephant Man*, produced better vocabulary learning results than the others, although they were still roughly of the same magnitude. All texts are not the same and this is a variable worth controlling and taking account of.

The Brown, Waring, and Donkaewbua (2008) study compared three treatments, reading-only, reading-while-listening, and listening-only using three graded readers at the 400 headword level using a roughly similar methodology using substitute words as in the Waring and Takaki (2003) study. The learners were tested using a multiple-choice test and a translation test three times, immediately after, a week later, and three months later. The immediate post-test results for the reading-only group were very similar to the Waring and Takaki (2003) study. The reading-while-listening mode gave similar results to the reading-only mode and these two were much better than the listening-only mode. The difference was most notable on the translation test where the listening-only scores were very low.

Most learners preferred the reading-while-listening mode, and if the number of learners involved had been much larger, it is likely that there could be a small but significant difference in vocabulary learning favoring the reading-while-listening mode over the reading-only mode. The disadvantage of reading-while-listening is that the speed of input is held back by the speed of spoken text and suggests that learners listening to graded readers should probably listen to books one or two levels lower than they are reading. As learners' proficiency develops, they should be able to read much faster than the speed of speaking. In the Brown, Waring, and Donkaewbua study, however, the reading and listening rates were very similar at around 100 words per minute (wpm). None of the learners preferred the listening-only mode. Whether this is a feature of Japanese learners remains to be seen. Repetition was also clearly related to learning.

The Brown, Waring, and Donkaewbua study confirmed the results of the Waring and Takaki study, adding the very useful finding of the value of reading-while-listening.

Extensive Reading and Enriching Vocabulary Knowledge (Pigada & Schmitt, 2006)

The Waring and Takaki (2003) and Brown, Waring, and Donkaewbua (2008) studies showed the importance of repetition in learning and thus indirectly the importance of extensive reading for strengthening and enriching knowledge of partially known words. The Pigada and Schmitt study directly addressed the issue of partly known words. This study is briefly discussed in Nation and

88 *The Most Important Studies*

Webb (2011, Chapter 6, pp. 103–104) because of its focus on multiple aspects of what it means to know a word, its focus on both new and partly known words, its use of more than one test, and its giving credit for partial knowledge as well as fuller knowledge of a word. It also involved a month of extensive reading and looked at a large number of target words.

The study involved just one learner who was learning French as a foreign language. The learner read several French graded readers totaling around 30,000 running words (four books over the period of a month) with no other concurrent exposure to French. He had an interview pre-test for knowledge of the form (spelling), meaning, and use (gender for nouns and prepositions for verbs) of each word. The same test was used as a post-test. The testing was very time-consuming. The spelling and meaning were each scored on a three-point scale (0, 1, or 2) for each word. Grammar was scored 0 or 2.

The most important finding was that a lot of vocabulary learning occurs during extensive reading but sensitive measures of different aspects of word knowledge are needed to show this. Knowledge of two-thirds of the 133 target words in the study was enhanced in some way through extensive reading. This two-thirds figure is slightly misleading in that some of the 133 words were shown to be already known in the pre-test (24 known for spelling, nine known for meaning, and ten for grammar) and so the proportion and the following percentages actually under-estimate the size of the increase. Pigada and Schmitt provide very detailed results for the three knowledge categories, for the various word frequency levels, and for the size of increase of knowledge. Overall, of the 133 target words:

> 66 (49.6%) were enhanced in one type of word knowledge, thirteen (9.8%) in two types, and eight (6.0%) in all three types of word knowledge. Adding these figures together, we find that some degree of learning was demonstrated for 87 out of the 133 target words, an impressive 65.4%, or a pick-up rate of about one of every 1.5 words tested.
>
> (Pigada & Schmitt, 2006, p. 17)

If this learning is put into words per hour, something was learned for 14.5 words per hour. Spelling made the greatest improvement, followed by knowledge of articles, with meaning the next, followed by knowledge of which prepositions go with verbs. Frequency of occurrence affected learning, but not in a straightforward way. Spelling required only a small number of meetings but knowledge of meaning required many more repetitions with around 20 repetitions being needed to be sure of improvement in all three aspects of knowledge. The learner did not use a dictionary although the books had occasional marginal glosses which were used.

Pigada and Schmitt make the point that their method of testing required recall, not recognition as in multiple-choice tests. It is likely that had the interview recall testing been accompanied by multiple-choice testing, then even more partial learning could be shown. This takes up a theme developed in the

The Most Important Studies 89

Waring and Takaki (2003) and Brown, Waring, and Donkaewbua (2008) studies, namely that the type of test used strongly affects the kind of knowledge that is measured. In addition, only nouns and verbs were tested and there was likely to have been learning of adjectives and adverbs which were not tested.

Pigada and Schmitt also stress that if only one kind of knowledge is measured and if there is no credit given for partial knowledge, then the vocabulary learning gains from extensive reading will be greatly under-estimated.

What can we take from the Pigada and Schmitt study?

1 Substantial learning of various aspects of word knowledge can result from extensive reading.
2 Repetition helps learning.
3 Knowledge of written form is most readily learned through extensive reading, and knowledge of the form-meaning connection and grammar also increases especially with repeated meetings with words.

These findings reinforce the idea that large quantities of extensive reading are needed to get the best results for vocabulary learning, because large quantities of input increase repetition and variety of context.

So far we have looked at three different kinds of studies – a large-scale classroom-based study with a control group (Elley & Mangubhai, 1981), a short experimental study with immediate and delayed post-tests (Waring & Takaki, 2003), and a detailed single-subject study looking at both previously unknown words and partially known words (Pigada & Schmitt, 2006). The next study is very different in that it describes what could happen rather than what did happen. It is important because it examines an important aspect of the feasibility of extensive reading. Is it possible to do enough extensive reading to make substantial vocabulary size increases?

How Much Extensive Reading Do Learners Need to Do? (Nation, 2014)

Cobb (2007, 2008) on one side and McQuillan and Krashen (2008; McQuillan, 2008) on the other have debated the feasibility of learning substantial amounts of vocabulary from extensive reading. In essence, they were arguing about different things. Cobb argued that the difficulty of the material and the small amounts of time available would make learning enough words through reading impossible. McQuillan and Krashen ignored the time and difficulty aspects and said that enough material could be read to meet words enough times to learn them.

Nation (2014) also put to one side the difficulty argument and used corpus analysis software (the *AntWordProfiler* program) and the BNC/COCA word family lists to see how many tokens (running words) would have to be read to meet most of the words at least 12 times at each of eight 1,000 word levels (the second 1,000 words to the ninth 1,000 words

90   *The Most Important Studies*

inclusive). The major assumptions were that the learners could read the material at a speed of 150 or 200 wpm, and that a minimum of 12 repetitions were needed to provide an opportunity for learning to occur.

The importance of this study, even though it does not measure actual learning from extensive reading, is that it examines whether extensive reading could possibly cover most of the vocabulary that learners need to learn within a manageable amount of reading time.

The conclusion was that at a slow reading speed of 150 wpm allowing between seven minutes per school day (for the second 1,000 words of English) and one hour and 40 minutes per school day (for the ninth 1,000 words), learners could read enough to have a chance of learning most of the words at each of the 1,000 word levels. Note that these estimates are based on reading five days a week for 40 weeks of the year (200 days) in order to learn 1,000 words a year. The period of time involved would be considerable, several years at 1,000 words a year, but this would match native speaker learning rates (Coxhead, Nation, & Sim, 2014). On the other hand, the commitment of learning time would only be a few minutes each school day (seven minutes per day for the second 1,000, ten minutes per day for the third 1,000, 17 minutes for the fourth 1,000, 33 minutes for the fifth 1,000, and so on). In addition, the figures only apply to learning from written input and additional spoken input and deliberate learning would increase the chances of learning and reduce the time needed for written input.

The justification for this optimistic view of learning from input comes from (1) the availability of large numbers of graded readers including the free mid-frequency readers which means that the reading material does not have to be difficult, and (2) the results of speed reading courses which show that EFL learners can achieve reading rates of well over 150 wpm (Chung & Nation, 2006; Tran, 2012). Note that in the Waring and Takaki (2003) study the untrained learners were already reading at close to 100 wpm which is close to the mean reading speed in a variety of EFL studies (McQuillan & Krashen, 2008).

After the publication of Nation (2014), Cobb (2016) responded to the article and to McQuillan (2016), restating his position. He fairly summarizes Nation's paper noting the six years at 1,000 words per year needed to get from around 3,000 words to 9,000 words.

It is important to stress here that Nation is not an advocate of solely learning through comprehensible input through reading. His unrelenting advocacy of the four strands shows this (Nation, 2007, 2013b). The purpose of the Nation (2014) research was to see what quantity of reading and how much time was needed to cover the high and mid-frequency words enough times to have a chance of learning them solely through reading.

The Nation (2014) study could be improved by using graded readers and the mid-frequency readers as the corpus, rather than out-of-copyright novels. Unfortunately, there are not enough mid-frequency readers yet to do this beyond the sixth 1,000 word level. Using such vocabulary-controlled material

The Most Important Studies 91

would give a more trustworthy result because it would be precisely the material that the learners would have to read to suit the conditions needed for manageable reading. It is highly likely that slightly smaller quantities of reading and thus smaller amounts of reading time for this vocabulary-controlled material would be needed than in the Nation (2014) study. Beglar and Hunt (2014) calculate the amount of extensive reading that learners with knowledge of the most frequent 1,600 words of English would have to do to develop reading fluency. Their estimate of 200,000 running words roughly agrees with Nation's calculation of around 170,000 running words for the second 1,000 words.

What can we take from the Nation study and the subsequent debate?

1   Learners would have to do large quantities of reading each year in order to have a chance of learning around 1,000 words a year.
2   This reading would require the use of vocabulary-controlled material.
3   The amount of time needed each school day for this reading is a feasible and manageable amount of time.
4   To reach the vocabulary sizes needed for largely unassisted reading of unsimplified texts, EFL learners would need to do this regular reading for several years.

There is no doubt that accompanying extensive reading with deliberate vocabulary learning, extensive listening, fluency development, and meaning-focused output would greatly increase vocabulary growth. However, the quantities of extensive reading that need to be done, at least for the most frequent 6,000 words of English, could comfortably fit within a well-balanced language course which also allows time for a range of other language-learning focuses.

It is also worth noting that there is substantial largely unpublished documented evidence from Akio Furukawa's SEG cram school and from other programs such as that at Toyota National College of Technology and Miyagi Gakuin University where many learners read close to a million words a year that learners can be motivated to do very large amounts of reading far in excess of what the Nation study suggests.

So far, the four studies we have looked at show that extensive reading courses are feasible, and result in substantial amounts of language learning, with minimum effort from the teacher. While the Elley and Mangubhai study looked at a range of language-related learning outcomes, the other three studies focused on vocabulary. In the following study, the focus moves to fluency.

Fluency, Graded Readers, and Extensive Reading (Beglar, Hunt, & Kite, 2012)

Beglar, Hunt, and Kite (2012) looked at the effect of extensive reading on reading fluency development. One striking feature of this study is that it looked at the effects of an extensive reading program that lasted a year. An

92   The Most Important Studies

additional reason for its inclusion in this list of important studies is that this report focuses on the effect of the extensive reading program on reading fluency. The pleasure reading groups (extensive reading) made greater fluency gains than the intensive reading group, and among the pleasure reading groups, the groups that made the largest fluency gains were those who read the most, and among those the greatest gains were made by those who read the most material written within a controlled vocabulary (graded readers). Comprehension was high on both the pre-test and post-test so fluency gains did not come at the expense of comprehension.

The classes met once a week for 90 minutes for 28 weeks, and the learners did reading outside class which was carefully monitored. The average amount of reading by the three pleasure reading groups was between 136,000 standard words and 200,000 standard words for the year. Around 63% of the words read by Groups 1 and 2 were in vocabulary-controlled texts, compared with Group 3's 85%.

The amount read and fluency gains were measured by using 'standard words' (six letter spaces equaling one word). The four pre-test and post-test passages for measuring fluency were well within the learners' vocabulary knowledge and each was accompanied by comprehension questions to ensure a focus on meaning. The initial reading rates were around 90 to 100 swpm (standard words per minute). The post-test reading rate gains were 2.97 swpm for the intensive reading group, 8.02 swpm and 12.84 swpm for the two pleasure reading groups who read 63% simplified text, and 16.85 swpm for the pleasure reading group who read 85% simplified text.

What should we take from the Beglar, Hunt, and Kite study?

1   Extensive reading of texts **at the right level** results in improvements in reading fluency.
2   The more you read, the more fluent you can become at reading.
3   Extensive reading programs should involve vocabulary level testing using the New Vocabulary Levels Test or the Updated Vocabulary Levels Test, so that learners and teachers can be best informed about what material they should be reading.

If we apply the principle of the four strands to fluency development in extensive reading, then about one-third of the time in an extensive reading program should be spent reading really easy material with the goal of reading it quickly (Nation, 2013b, p. 16).

Although the Beglar, Hunt, and Kite study shows the positive effect of pleasure reading and especially vocabulary-controlled pleasure reading on reading fluency, the fluency gains are much less than those that would be made in a speed reading course where learners read 20 vocabulary-controlled passages around 500 words long followed by comprehension questions (Chung & Nation, 2006; Macalister, 2008b, 2010b; Tran, 2012). Such a course typically takes less than ten minutes per session for 20 sessions, a total of less than three and a half hours.

The purpose of this comparison is not to criticize the effect of extensive reading on reading fluency, but to point out that the effectiveness of extensive reading over a range of learning outcomes is likely to be substantially increased by including a targeted fluency development course as part of the extensive reading program. An extensive reading program involving vocabulary-controlled texts is also highly likely to reinforce the gains made by a speed reading course.

Reading Fluency and Extensive and Intensive Reading (McLean & Rouault, 2017)

Very well conducted research studies consider the weaknesses and strengths of previous studies and use this knowledge to carefully design research that builds on the strengths and avoids the weaknesses. McLean and Rouault's (2017) study of fluency development from extensive reading does this. Their study was conducted over one academic year (two semesters) making it long enough to be a realistic study of extensive reading. The learners did large amounts of extensive reading. The learners doing extensive reading were compared with learners doing intensive reading. The experimental group (extensive reading) and the control group (intensive reading) spent the same amount of time on their treatments, so the important variable of time on task was controlled for. The measures of fluency were practiced in both treatments to avoid a practice effect favoring the experimental group. A standard unit of measurement (standard words) was used to ensure accuracy in measuring reading speed. A comprehension measure was included to make sure that reading speed was accompanied by adequate comprehension. The reading was monitored to make sure it was actually done. The pre-test and post-test measures were identical so that gains could be confidently attributed to the treatment and not to pre-test/post-test format or content differences. The study involved an experimental research design where the learners were individually randomly assigned to treatments.

The study involved Japanese learners of EFL at first year university level. The two treatments were done as homework but were carefully monitored for the time taken and to ensure that the work was actually done. The extensive reading group had a minimum reading target of 4,000 running words per week, which would occupy around 60 minutes per week. Comprehension was monitored using MReader. The intensive reading group spent a similar amount of time on their grammar-translation reading.

By the end of the academic year, the extensive reading group had increased their reading speed from just under 100 swpm to just over 130 swpm, or an increase in reading speed of 33.74 words or 30.96 swpm. The intensive reading group made a small reading speed gain of 5.68 words or 5.15 swpm.

What should we take from the McLean and Rouault study?

94   *The Most Important Studies*

1   Extensive reading is an efficient and effective way of developing reading fluency.
2   Reading fluency increases can be accompanied by good levels of comprehension.
3   There are benefits in accompanying extensive reading fluency practice with a timed reading course.
4   Good research is built on careful critical evaluation of previous research.
5   Experimental extensive reading studies, which control for the critical factors of a study, are possible in pedagogical settings over an academic year.

The Beglar, Hunt, and Kite (2012) study and the McLean and Rouault (2017) study confirm that extensive reading using material which is at the right level for the learners results in reading fluency improvement. This is a very important finding, because reading fluency also involves good comprehension. Reading fluency underlies efficient and effective learning from reading. A fluent reader can read a lot, understand a lot, learn a lot, and gain a lot of enjoyment from reading.

How Much Vocabulary Can Be Learned Through Extensive Reading? (Pellicer-Sánchez & Schmitt, 2010)

Pellicer-Sánchez and Schmitt (2010) looked at vocabulary learning from an unsimplified text (*Things Fall Apart*) by 'relatively advanced' learners of English. The novel contained some words of an African language which would not be known to the learners reading the novel. These words were the focus of the research on vocabulary learning from extensive reading. This well-known novel is around 67,000 words long, so involved a substantial amount of reading. The learners were tested on knowledge of spelling, word class, meaning recall, and meaning recognition for 34 of the words. Note that this does not include all the words likely to be unknown in the novel for each learner. The largest gains were on meaning recognition (43% of the words), followed by spelling (34%), word class (20%), and meaning recall (14%). Learning was largely related to frequency of occurrence.

This study is in the tradition of the *Clockwork Orange* study (Saragi, Nation, & Meister, 1978) where foreign words which are part of an English text are the focus of the research. The Pellicer-Sánchez and Schmitt study is the best of those studies with its careful design and multiple-measures of vocabulary knowledge. The Saragi, Nation, and Meister study was done with native speakers of English. In the Pitts, White, and Krashen (1989) study, in spite of 50% of the learners not finishing the reading, there were still vocabulary gains. Although there is mention of *Clockwork Orange* in the title, the Horst, Cobb, and Meara (1998) study deliberately follows a different methodology. A weakness of the *Clockwork Orange* studies is that the target words appearing in the text would most likely appear in helpful contexts because the writer of the novel would be very aware that the readers would not know the words. Nonetheless, they do show the effects of incidental vocabulary learning and control well for previous knowledge or learning from outside the text.

What should we take from the Pellicer-Sánchez and Schmitt study?

1   Vocabulary learning involves learning previously unmet words and enriching knowledge of previously met words.
2   Sensitive tests are needed to pick up learning from extensive reading.
3   Extensive reading develops multiple aspects of vocabulary knowledge and at different rates.

Balancing Ecological Validity and Control (Suk, 2017)

Suk (2017), in a 15-week quasi-experimental study which took steps to control as many factors as possible, compared (1) intensive reading involving 100 minutes per week in class and two to three hours intensive reading activities outside class with (2) intensive reading (70 minutes per week) plus extensive reading (30 minutes per week made up of 15 minutes reading and 10–15 minutes of related activities) in class and two to three hours extensive reading outside class. The participants doing extensive reading were expected to read 200,000 words during the semester and sat online MReader quizzes on the books they read. The difficult part of this study to control is the out-of-class work. The researcher was aware of this and used a variety of techniques to make sure that the out-of-class work was being done.

The measures involved in the study covered reading speed and comprehension, and vocabulary learning. The vocabulary test drew on the corpus of graded readers used in the study (see Horst, 2005 for a similar methodology) so that all the tested words had a high chance of having been met in the extensive reading.

Suk found gains in reading comprehension, reading fluency, and vocabulary knowledge.

Controlling the variety of confounding factors likely to be involved in an ecologically valid extensive reading study lasting a whole semester is very difficult. The study by Suk (2017) is notable for the determined efforts made to take account of the weaknesses revealed in earlier studies of extensive reading. In this respect it is similar to the Waring and Takaki (2003) and McLean and Rouault (2017) studies where the errors in previous research were carefully examined and then all efforts were made to make sure they did not occur in the current study.

The vocabulary test was a translation recall test (the learners had to provide a translation for the tested word). Compared to a multiple-choice recognition test, this is quite a tough test and may under-estimate the gains made. Nagy,

96   *The Most Important Studies*

Herman, and Anderson (1985) found that to measure successful guessing from context, they had to use sensitive recognition tests not recall tests.

What should we take from the Suk study?

1   It is possible to control most of the critical factors such as time on task, relevance of tests, equality of groups, and fidelity of the treatments in a prolonged extensive reading study.
2   Extensive reading results in gains in reading comprehension, reading fluency, and vocabulary knowledge.
3   The vocabulary test used to measure vocabulary gains from extensive reading should contain words that are highly likely to be met in the extensive reading. It would also be good to check that such words were likely to occur in the control treatment.
4   Extensive reading is part of a well-balanced language course and is not intended to be a total replacement for intensive reading or other language-focused activities. Each contributes to learning in its own way and they should be seen as complementing each other not as alternatives.
5   Extensive reading can usefully be done both in class time and out of class time.

The Suk study could be improved by using a recognition test of vocabulary knowledge in place of, or as well as, a recall test as in the Pellicer-Sánchez & Schmitt (2010) study. This would show gains in partial knowledge as well as more strongly established knowledge. It may be better to have a separate fluency measure where the focus is clearly on fluency and not have the conflicting demands of comprehension accuracy and reading fluency in one measure. Having said that, the fluency measure did show fluency gains and it could be argued that a fluency measure primarily focusing on comprehension is a more valid measure than one which prioritizes fluency.

This chapter has reviewed the studies that someone advocating extensive reading could most confidently mention when attempting to show the value of extensive reading. They show some of the range of knowledge that can be gained from extensive reading, how easy it is to implement extensive reading, the feasibility of extensive reading for providing opportunities for increasing language knowledge, and the substantial increases that can be made if there is plenty of extensive reading.

These studies provide a useful research base but by themselves they are not enough to cover the many aspects of extensive reading. In the following chapters we will look at this broader research base.

7 Research Findings

Motivation and Pushing Learners to Read

Learners of English as a foreign language can differ widely in their enthusiasm for reading English (Takase, 2007). A lack of enthusiasm may come from the perceived difficulty of the task. It may also come from a lack of interest in reading in general in both the first language and foreign language, although Takase found that enthusiasm for reading in one language was not necessarily mirrored by enthusiasm for reading in the other language. As Brantmeier (2005) shows, interest in reading is a complex issue and is affected by a wide range of variables. Learners' attitudes towards extensive reading are important because extensive reading works when learners read large quantities of material. Learners are unlikely to read a lot unless they enjoy doing it and see some value in such reading.

The attitude that matters in extensive reading is the willingness to do a lot of reading. There are many factors that can motivate this willingness (Mori, 2002; Yamashita, 2013) and researchers have provided convincing evidence of the complex nature of motivation. The strength of the various sources of motivation (and distraction) changes as learners' experience and skill in reading develop (McLean & Poulshock, 2018; Mikami, 2017). The case studies conducted by de Burgh-Hirabe and Feryok (2013), Judge (2011), Nishino (2007), and Ro (2013) provide valuable insights into the changing motivations and factors affecting commitment to extensive reading. Case study research seems particularly revealing for investigating attitudes to extensive reading, possibly because the complex and changing nature of motivation provides a lot to talk about. The many different kinds of motivation that researchers identify can be usefully related to actions that teachers can take to encourage and support learners' willingness to do a lot of reading, and in this chapter we will relate the kinds of motivation to actions the teacher can take to encourage motivation.

Motivation is a complex issue especially when we wish to link causes to motivation. Mori (2002) examined possible aspects of motivation, and found that Gardner's (2001) integrative motivation (wanting to be part of a native-speaker community) was not an important factor in the motivation to read for Japanese university level foreign language learners of English. The factors that seem to be at work are fortunately more closely related to

98 *Motivating Learners to Read*

the immediate task of reading, and so are more easily influenced by the teacher or course-designer running an extensive reading program. These factors include the pleasure of reading, the reward of success in reading, the satisfaction of obvious progress, the virtuous feeling of doing something of value, and the power of independence and control. Let us look at each of these to see how they can be encouraged and supported.

The Pleasure of Reading

If learners enjoy reading then they are likely to keep on reading. Enjoyment of the task for its own sake is a kind of intrinsic motivation. Virtually all studies looking at motivation and extensive reading identify this factor. Nishino (2007) found that his two subjects read for a much longer time in a session at points where the books they were reading became really exciting. They were surprised at how much time they had spent because they had experienced 'flow' (Csikszentmihalyi & Nakamura, 1989) and lost track of time. Pleasure had taken control of them. Their interest in the Harry Potter books they were reading made them lose interest in the less exciting graded readers. Kirchhoff (2013) found that Japanese learners of English often experienced flow during extensive reading, but often experiencing flow did not correlate with greater amounts of time spent reading, possibly because experiencing pleasure while reading is only one of a range of factors affecting quantity of reading. As Kirchhoff notes, the conditions favoring flow are very similar to the conditions favoring extensive reading.

The goal of enjoyment lies behind the idea that learners should choose what books they want to read.

The Reward of Success

Another kind of intrinsic motivation that has been identified in several studies (de Burgh-Hirabe & Feryok, 2013; Judge, 2011; Nishino, 2007) is a feeling of success in being able to perform a challenging skill. This feeling can occur when learners successfully read a book in a foreign language from the beginning to the end with good comprehension. For this kind of motivation, the content of what learners read need not be interesting or engaging (although it helps if it is), but should be accessible for the learners. The feeling of success is its own reward which makes it a kind of intrinsic motivation. This feeling of success encourages self-efficacy (Bandura, 1977), which is the feeling that you are capable of performing a task successfully. Burrows (2013) developed a very useful measure for reading self-efficacy for L2 learners, and showed that extensive reading over a sustained period increases feelings of positive self-efficacy, although not as much as work on reading strategies, or work on reading strategies combined with extensive reading.

The goal of successful reading lies behind the idea that learners should read books that are at the right level for them. This goal can also be reached by providing some well-focused advice and strategy-training, perhaps through individual counselling on reading difficulties.

The Satisfaction of Obvious Progress

The satisfaction of obvious progress is connected to the previously discussed motivations of the reward of success, and the virtuous feeling of doing something of value. The difference, however, lies in the longer-term nature of the satisfaction of obvious progress. Learners may feel the reward of success after the completion of the book, but the satisfaction of obvious progress comes when they realize that they are now reading more fluently than they read before, that comprehension is easier, and that they are now reading books at a higher level of proficiency than they read before.

The way to tap into this motivation is for the learner and the teacher to keep records of the number of books and running words read, of the time taken to read each book, of the learners' reading speed, and of the learners' performance on comprehension tests based on the books. Electronic extensive reading programs like Xreading provide a wealth of such information that is readily accessible to both the teacher and the learners. The learners should be told to expect such improvement and to look for it. Tabata-Sandom (2017) found that learners of Japanese as a foreign language enjoyed pleasure reading and saw that it had positive effects on their proficiency.

The Virtuous Feeling of Doing Something of Value

The motivation of doing something useful is probably a kind of extrinsic motivation as it sees the task eventually accomplishing a worthwhile goal. We get the same feeling from knowingly eating healthy foods and avoiding those considered unhealthy. Lipp (2017) found that developing learners' metacognitive knowledge of extensive reading had positive effects on reading. This metacognitive knowledge involves reflecting on progress made and future benefits, reflecting on the enjoyment of the reading, and the deliberate application of strategies such as finding a good time and place to read, making time for regular reading, and setting reading goals.

The research shows the values of extensive reading for developing the reading skill, for receptive vocabulary growth, and for benefitting a range of other language-related factors. When learners know of these benefits, they can experience a feeling of virtue when they read. This motivation is enhanced by informing the learners of the benefits, by the learners keeping records of how much they read, and by the teacher giving grades for doing extensive reading.

The Power of Independence and Control

Being in control of what you are doing without the need of support from others gives a feeling of independence and control. Extensive reading is

100 *Motivating Learners to Read*

essentially an individual activity, and being able to decide what you read, when you read, what words to look up, and whether to do the activity at all can provide a satisfying feeling of control. Judge (2011) found that several of the learners he interviewed expressed a feeling of satisfaction with being able to do this. He called it the 'lure of autonomy'.

This aspect of motivation can be enhanced by letting the learners choose what they read, by informing the learners how to choose books at the right level and how to manage their reading, by encouraging dictionary use when it is needed, and encouraging at least some of the reading to be done outside of class time. Table 7.1 summarizes the major motivational factors in extensive reading and suggests ways of enhancing them.

Factors Discouraging Extensive Reading

Just as there are sources of motivation that encourage learners to do extensive reading, there are factors that discourage it. Several of these are the reverse of the positive factors we have already looked at – not gaining pleasure from reading, finding the reading too difficult, not experiencing any progress in developing the skill of reading, seeing no point in doing the reading, and being forced to do what you do not want to do. In Mikami's (2017) study, difficulty factors (hard to understand the books) and ability factors (my English is bad) were by far the most common factors cited for not wanting to do extensive reading. Huang (2015) found that although

Table 7.1 Enhancing the Various Motivations to Do Extensive Reading

Motivation	*Enhancing the motivation*
The pleasure of reading	Let learners choose what they read Help learners choose books at the right level Have a reading time where there are no distractions
The reward of success	Help learners choose books at the right level Have a fluency component as part of the extensive reading course where learners read really easy books Encourage learners to read books where they have background knowledge such as having seen the movie
The satisfaction of obvious success	Keep accessible records of progress across a wide range of factors involved in reading – a reading speed graph, a cumulative record of the amount read, and comprehension scores Display signs and milestones of progress
The virtue of doing something good	Keep learners informed of the nature of the benefits of extensive reading
The power of independence and control	Let learners choose what to read Allow dictionary use Encourage reading outside of class

learners enjoyed extensive reading, they found it time-consuming and considered it not efficient enough for exam preparation.

Another major factor is distraction, especially when extensive reading is set as homework. There are so many other things to do. One of the reasons for the success of Akio Furukawa's SEG language schools (Chapter 3) is that they provide a fixed time where the only thing to do is to read. Learners could do this at home, but they generally say that they cannot find the time or lack the discipline. Although extensive reading can bring pleasure and enjoyment, there are many other things that also do that for much less effort.

Ro (2013) noted that when his learner was in an environment where she did not feel comfortable or relaxed, it was difficult to get the reading done, suggesting that not only distraction but emotional reactions to a situation can be a hindrance. This suggests that learners should be advised to find their 'happy place' to do extensive reading, where interruptions are minimalized (cell-phones are turned off, no-one else is around) and there is nothing else to do but read.

Pushing Learners to Read

In order to enjoy reading, to experience success, to experience doing something of value, to see obvious progress, and to feel in control, learners need to actually do the reading, and they may need to be pushed to do this. Yamashita (2013) and Stoeckel, Reagan, and Hann (2012) found that doing 15 weeks of extensive reading, involving roughly a graded reader a week, increased comfort, reduced anxiety, and positively increased learners' view of the theoretical value of extensive reading. Cheetham, Harper, Elliott, and Ito (2016) found that extrinsic goals, such as the challenge to read a certain number of books or words, had positive effects on learners' attitudes to extensive reading. There is evidence from other languages besides English that doing extensive reading increases motivation for such reading (Hardy, 2016 for Spanish; Dupuy, 1997 for French; Hitosugi & Day, 2004 for Japanese).

McLean and Poulshock (2018) compared three groups under three different types of requirements to read. One group was required to read a certain number of words of extensive reading texts outside class time each week for eight weeks. They received a grade for doing this reading. Another group did in-class reading and was required to read a book a week outside class. The third group was encouraged to read a book a week outside class. The comparison was between the effects of (1) in-class reading, (2) word targets, and (3) verbal encouragement. All groups received credit for reading at least one book a week, which was typically much less than the word target group's goal of 2,500 words per week. Even after the word targets had been removed, learners in the word target group continued to do extensive reading. The word target group read longer books to reach their word targets and after the targets were removed they still tended to read longer books because, as they said in follow-up interviews, the longer

102 *Motivating Learners to Read*

books were more interesting. The McLean and Poulshock study shows that pushing learners to read and giving them ambitious targets pays off.

There are several ways in which learners can be pushed to read. These include setting aside time in class to do the reading with the teacher carefully monitoring that the reading is done, requiring each learner to sit a comprehension test after reading each book, making the amount of reading done (words read rather than the more variable measure of books read) a component of the grade for the course, and making sure that the learners are aware of the positive benefits of doing the reading. Requiring students to read a certain number of books and pass the MReader quizzes is a stricter form, but leads to a lot more reading being done because of the dual requirement of reading volume *and* demonstrating comprehension. Suk (2017), drawing on experience from a carefully controlled study of extensive reading, suggested five things that teachers can do to make sure that extensive reading is actually done:

1   set clear quantity of reading goals, preferably in words rather than books read;
2   use some class time to do extensive reading related activities such as reading book blurbs, quickwriting, and scaffolded silent reading to keep the learners focused and motivated to do the reading;
3   read and know a lot about the graded readers in the library so that learners can be directed to enjoyable, manageable books;
4   monitor learners' progress using MReader or Xreading or check their reading logs;
5   provide ongoing assistance by talking to the learners about difficulties they face in their reading and helping them overcome them.

There also needs to be a move to help extensive reading be seen as a crucial and legitimate learning activity. Brown (2009) suggests that textbooks should promote extensive reading by explicitly recommending that learners do it, by each unit in the textbook including recommendations for extensive reading, by including reading logs, by including excerpts from graded readers in the textbooks to tempt learners to read more including serializing a graded reader, by making learners aware of the range of topics covered by graded readers and getting the learners to follow a flow chart to help them find books that would interest them, and by including activities that involve discussing books read. Robb and Kano (2013) provide evidence that making the amount of extensive reading done contribute to a substantial part of the grade for a course has positive effects on the amount read. Teachers have to be careful not to assign all learners the same grade for reaching the minimum of, say, 60,000 words as this will likely demotivate the learner who read 140,000. The method with the most success seems to be where a minimum amount is set to pass the class, e.g. 60,000 words. To get higher grades, learners would need to read increasingly more material such as a C might be 75,000, a B, 100,000, and an A, 150,000.

Although short quizzes on each book read can be used to check that the reading has been done, such quizzes have little if any effect on learners' attitude to reading (Stoeckel, Reagan, & Hann, 2012). That is, the quizzes do not turn learners off reading but neither do they make them more enthusiastic about reading. So, if teachers want to use such quizzes as a way of making sure the reading is done, then they can be used without the fear of causing negative attitudes to reading. Robb (2015) also presents compelling arguments for making use of such quizzes, especially where learners may need to be pushed to read. Cheetham, Harper, Elliott, and Ito (2016) noted that some learners valued the feedback from quizzes which confirmed that they had read well.

A Coherent Approach to Motivating Learners to Read

We have looked at a variety of ways of motivating learners to do extensive reading. It is useful to consider how these ways could fit into some kind of framework that organizes them in a memorable and logical way and that might suggest additional ways.

Trying to motivate learners is trying to change their behavior, knowledge, and attitudes. Chin and Benne (1970) suggested a general framework for doing this. This consisted of three strategies – *law, reason,* and *involvement* (Chin and Benne called them *power-coercive, rational-empirical,* and *normative-re-educative*).

Law-based strategies involve forcing learners to change because of rules and requirements. For extensive reading this can include running some extensive reading in class time so that learners have to do it. It also can include quantity or assessment requirements such as having to read a certain number of words each week.

Reason-based strategies involve changing people's knowledge so that they understand things that they did not know before. When their knowledge changes, their attitudes may also change as a result. For extensive reading, this involves learning about graded readers and the benefits of extensive reading, learning about how extensive reading fits into a balanced learning program, and observing an extensive reading program in action.

Involvement strategies involve learners experiencing things first hand, talking about their experiences, and making their own decisions. The danger of using involvement strategies is that learners' involvement may give them insights and experiences that do not agree with the ones that the change-manager (in our case, the teacher) wants to encourage. However, involvement strategies can be very effective because they may give rise to intrinsic motivation, that is, the motivation that comes from within the learner not from outside. For extensive reading, involvement strategies include doing extensive reading and seeing what it is like, negotiating with the teacher about the amount of reading to be done or setting personal goals, and sharing experiences with each other.

As we have seen, motivation is a complex construct and bringing about change in a complex area requires using a variety of change strategies.

8 Research Findings
Does Extensive Reading Result in Reading Fluency and Comprehension Improvement?

By reading fluency we mean the speed at which learners read text while maintaining adequate comprehension of the text. As we saw in Chapter 6, Beglar, Hunt, and Kite (2012) found a relationship between comprehension and fluency, and it makes sense that fluency needs to involve comprehension to be meaningful. Similarly, comprehension should be accompanied by some reasonable degree of reading speed.

The Nature of Reading Fluency

Fluency is used with several meanings (Fillmore, 1979), and teachers may be unsure what sense is being used (Tavakoli & Hunter, 2018) when they hear or use the word. In this chapter, reading fluency refers to reading speed and it is typically measured in words per minute, or more accurately, in standard words per minute where the number of letter spaces in a text is divided by six (letters, punctuation, blank spaces between words). There is clear evidence that substantial amounts of extensive reading result in increases in reading speed, especially if the extensive reading involves reading material that is at the right level for the reader (see Beglar, Hunt, & Kite, 2012 in Chapter 6). Carver's (1976) data suggests that native speakers read material at their own level and material much easier than that at around the same speed. The reading speeds of Carver's subjects, however, were well above 200 words per minute. Non-native speakers of English whose speeds are much less than this are likely to gain a lot of benefit from reading very easy material.

Struggling with difficult reading material is not an effective way of improving reading fluency. This is largely because fluency involves making the best use of what you already know. Struggling with unknown words and unfamiliar grammatical constructions and ideas does not set up the ideal conditions for fluency development or for the measurement of what you can do with what you know.

Fluency Gains From Extensive Reading

Several studies have found that extensive reading results in fluency improvement as measured by speed in (standard) words per minute (Al-Homoud &

Schmitt, 2009; Beglar, Hunt, & Kite, 2012; Beglar & Hunt, 2014; Bell, 2001; Huffman, 2014; Iwahori, 2008; Lai, 1993; Lao & Krashen, 2000; Mason & Krashen, 1997; McLean & Rouault, 2017; Nishino, 2007; Robb & Susser, 1989; Sheu, 2003; Taguchi, Takayasu-Maass, & Gorsuch, 2004). Often the control group has been doing intensive reading (Al-Homoud & Schmitt, 2009; Bell, 2001; Huffman, 2014; McLean & Rouault, 2017; Robb & Susser, 1989), although in Beglar, Hunt, and Kite (2012) and Sheu (2003), there was a comparison between vocabulary-controlled and uncontrolled texts. Huffman's (2014) and McLean and Rouault's (2017) extensive reading courses also included some timed speed reading training. Karlin and Romanko (2010) found only small increases in fluency, but they suggest that the measurement of fluency increases may have been affected by multiple comprehension measures which could have encouraged learners to read more slowly and carefully. See Beglar, Hunt, and Kite (2012), Beglar and Hunt (2014), McLean and Rouault (2017), Nakanishi (2015), and Huffman (2016) for critiques of the extensive reading and fluency research.

The results showing the positive effect of extensive reading on reading fluency certainly support common-sense. We would expect doing plenty of reading at the right level to result in improvements in reading skill of which reading fluency is an important part. The most convincing evidence is provided in the studies by Beglar, Hunt, and Kite (2012) and by McLean and Rouault (2017). Both of these studies involved learners doing extensive reading over many months, and doing substantial amounts of reading. In the Beglar, Hunt, and Kite study, the learners who did the most extensive reading made the greatest fluency gains. Among the learners who did the most reading, the greatest gains were made by learners who read the most graded readers, that is, the reading material that was most likely to present them with the smallest amount of unknown vocabulary and unfamiliar grammatical constructions. In Chapter 10 of this book we look at the nature of reading fluency and at the nature of fluency development activities. The number one requirement for a fluency development activity is easy, familiar material and the Beglar, Hunt, and Kite study confirms this.

In a further detailed analysis of the Beglar, Hunt, and Kite (2012) data, Beglar and Hunt (2014) present evidence to show that **large** amounts of reading at the right level are needed for fluency improvement, suggesting around 200,000 standard running words per academic year for learners reading comfortably around the 1,600 headword level. Greater reading rate gains occur among learners who read graded readers that are well within their proficiency level. Their findings strongly support the idea that a well-balanced extensive reading course should contain a fluency development strand which involves reading material that is well within the learners' proficiency level, as well as a meaning-focused input strand that includes small proportions of unfamiliar vocabulary which contributes to vocabulary knowledge growth.

McLean and Rouault (2017) is the most thoroughly controlled study of the effect of extensive reading on reading fluency development. The controls

106 *Fluency and Comprehension Improvement*

included random assignment to treatments, time on task, participation, the use of a standardized text length unit (standard words), and familiarity with the measures (practice effect). An interesting feature of the study was that learners in both treatments regularly did targeted traditional speed reading courses (timed vocabulary-controlled passages with comprehension questions). One reason for this was because some texts from the speed reading course were used as the pre-test and post-test fluency measures and familiarity with this kind of measure was thus controlled for. Another positive feature of this is that Nation (2013a) recommends that reading courses should contain traditional targeted fluency training. Including such a course in the experiment allowed the separation of the effects of targeted training from incidental fluency development from extensive reading. It also had the effect, however, of making the comparison of fluency gains from extensive reading and intensive reading less striking because of the fluency increases caused by timed reading in the intensive reading group. However, this might be seen as a benefit as this helps isolate the effect of extensive reading, which is expected to have longer lasting effects on reading rate gains.

The gains in reading rate from the extensive reading in the Beglar, Hunt, and Kite (2012) study are not as great as the gains that can be made in a focused speed reading course (Bismoko & Nation, 1974; Chang & Millett, 2013; Chung & Nation, 2006; Cramer, 1975; Macalister, 2008a, 2010b; Tran, 2012). This is not surprising because courses focused on one skill or one aspect of a skill will usually result in more gains in that skill than courses which are more widely focused. There is evidence that the fluency gains made in focused speed reading courses transfer outside the speed reading course to other reading (Macalister, 2010b; Tran, 2012).

Reading speed gains from extensive reading come largely from the amount of material read (Beglar, Hunt, & Kite, 2012; Beglar & Hunt, 2014; McLean & Rouault, 2017). Reading speed gains from a traditional speed reading course are likely to also come from a sense of urgency in the reading and the confidence gained from reading faster with a demonstrably good level of comprehension. We would expect the fluency gains from extensive reading to be more enduring because of the substantial reading experience underlying those gains. However, because of the relatively small investment of time involved in a traditional speed reading course, a well-designed extensive reading program should include an early component dedicated to improving reading fluency (see Huffman, 2016 for a similar suggestion). There should also be time during the extensive reading program where learners read books that they have read before and books that are way below their usual reading level. The traditional speed reading course will provide a quick and substantial increase in speed that will allow more to be read in the same time during the extensive reading program, and the reading of easy familiar texts will ensure transfer from the speed reading course to other reading in the extensive reading program.

Most studies of extensive reading that measure fluency find a significant improvement. The size of the improvement depends on the amount read, the familiarity of the language in the reading material, and the kinds of tests used to measure fluency.

Issues in Measuring Fluency

The measurement of reading speed is an issue in studies of extensive reading. In traditional speed reading courses for learners of English as a foreign language (see Chapter 10 of this book), the training materials are vocabulary-controlled materials and the measurement of the improvement in reading speed uses the data from these vocabulary-controlled materials. The philosophy behind this is that fluency involves making the best use of what you already know, and so training materials and measures of speed should use material that is well within the proficiency level of the learners. Using texts that contain vocabulary and grammatical features that are outside the level of the learners confounds fluency and general proficiency because the unknown vocabulary and other unfamiliar language features create obstacles to fluency. Choosing texts using readability measures intended for native speakers, such as the Flesch-Kincaid index, does not solve this problem, because such measures do not involve the strict vocabulary control which is important for learners of EFL who have much smaller vocabulary sizes than native speakers.

The Number and Size of Measures

There are several issues to consider when comparing reading speed increases from extensive reading with reading speed increases from a speed reading course. In a traditional speed reading course for learners of EFL (Fry, 1965, 1967; Millett, 2005; Quinn & Nation, 1974), the practice texts and the measures of reading speed are the same texts. This familiarity with the measures provides advantages for the learners. Chung and Nation (2006) compared three ways of using the scores from the texts in a traditional course to measure speed increases – (1) the increase between the average of the first three and the average of the last three texts (the average scoring method); (2) the increase between the highest and the lowest score (the highest minus lowest scoring method); and (3) the increase between the first and the last text (the 20th minus the 1st scoring method). Method (1) is the most conservative because unusually high or low scores become part of an average, and because the average starting score is usually higher than the score on the first text. However, it has the advantages of allowing learners to become familiar with the nature of speed reading and increases reliability by using the average of three measurements. It thus does not exaggerate speed increases. McLean and Rouault (2017) were even more conservative in their use of timed texts, allowing for two practice texts before learners read the texts used to measure reading speed. This idea of excluding scores on the first two passages or at least the first passage is a sensible idea and will help remove the unfamiliarity effect that makes initial reading slow.

108   *Fluency and Comprehension Improvement*

If the measures for reading speed before and after extensive reading are single measures of short duration such as a one-minute reading probe (Iwahori, 2008), reliability is likely to be affected by the use of such a short, unfamiliar measure and a single measure which may under-estimate reading speed. In addition, if the texts contain unknown words, this will also under-estimate fluency increases. Some extensive reading measures of fluency involve measuring the speed taken to read a whole book (Sheu, 2003). While this has the advantage of ecological validity, it allows for the intrusion of other variables such as distraction and fatigue, and usually involves the uncertainty of self-reporting. Al-Homoud and Schmitt (2009) chose texts within the learner's proficiency level and got them to read for three minutes marking the word they had reached in that time. The learners did this with three texts and the average number of words read was used. The use of long texts and several measures is likely to increase the reliability of the measure.

Standard Words

Different texts with the same number of words in each text can differ according to the number of characters in a text (or the number of standard words in a text). The number of standard words is the total number of characters divided by six. The total number of characters includes letters, spaces, and punctuation, which are often counted in most writing software. In MS-Word the total number of characters can be found by double-clicking on Words in the status bar at the bottom of the screen. Carver (1976) recommended the use of standard words rather than words as a more precise measure of text length or reading speed.

Kramer and McLean (2013, 2019) conducted two studies which showed that the number of standard words in a text (the number of character spaces in a text) was a better predictor of the time needed to read a text than the number of words. One study involved text which was adjusted to particular character lengths, and the other involved unadjusted text. Doing two studies countered possible criticisms for using character-adapted texts and re-reading of the same content because of the Latin-squares design. One study involved four pieces of reading (two texts with two versions of each text), and the other involved 13 texts read over a period of 13 weeks.

Kramer and McLean recommend including both word and standard word counts in studies of reading fluency and amount of reading, but it is clear from their research that at the very least it is essential to use standard word calculations. It may be sensible to use characters rather than words or standard words as the measure, because measuring standard words is essentially measuring characters. It may, however, be too big a step from the familiar words per minute measure to attract many supporters. The number of words does not affect the difficulty of a text, simply its length.

Fluency development is a very important part of an extensive reading program. If traditional speed reading training is provided early in an extensive

Fluency and Comprehension Improvement 109

reading program, it can increase confidence and can substantially increase the amount of reading that learners are able to do within a set time. If some of the extensive reading program includes the reading of very easy material, then fluency development can be a thoroughly worthwhile goal of the extensive reading program.

Extensive Reading and Comprehension

Developing fluency in reading involves reading faster, but it makes no sense to read faster if you do not really understand what you read. If extensive reading is done properly with learners reading material which is at the right level for them, we should expect to see some improvements in comprehension, but these improvements may be at least partly hidden as learners move on to material that will still provide only a small challenge for them.

In some of the studies cited here, the gains from extensive reading were compared with gains from intensive reading (Al-Homoud & Schmitt, 2009; Bell, 2001; de Morgado, 2009; Suk, 2017). This kind of comparison is ethically sound as it gives learners in either treatment a chance to improve in reading. In a well-balanced language course, it is good to have both extensive reading and intensive reading as both can contribute in different ways to growth in language proficiency. However, following the principle of the four strands (Nation, 2007), the time spent on extensive reading (meaning-focused input and fluency development) should be three times that spent on intensive reading (language-focused learning), with all kinds of reading making up about one-quarter of the total course time (see Figure 8.1). This time includes extensive reading, intensive reading, reading strategy development, and deliberate reading instruction.

Listening	Speaking	Reading		Writing
		Extensive reading	Intensive reading Strategy training	

Figure 8.1 Time Spent on Extensive Reading and Intensive Reading in a Well-Balanced Course

How Do You Measure Comprehension?

Comprehension is notoriously difficult to define, and this is partly reflected in the variety of measures that have been used to measure comprehension. Some studies have measured comprehension change by using a standardized measure such as the reading section of TOEIC (Carney, 2016; Storey, Gibson, & Williamson, 2006), TOEIC scores (Mason, 2011; Nishizawa, Yoshioka, & Fukada, 2010; O'Neill, 2012), the Cambridge Preliminary English Test and Pre-TOEFL (Al-Homoud & Schmitt, 2009), the reading section of TOEFL

110 *Fluency and Comprehension Improvement*

(de Morgado, 2009), the reading section of STEP (Tanaka & Stapleton, 2007), or other independently-made measures (Lai, 1993; Lituanas, Jacobs, & Renandya, 2001; Robb and Susser, 1989; Yamashita, 2008). Some have used in-house measures (Robb & Kano, 2013), or multiple-choice measures specifically designed for the study or series of studies. De'Ath (2001) used a 35-item multiple-choice sentence completion test, and a similar test was also used as a pre-test in the Elley and Mangubhai (1981) study. Elley and Mangubhai also used a set of six passages and 32 multiple-choice items as a reading comprehension post-test. A similar kind of test seems to have been used in the Singapore REAP study (Elley, 1991). Mason and Krashen (1997) also used a text with multiple-choice questions in their third study. Bell (2001) used three texts, one accompanied by modified cloze, one by true/false, and one by multiple-choice questions.

Suk (2017) similarly developed her own tests of reading comprehension, using four reading passages. Each passage was accompanied by eight multiple-choice questions. She gave careful thought to the topics of the texts, the balance of narrative and factual texts, and the difficulty levels of the texts. The measures were well-trialled. Huffman (2014) used the comprehension questions accompanying each speed reading text (Quinn & Nation, 1974) as the comprehension measure. Mason and Krashen (1997) used a specially prepared 100-item cloze test as their measure of reading skill in all three of their studies. Lee (2007) used the same test. The use of a cloze test raises interesting questions about what is being measured. The cloze test was originally created as a measure of text readability (Taylor, 1953). It then was used as a measure of text comprehension (Anderson, 1971), with John Oller (1979) later proposing it as a test of overall language proficiency. It seems reasonable to use it as a test of comprehension. Rodrigo, Krashen, and Gribbons (2004) also used a cloze test, but found that although the traditional group did not score well on the test, the differences between the extensive reading, reading with discussion and traditional groups were not significantly different on this measure. Singh (2001) used a cloze test as a measure of comprehension in his Book Flood study, finding that the experimental group gained much higher scores than the traditional aural-oral group. Yamashita (2008) used a version of the cloze test which was not fixed deletion, but she considered it as a measure of linguistic ability rather than comprehension.

Oral reading has also been used as a measure (Lituanas, Jacobs, & Renandya, 1999), and learners doing extensive reading out-performed intensive reading groups on this measure.

The Effects of Extensive Reading on Reading Comprehension

Some studies have found little or no superiority for extensive reading on reading comprehension. Carney (2016) found no convincing relationship between scores on the reading section of TOEIC and extensive reading.

Fluency and Comprehension Improvement 111

Huffman (2014) found no differences in comprehension scores between his intensive reading group and the extensive reading group, but the pre-test comprehension scores were already high at close to nine out of ten correct, allowing little room for improvement. Lai (1993) used a standardized reading test involving multiple-choice cloze, deduction of meaning, deletion of extra words, and vocabulary recognition. He found no major difference in comprehension between his extensive reading group and the traditionally taught group. Al-Homoud and Schmitt (2009) found increases in comprehension but no major differences between the intensive reading group and the extensive reading group. Certainly, comprehension was not negatively affected by extensive reading or intensive reading. When you consider that intensive reading is deliberately focused on various aspects of text comprehension, then it is quite an achievement for extensive reading, which relies on incidental learning, to help comprehension to an equal degree. De Morgado (2009) found a small but significant improvement for the extensive reading group but none for the intensive reading group.

Suk (2017) found significant, slightly greater improvement in reading comprehension for her extensive reading group over the intensive reading group. However, the pre-test scores were already high (around 26 out of 32) with some learners gaining maximum scores leaving little room for improvement and the possibility of a ceiling effect for some learners. As mentioned earlier in this book, this is what extensive reading should be like – reading at the right levels with opportunity for not too burdensome gains to be made.

Some studies have found more striking improvement in comprehension. Bell (2001) using cloze, true/false, and multiple-choice measures found that his extensive reading group made greater gains in comprehension than his intensive reading group on all measures. The gains were substantial and were not limited by ceiling effects.

Several of the classes in De'Ath's (2001) study who were involved in the Book Flood program had higher scores on the comprehension test than those following the oral-aural program, and Elley and Mangubhai's (1981) study showed superior comprehension scores for the extensive reading groups. Robb and Kano (2013) found good increases for the extensive reading treatment groups on their 32-item in-house reading measure, but there is no description of the types of items in the measure. Mason and Krashen (1997) found greater increases in scores on their 100-item cloze test in all three of their studies for the extensive reading group compared to the more traditionally taught group. In their third study, the extensive reading groups also performed better on the reading comprehension test. Yamashita (2008) found improvement on her question-based comprehension measure, but not on her cloze test. Lituanas, Jacobs, and Renandya (1999) used a standardized oral reading test (the Gray Standardized Oral Reading Test) and the Informal Reading Inventory and found substantial increases in reading skill for the extensive reading group.

112 *Fluency and Comprehension Improvement*

Measuring the effect of extensive reading on reading comprehension is highly dependent on the difficulty level of the measures used. If a measure is too easy, then there will be a ceiling effect on the scores with little opportunity for learners to show improvement. There is also a need to make sure that the type of work done in the intensive reading or the traditional classes does not involve the same exercises used in the comprehension measure.

Overall, extensive reading seems to at least match the effects of intensive reading on comprehension and because of the quantity of reading done, it is likely to have even more positive effects on comprehension. Focusing on large quantities of reading at the right level and focusing on reading fluency do not negatively affect comprehension and are more likely to improve it.

Extensive Reading and Language Proficiency

The positive effects of extensive reading are not limited to vocabulary growth, fluency, and comprehension. Jeon and Day (2016) in their meta-analysis of extensive reading studies grouped reading comprehension, reading rate, and vocabulary as reading proficiency, finding a small to medium positive effect size for extensive reading. Krashen's (2007) meta-analysis of extensive reading studies found strong positive effects on comprehension as measured by multiple-choice and cloze measures.

Studies that used cloze tests as measures could be considered as measuring overall language proficiency, but we have included these studies as dealing with comprehension. They have generally shown a positive effect from extensive reading. Krashen and Mason (2015) used total scores on the TOEIC test as a measure of language proficiency, finding that the quantity of reading done by each of their seven readers was a good predictor of individual gains on the TOEIC test. Sheu (2003) used the Cambridge Key English Test which uses a mixture of question focuses (vocabulary, grammar, reading comprehension) and found a substantial increase by the reading groups over the traditionally taught group. Iwahori (2008) used a 100-item C-test involving several short texts as a test of overall proficiency (Klein-Braley, 1997), finding a significant but small increase in C-test scores over the seven-week course. The study did not involve a control group.

Extensive Reading and Writing

There have also been studies that show the effect of extensive reading on writing. Lai (1993) found an increase in the amount written, and a small increase in error-free T-units and writing style by one of his experimental reading groups. Tsang (1996) used Jacobs, Zingraf, Wormuth, Hartfiel and Hughey's (1981) ESL Composition Profile to measure writing skill. This profile covers content, organization, vocabulary, language use, mechanics, and overall impression with a different range of points available for each of those factors. Surprisingly, the extensive reading program learners out-

Fluency and Comprehension Improvement   113

performed the writing program learners, but this may have been because the writing program focused on output and provided minimal corrective feedback. Lee and Hsu (2009) and Mermelstein (2015) also used the Jacobs et al. ESL Composition Profile to measure writing improvement. In Mermelstein's study, the control group and the extensive reading followed essentially the same program over one academic year, except that the extensive reading group had part of the program replaced by extensive reading. The extensive reading group also did out-of-class reading. While both the control group and the extensive reading groups made significant gains in writing, the extensive reading group made the greater gains.

Lee and Hsu (2009) found significant gains in most of the factors (with the addition of fluency operationalized as the total number of words written) in the Jacobs et al. Profile.

Some of the Book Flood studies (Elley & Mangubhai, 1981; Schollar, 2001) used a writing measure. Schollar used a picture writing task involving measures of grammatical correctness and coherence. Elley and Mangubhai considered content, sentence sense, and mechanics. The extensive reading groups did better than the oral–aural groups on these measures. Elley and Mangubhai suggest caution in interpreting these measures as a large proportion of their learners achieved zero scores in written composition. The Book Flood studies also included measures of English structures (grammar) which showed small but consistent differences in favor of the extensive reading groups. Hafiz and Tudor (1989, 1990) and Tudor and Hafiz (1989) looked at the effect of extensive reading on writing, using second language learners in England and learners of EFL in Pakistan. They found improvement in writing.

Lightbown, Halter, White, and Horst (2002), however, caution against reliance on a solely comprehension-based program for developing writing skills. We need to see extensive reading programs and other comprehension-based programs as effective because essentially they provide large quantities of input. The interesting input engages learners and helps develop receptive knowledge of the language. It does not provide some magical means of developing high levels of proficiency in the productive skills. We learn what we give attention to (Barcroft, 2015), and if we do not read like a writer and actually do writing, our writing skill does not get the best opportunity to develop. Extensive reading should be a very important part of a well-balanced language program, not the whole program.

The research shows that extensive reading affects a wide variety of aspects of language proficiency, and in many studies it does this more effectively than intensive reading and traditional language-focused teaching. Large quantities of input provide opportunities for meeting a variety of language features and for repetition of these features. If the material used is at roughly the right level for the learners, then these opportunities can bring about a range of types of language development.

9 Research on Vocabulary Learning From Extensive Reading

It is important to see vocabulary learning through extensive reading as being just one of the many kinds of learning that can occur through extensive reading. It is also important to see the deliberate learning of vocabulary as not being in competition with vocabulary learning through extensive reading, but as a support and supplement to vocabulary learning through extensive reading (Laufer, 2003, 2009). However, as Laufer (2003), Cobb (2007), and Nation (2014) show, unless learners do very large amounts of extensive reading, it is likely that most EFL vocabulary learning will come from deliberate study. An important aim of this book is to encourage course-designers and teachers to set up the conditions for extensive reading to be a major contributor to growth in language proficiency including vocabulary growth.

The vocabulary learning effects of extensive reading are most likely to be noticeable in extended extensive reading courses. This is because of the repetition effects of substantial amounts of input. Not only are more different words met as more material is read, but there is much more opportunity for words to be repeated (Nation, 2014).

Does Extensive Reading Result in Vocabulary Learning?

There is clear evidence that extensive reading in a foreign language results in vocabulary learning. This evidence is mainly from two types of studies – studies involving the reading of a single text (Brown, Waring, & Donkaewbua, 2008; Horst, Cobb, & Meara, 1998; Pellicer-Sánchez & Schmitt, 2010; Waring & Takaki, 2003; Zahar, Cobb, & Spada, 2001), and studies involving learning from an extensive reading program (Al-Homoud & Schmitt, 2009; Horst, 2005; Pigada & Schmitt, 2006; Suk, 2017; Uden, Schmitt, & Schmitt, 2014; Webb & Chang, 2015). The single text studies attempt to carefully control as many variables as possible, while the reading program studies aim to keep the reading as normal as possible.

The results of these studies partly depend on how many measures of vocabulary knowledge of the same words were used. Where a single measure of vocabulary is used as in Zahar, Cobb, and Spada (2001) or the emphasis is placed on a single measure as in the Waring and Takaki (2003)

Research on Vocabulary Learning   115

report, the amount of vocabulary learning is seen as being rather small. Where multiple measures of the same words are used, we can see evidence of larger amounts of vocabulary learning at different strengths of knowledge (Waring & Takaki, 2003), and of different aspects of word knowledge (Pigada & Schmitt, 2006). Nonetheless, if we view extensive reading simply as a way of learning vocabulary, it is not as efficient as decontextualized vocabulary learning from flash cards (Qian, 1996; Nozaki, 2007; Webb, 2009). There are several reasons for this (Laufer, 2003). First, during extensive reading a reader's attention is primarily on following the story of a fiction text or the content of a non-fiction text. Because we tend to learn what we focus on (Barcroft, 2015), this means that incidental vocabulary learning is typically small because the words do not get a sustained deliberate focus during reading. There are so many other aspects of reading besides vocabulary requiring attention. Second, vocabulary learning during reading depends to some degree on guessing from context. Such guessing may not be successful, and when successful typically only adds small amounts of knowledge about a word because each context contributes only partial knowledge (Nagy, Herman, & Anderson, 1985). In addition as Mondria (2003) has shown, the guessing process itself does not contribute much to the quality of learning. Third, learning vocabulary from extensive reading requires substantial amounts of reading to get the amount of repetition needed for learning (Nation, 2014). Deliberate attention to word cards can quickly provide substantial amounts of repetition.

It is easy to see these points as criticisms of extensive reading, when, in fact, studies measuring vocabulary gains from intensive study measure words learnt directly. By contrast, extensive reading is not *primarily* a vocabulary learning task but one to build fluency, a sense of language, and reading speed. As we have seen, extensive reading can only be done if the text is relatively easy and the learner is focused on comprehending the text, not working out what words mean. This means that only two out of 100 words may be available for learning whereas in intentional vocabulary learning, there are many more words to learn. Moreover, this comparison is measuring outcomes using the same criteria for success when the learning is different. As we saw earlier, if a word is not met 10–12 times while reading extensively, it will not meet the criteria for being learnt as determined by the successful completion of a test question and will under-represent the partial knowledge gained in extensive reading. In the same vein, it doesn't seem to make much sense to compare intensive reading (such as studying for TOEIC or grammar-translation reading) to extensive reading.

However, extensive reading is a very important means of vocabulary learning, and this is especially so if the extensive reading program involves large amounts of reading at the right level for the learner. Although we have been comparing deliberate learning with learning from reading, deliberate vocabulary learning is not in competition with extensive reading but should be seen as a support for extensive reading and a very useful part of a balanced learning program.

Vocabulary Learning in Single-Text Studies

One advantage of investigating vocabulary learning from a single text is that it is possible to control other possible sources of input so that we can be sure that the learning that occurred was a result of the reading of the text. Another very important advantage is that it is much easier to base the vocabulary tests that measure learning on the actual vocabulary that occurred in the text, so that they are not testing words that the learners did not meet and so had no chance of learning.

In Chapter 6 on the most important research studies on extensive reading, we looked at the studies by Waring and Takaki (2003) and Pellicer-Sánchez and Schmitt (2010) which looked at vocabulary learning from a single text. All found evidence of substantial amounts of vocabulary learning.

The Waring and Takaki (2003) study showed that when multiple measures of the same words are used we can see evidence of substantial amounts of vocabulary learning at different strengths of knowledge. The study also showed the importance of repetition in learning.

Pellicer-Sánchez and Schmitt (2010) looked at vocabulary learning from an unsimplified text (*Things Fall Apart*, which was 67,000 words long) by 'relatively advanced' learners of English. Several different kinds of tests of the same words were used which also enabled gains in knowledge of partly known words to be measured. The largest gains were on meaning recognition (43% of the words), followed by spelling (34%), word class (20%), and meaning recall (14%). Learning was largely related to frequency of occurrence. The study showed that when several tests including sensitive tests are used, we can see gains in vocabulary knowledge of many different strengths and types. Hatami (2017) measured knowledge of 16 target words on several measures of the same words. One experimental group read the text and the other listened to the text. The control group did not encounter the text at all. As Brown, Waring, and Donkaewbua (2008) found, vocabulary was learned through reading and through listening, but the reading group learned more than the listening group, except on the test of recognition of spoken form where the scores were similar. The learning occurred across a range of aspects of vocabulary knowledge.

Horst, Cobb, and Meara (1998) used an unusual treatment methodology of getting the learners to quietly read a simplified version of *The Mayor of Casterbridge* (just over 20,000 words long) while it was also read to them over six classroom sessions of about an hour each. No unfamiliar vocabulary was explained to the learners. Brown, Waring, and Donkaewbua's (2008) study provides support for the effectiveness of reading-while-listening with vocabulary learning results similar to just reading, and the same technique was used in Zahar, Cobb, and Spada (2001). The learners in the Horst, Cobb, and Meara study sat a 45-item multiple-choice vocabulary test and a 13-item association test, both used as pre-tests and post-tests. The post-test multiple-choice score of 26.26 out of 45 showed a gain of 4.62 over the pre-test score of 21.64. The association test also showed a gain (pre-test 5.53

out of 13, post-test 6.71). These are small but significant gains which with a more elaborate testing methodology (Waring & Takaki, 2003; Pigada & Schmitt, 2006) would probably have been higher.

The Zahar, Cobb, and Spada (2001) study looked beyond how many words can be learned from reading a text to the much broader question of, "Is it possible to learn enough vocabulary from reading to have a functional reading lexicon?" The learners were given a recognition matching pre-test on 30 words in the short text, *The Golden Fleece*, then several days later did reading-while-listening immediately followed by the opportunity to quietly re-read the text a few times. Two days later they sat the same test as a post-test. The average learning gain was 2.33 words which was a reasonable gain given the high pre-test scores and the short treatment. They found an effect for frequency of occurrence in learning and concluded that on a scale of contextual richness from one to five, repeated words tended to average out at around 2.5 indicating that there will be some contexts that help quite a lot and others that are less supportive. Repetition seems to make contextual richness a non-issue.

Using the results of their study, Zahar, Cobb, and Spada (2001) calculated that "in a school year of roughly 40 weeks, learners would acquire only 70 new words a year [through reading], and at this rate 2,000 new words would be learned in just under 29 years" (p. 558). Zahar, Cobb, and Spada make the case for deliberate learning and lexically supported reading. These are useful suggestions, and there is also a strong case to be made for also having much more extensive reading as we saw in Chapters 4 and 5.

Studies of learning from a single text provide evidence of learning or the lack of it, but an extensive reading program involves the reading of very many texts. Projecting learning from a single text does not allow for the effects of repetition and the greater number of unknown words that occur in an extensive reading program.

Vocabulary Learning in an Extensive Reading Program

Nakanishi (2015) in a meta-analysis of 34 studies of extensive reading found that overall, learners in an extensive reading program out-performed other learners. There was a large effect for vocabulary learning in pre-/post-studies, but the number of studies involved was not large. Several of the studies that follow in this section were not in the Nakanishi meta-analysis possibly because they did not meet his definition of extensive reading.

In Chapter 6 on the most important research studies on extensive reading, we looked at the studies by Brown, Waring, and Donkaewbua (2008) and Pigada and Schmitt (2006), which looked at vocabulary learning from reading several texts. Both found evidence of substantial amounts of vocabulary learning. In Chapter 6 we also looked at the study by Suk (2017) which examined vocabulary learning in an extensive reading program.

The Brown, Waring, and Donkaewbua (2008) study compared three treatments: reading-only, reading-while-listening, and listening-only using three

118   *Research on Vocabulary Learning*

graded readers. The reading-only and reading-while-listening produced more vocabulary learning than listening-only, and the two measures of vocabulary learning gave results similar to the Waring and Takaki (2003) study showing different types of learning. The Pigada and Schmitt (2006) study involved one learner reading four French books totaling 30,000 running words, and involved recall tests of vocabulary form, meaning, and use. The study found that knowledge of two-thirds of the target words was added to in some way, and that there were improvements in word knowledge of various types in around 14.5 words per hour. Meaning and use knowledge required many more repetitions than form (spelling) knowledge. A notable feature of the Suk (2017) study was the attempt to control a range of potentially influential factors while still running a realistic extensive reading program. The learners read around 150,000 running words. The extensive reading groups easily out-performed the intensive reading group on vocabulary learning.

While the studies just described used specially constructed vocabulary measures based on the vocabulary occurring in the texts that the learners read, several studies have used the Vocabulary Levels Test (Schmitt, Schmitt, & Clapham, 2001; Lee 2007) as a vocabulary growth measure. Al-Homoud and Schmitt (2009) used the 2,000, 3,000, and AWL levels of the Vocabulary Levels Test. Both the intensive reading and extensive reading groups made similar substantial gains of around six to seven out of 30 at the 2,000 level, around 200 words. The two groups made smaller but equal gains at the 3,000 level, and even smaller but equal gains at the AWL level. Although intensive reading involves a deliberate focus on vocabulary, at all levels the extensive reading group matched the intensive reading group's vocabulary gains.

Lee (2007) did three consecutive studies, each a year long. Each time the administration of the extensive reading program was improved, and each time the learners in the extensive reading groups made greater gains on the Vocabulary Levels Test and a cloze test (Mason & Krashen, 1997). The gains from extensive reading were consistent but not large. This was probably because the amount of extensive reading done was modest involving less than a book a week, and the vocabulary measure was not targeted at the words met in the reading. The strengths of the study are its length (each treatment was one year long) and the use of several comparison control groups following the regular program.

Kweon and Kim (2008), using a self-report yes/no test and testing large numbers of words that occurred in the texts, found evidence of large amounts of vocabulary learning that continued to be retained on a delayed post-test four weeks after the immediate post-test. Rodrigo, Krashen, and Gribbons (2004) also used a self-report vocabulary test but directed at the learning of Spanish through extensive reading. They found that the extensive reading group and the reading with discussion group learned more words than the traditional group. Yamamoto (2011) found no great increases in vocabulary size through getting the learners to read five graded readers over a semester. This could have been partly the result of using the old Vocabulary Levels Test as the vocabulary measure rather than a vocabulary test based on the words in the books that the learners read. Cho, Ahn, and Krashen (2005) and Cho and Krashen (1994) found that all the learners in their studies learned vocabulary from their reading.

The Book Flood studies (De'Ath, 2001; Elley & Mangubhai, 1981; Ng & Sullivan, 2001; Ng, 2001) did not include a measure of vocabulary growth but did include word recognition measures which involved reading isolated words aloud. The extensive reading groups out-performed the oral teacher-fronted classes on that measure.

In terms of the quantity of vocabulary learning, studies involving several texts have shown greater learning than those involving single texts.

How Much Vocabulary Can Be Learned From Extensive Reading?

It is difficult to calculate how much vocabulary learning can occur from extensive reading, because learning will depend at least partly on the number of repetitions and this will depend on the amount of text read. In Chapter 5 we looked at two analyses of repetition and the amount of input needed to learn around 1,000 words a year. This research showed that such amounts of input are feasible but they involve persistent and long-term involvement in extensive reading. In a study of first language learners of English, Nagy, Herman, and Anderson (1985) calculated if learners read around one million running words of text a year, they would be likely to increase their vocabulary size by 1,000 different words per year. Even with a substantial extensive reading program, it would take learners several years to reach the vocabulary sizes of 5,000 words or more needed to comfortably deal with unsimplified texts.

Some studies involving reading in EFL have shown only very small gains in vocabulary knowledge (Horst, Cobb, & Meara, 1998; Zahar, Cobb, & Spada, 2001). The amount of vocabulary shown to be learned in an experimental study depends on a range of factors:

1   The level of the material being read in relation to the learners' vocabulary and grammatical knowledge: Texts which are too difficult and texts which are too easy provide little opportunity for vocabulary growth. Having texts at the right level is one of the critical factors in learning from extensive reading. If the texts are too easy, as seems to be the case in the Hafiz and Tudor (1989) study, then there is little to learn. If the texts are too difficult, as in the Pitts, White, and Krashen (1989) study, then the high density of unknown words makes learning difficult.
2   The sensitivity of the tests used: As the Waring and Takaki (2003) study, and numerous other studies (Laufer, Elder, Hill, & Congdon, 2004; Laufer & Goldstein, 2004; Nation, 2013a Chapter 13) have shown, the format of the tests (receptive vs productive, recognition vs recall, immediate vs delayed) directly affects the size of the result. Learning involves moving from no knowledge to various degrees of

120 *Research on Vocabulary Learning*

partial knowledge to strong knowledge. When measuring vocabulary learning from extensive reading we need to take account of this by allowing learners to demonstrate these various degrees of knowledge.

3   The aspect of vocabulary knowledge being measured: It is easier to show gains in knowledge of word form than it is to show gains in meaning or use (Pigada & Schmitt, 2006; Waring & Takaki, 2003).

4   The amount of input and repetition: The amount of input and repetition are related because a larger amount of input provides greater opportunities for repetition to occur, and all studies that have isolated repetition as a variable have shown a consistent but not perfect relationship between repetition and learning. The more repetitions there are, the more likely a word is to be learned (Kweon & Kim, 2008; Pellicer-Sánchez, 2016; Pellicer-Sánchez & Schmitt, 2010; Saragi, Nation, & Meister, 1978; Waring & Takaki, 2003). In addition, the more words there are to learn, the more words likely to be learned, as long as the density of unknown words is low. Some studies tested only a few words (Sheu, 2003), while others tested very large numbers (Horst, 2005; Kweon & Kim, 2008; Pigada & Schmitt, 2006; Rodrigo, Krashen, & Gribbons, 2004).

5   The availability of dictionaries or glosses: If vocabulary learning is solely reliant on successful guessing from context, then the amount of vocabulary learned is likely to be smaller than if learners can check their guesses and find the meanings of words which have occurred in unhelpful contexts. The research surveyed in this book (see especially Mondria, 2003) suggests that learners should be encouraged to do dictionary look-up during reading as long as the texts they are reading are at roughly the right level for them.

Nonetheless, vocabulary learning from extensive reading is a fragile process and will be mainly incidental learning. We can only expect large amounts of stable learning if there are large quantities of input at the right level for the learners.

Horst (2005) examined the feasibility of allowing the learner's choice in their reading and still directing the vocabulary growth measures at words that they were likely to have met in their reading. Horst's study is important because it not only looks at vocabulary learning through extensive reading, but proposes and trials a methodology for investigating such learning. Horst identified three methodological challenges in measuring vocabulary growth from extensive reading:

1   Identifying vocabulary that occurred in participants' reading. That is, choosing words to test that they had met in their reading.

2   Distinguishing between extensive reading and other sources of L2 input. Making sure that the vocabulary learning came from extensive reading.

3   Providing ample opportunity to demonstrate growth. Having a large enough test.

Research on Vocabulary Learning   121

She solved these problems by scanning and analyzing large numbers of graded readers, by using vocabulary profiling to identify topic words likely to have occurred only in particular texts, and by using a yes/no test format to quickly test lots of words. Each learner in the study had their own individualized vocabulary test (100 words) based largely on the books that they read.

The 21 learners in the extensive reading program varied greatly in the amount they read. The reading was done outside class but around an hour a week was spent on activities involving and supporting the reading. Over the six weeks of the program, the learners averaged a gain of 17 words on the 100 items sampled for the tests (words which occurred only once in the texts were not chosen for testing). This does not mean that learners learned only 17 words during their reading, because the test words were sampled from a much larger population. Knowing the size of that population would allow a calculation of the total number of words learned, but that was not possible in this study. However, it seemed that learners learned something of around half of the unknown words they met.

Webb and Chang (2015) looked at vocabulary learning from ten graded readers as result of reading-while-listening over a 13-week period in class for four hours a week, at the rate of one graded reader per week. The reading was followed by learner-led discussion of the text just read. A control group followed a more form-focused course for the same time. The learners sat the same pre-, post- (after one week), and delayed-post-test (after three months) testing 100 words. Between the post-test and the delayed post-test, there were five weeks of vacation and seven weeks of classes which involved more reading-while-listening for the experimental group.

There was a striking difference in vocabulary gains between the experimental and control groups, with the experimental group making a 44% relative gain (19.72 words) and the control group a 5% relative gain (4.43 words) on the post-test. The experimental group's gains were largely maintained on the delayed post-test. The vocabulary test favored the experimental group because all the words in the test were met in the graded readers. The use of a single test for each word, however, probably under-estimated the gains. Nonetheless, this study showed strong evidence of vocabulary learning from audio-assisted reading and subsequent discussion activities.

Guessing From Context, Look-Up, and Deliberate Learning

As Laufer (2003) shows, there are numerous subskills required to learn vocabulary incidentally from extensive reading. One of these is skill in guessing from context. The Mondria (2003) study is not a study of extensive reading as it did not look at learning from texts but from single sentences. However, it is looked at here because it provides an answer to the question, "Should learners be able to look up the meanings of words while reading?" This is an important question because meaning look-up is not always recommended, but if look-up greatly enhances vocabulary learning

122   *Research on Vocabulary Learning*

without unduly interfering with reading comprehension and the pleasure of reading, then it is worth doing. The study also provides a comparison between incidental learning and deliberate learning of vocabulary. We could see this comparison as a kind of comparison between learning through extensive reading and the deliberate study of vocabulary.

Mondria (2003) compared learning from inferring (guessing from context) with learning from inferring and verifying (looking up the meaning). He also compared two deliberate learning conditions, (a) inferring the meaning, verifying, and memorizing, and (b) memorizing a given meaning with no inferring or verifying. This second comparison allowed him to check if inferring added a depth of processing effect enhancing the learning. Because the same learners did all four kinds of learning, he was able to compare the deliberate learning with the incidental learning. He not only compared the amount of learning using a translation recall test two weeks after learning but also measured the amount of time needed for each kind of learning. This allowed him to examine both the effectiveness and the efficiency of the different kinds of learning.

In the deliberate learning part of the study, the inclusion of inferring did not provide a consistent positive effect and took more time. Having to infer before memorizing does not produce better results than simply being given the word and meaning to learn. Guessing from context does not seem to add a strong depth of processing effect enhancing learning. As would be expected, deliberate memorization of vocabulary resulted in much more learning than inferring or inferring plus verifying. Deliberate learning also took much more time.

The Mondria study shows that guessing from context (inferring) results in learning, and looking up the meaning (verifying) adds to that learning. Looking up a word after having a guess will substantially increase vocabulary learning. If vocabulary learning is one of the goals of extensive reading, learners should use dictionary look-up or consult a gloss. Deliberate learning of vocabulary is thus a very useful accompaniment to extensive reading.

Deliberate learning and extensive reading should not be seen as alternatives for vocabulary growth but should be seen as useful partners. While deliberate learning is very effective, extensive reading achieves a wide range of learning goals incidentally and reinforces and enriches deliberate learning.

10 Developing Reading Fluency

This chapter describes the visual nature of the reading process as it relates to reading speed. It points out that there is a physical limit on normal reading speed and beyond this limit the reading process will be different from normal reading where almost every word is attended to. The chapter describes a range of activities for developing reading fluency, and suggests how the development of fluency can become part of an extensive reading program.

A Reading Fluency Activity

"Are you ready? Go!"

At this command, 18 heads dip down and the learners begin reading in earnest. At the same time the teacher is pointing to minutes and seconds written on the board, indicating how much time has passed since the learners began reading.

Minutes	Seconds
0	00
1	10
2	20
3	30
4	40
5	50

As each learner finishes reading the short text, they look up at the board, note down the time it took them to read it, and then turn over the text and start answering the ten comprehension questions on the back of the sheet. When they have answered the questions, they get their answer key and mark their own answers. They look at the conversion chart and convert their time into words per minute. They enter their speed in words per minute onto the speed graph and they enter their comprehension score out of ten onto the comprehension graph. The teacher moves around the class looking at graphs and giving comments and encouragement to the learners.

124   *Developing Reading Fluency*

The whole activity has taken about seven minutes. The same activity will happen two or three times more in the same week and will continue for a total of around seven weeks until all of the 20 texts have been read. This is a typical lesson in a speed reading course for non-native speakers of English.

The Nature and Limits of Reading Speed

It is sometimes claimed that with speed reading training, readers can read whole books in a very short time. As we shall see, these claims are greatly exaggerated, and do not involve what we might call normal reading. Here we are interested in getting learners to read at a rate that is comfortable and is not too far from the rate that a typical young native speaker might read at.

To see what reading speed goals it is sensible to aim for, we need to understand the physical nature of reading and how this relates to reading speed. There are many misconceptions about reading faster, particularly about how fast people can read, and these can be cleared up by looking at the physical nature of reading. When people read, three types of action are involved – fixations on particular words, jumps (saccades) to the next item to focus on, and movements back to an item already looked at (regressions). This means that while reading the eyes do not move smoothly along a line of print, but jump from one word to another. There has been a great deal of research on eye movements while reading, and recent improvements in eye tracking technology have confirmed the following findings (Rayner, 1998):

1   A skilled reader reading at around 250–300 words per minute (wpm) makes around 90 fixations per 100 words. Most words are fixated on, but some very frequent function words like *the* and *of* are fixated on much less often than content words. The longer the word, the more likely it is to receive a fixation. If a word is really long, it may receive two or even three fixations. Around 200 milliseconds are spent on each fixation (about five per second). The length of these fixations varies a lot depending on how difficult a word or sentence is to read.
2   Each saccadic jump is around 1.2 words in English. This is about eight letters. In Finnish, where words are longer, the average jump is ten letters. This is around the maximum number of letters that can be seen clearly in one fixation. During the jump no items can be focused on because the eyes are moving. A jump takes about 20 milliseconds. The basic unit in the jump is the word and languages with quite different writing systems (for example English and Chinese) all tend to have an average of one jump for every 1.2 words.
3   A skilled reader makes around 15 regressions in every 100 fixations. Regressions occur because the reader made too big a jump (many regressions when reading in English are only a few letters long), and because there were problems in understanding the text.

Developing Reading Fluency 125

What this research shows is that in normal skilled reading most words are focused on. Because there are limits on the minimum time needed to focus on a word and on the size and speed of a jump, it is possible to calculate the physiological limit on reading speed where reading involves fixating on most of the words in the text. This is around 300 words per minute. (Five fixations per second times 1.2 = six words per second times 60 = 360 wpm. If regressions are considered, this reduces the forward movement through the text to around 300 wpm.) If someone is reading at a speed of 400+ wpm, then that person is no longer fixating on most of the words in the text. In Urquhart and Weir's (1998) terms, that person is no longer doing careful reading, but instead is doing 'expeditious reading' which includes skimming and scanning. Unless such readers bring a great deal of background knowledge to their reading, they will usually be unable to answer detailed questions on parts of the text not fixated on.

Many non-native speakers of English and some native speakers read at speeds which are well below 300 wpm. They could benefit from doing a speed reading course, and should be aiming for speeds higher than 150 wpm and preferably around 250 wpm on easy material. Research on speed reading with non-native speakers of English shows that they can easily reach such speeds (Chung & Nation, 2006; Cramer, 1975; Tran, 2012).

In Chapter 8 on research on extensive reading and reading speed, we looked at research (Carver, 1976; Kramer & McLean, 2013) which suggested that using the number of characters or using standard words (six letter spaces equals one standard word) is a more valid measure of reading speed. In this chapter, we will continue talking about words per minute but for research purposes it is better to use standard words per minute.

About one-quarter of the time in a well-balanced language course should be spent on helping learners become more fluent in using the language they already know, that is, making the best use of what they have already learned. This fluency development needs to cover each of the four skills of listening, speaking, reading, and writing and needs to involve substantial amounts of input and output (Nation, 2007, 2013b). In an extensive reading program, about one-third of the time should be spent on fluency development work, most of it involving reading easy graded readers. A small proportion of this fluency time, however, should include at least one speed reading course.

The physical symptoms of slow reading are (1) fixating on units smaller than a word (word parts, letters, parts of letters) and thus making several fixations per word, (2) spending a long time on each fixation or on some fixations, and (3) making many regressions to look back at what has already been read. Increasing speed will result in a change in these symptoms.

Reading speed is affected by a range of factors including the purpose of the reading, and the difficulty of the text. The difficulty of the text is affected by the vocabulary, grammatical constructions, discourse, and background knowledge. A reasonable goal for second language learners who are reading material that contains no unknown vocabulary or grammar and that

126　*Developing Reading Fluency*

has easy content is around 250 wpm. Let us now look at how learners can be helped to reach this reading speed.

The Nature of Fluency Development

We have looked briefly at the physical aspects of reading and how these change as fluency develops. But these signs are the result of mental processes. One of the mental processes involved in reading is decoding, that is, turning the written form of a word into a familiar spoken form with a known meaning. Readers develop skill in decoding in two related ways. First, through practice they become faster at recognizing the unit they are working with, and second, they change the size of this basic unit. When someone begins to read an unfamiliar written script there are many things to notice. Imagine, for example, a Thai speaker is learning to read English. Because Thai uses a different script from English, learning to read the English letters *p, b, d*, and *g* is quite difficult because although the letters have some similarities, there are important differences. Where is the circle part of the letter, at the bottom as in *b* or at the top as in *p*, on the right of the stalk as in *b* or on the left as in *d*? The letters *p, b*, and *d* have straight stalks, *g* has a curved stalk. At a very early stage of reading English, each part of a letter is an important piece of information. With practice, fluency in recognizing the different letters develops and soon the basic unit that the reader is working with is no longer the parts of the letters but the letters themselves. With further reading experience the basic unit that the learner is working with will change from letters to word parts and words. At early stages of word recognition, learners may rely on only some of the letters, usually the initial letters, for word recognition. As they become more accomplished readers, they may no longer need to notice each letter but can recognize whole words and, if necessary, apply rules or use analogy to quickly decode unfamiliar words. What this means is that fluency development involves not just becoming faster, it also involves changing the size and nature of the basic unit that the reader is working with. Another way of putting this is to say that fluency develops when complex activities like reading are made less complex by the fluent mastery of some of the subskills involved in the activity.

There are two main paths to fluency. One could be called *the well-beaten path*. A repetitive activity, like re-reading, is an example of this. In such activities, repetition of the same material is used to develop fluency. By doing something over and over again you get better at doing it. The second path to fluency could be called *the rich and varied map*. In such activities, the learners do things which differ slightly from each other but which draw on the same kind of knowledge. A good example of this is easy extensive reading where learners read lots of graded readers at the same level. The stories differ but the same vocabulary and grammatical constructions reoccur and the learners develop a rich range of associations with the same words and constructions.

This is a bit like going to school on the first day when you know no-one. Then after a while, you learn a few names and then the connections between

Developing Reading Fluency 127

friends, by the end of the semester you know all the classmates and the inter-relationships. Knowledge of words develops in a similar kind of way.

The Nature of Fluency Development Activities

If an activity is going to contribute effectively to fluency development then it needs to meet certain conditions. Let us look at a very useful fluency development activity for reading aloud to see what these conditions are.

Repeated reading has been used with good results with first language readers to help reach a good degree of oral reading fluency (Dowhower, 1989; Rasinski, 1990; Samuels, 1979; Sindelar, Monda, & O'Shea, 1990). The learner reads a text (about 50–300 words long) aloud with help where necessary, while the teacher or another learner listens. Then the text is re-read reasonably soon after (within a day). Then the text is read again a day later. The text should only be a little bit above the learner's present level. Most of the running words should be easily recognized. The optimal number of repetitions is around three to five. Using texts intended to be read aloud, like poems, plays, jokes, or stories, can increase the purposefulness of the activity. Repeated reading and repeated reading while listening to a taped passage give similar positive results.

There are four conditions that need to be met for an activity to truly be a fluency development activity. The first and most important condition is that the material should be easy. It is important to choose texts for repeated reading where all the vocabulary is known and there are not too many irregularly spelt words. The second condition for a fluency activity is that there should be some pressure to perform at a faster than normal speed. In the repeated reading activity, the repetition provides this encouragement. To strengthen this condition, the time taken to read the text could be noted for each reading and the reader should be trying to beat her previous speed for the same text. The third condition needed for a fluency development activity is that the learners should be focused on the message. In repeated reading, this condition is met by having a listener. The reader is trying to communicate the message of the text to the listener. The fourth and final condition is that there should be quantity of practice. In repeated reading, the text is not very long but the repetitions mean that there is quite a lot of reading practice.

Let us now look at a range of reading activities that meet these conditions and that are thus very useful for developing reading fluency. The activities are divided into three groups which are in order of development. The first group of reading fluency activities involves reading aloud. Such reading is a very important first step towards the second group of activities which involves careful silent reading. The third group involves expeditious reading or skimming and scanning very quickly to get a particular piece or a particular type of information. Skill in careful silent reading is an important prerequisite to most skimming and scanning.

128 *Developing Reading Fluency*

Increasing Oral Reading Speed

In the first language classroom, reading aloud to the teacher or to a peer is a very important step towards gaining fluent decoding and comprehending skills which are a necessary preparation for fluent silent reading. There are several useful activities for working on oral reading and they have just as much value in the foreign language class as in the first. What all these activities have in common is a learner reading aloud, trying to convey the message of the text to a sympathetic and interested listener. In small classes this may involve a learner reading to the teacher, but in most classes it will involve pair work where a learner reads to a classmate. This kind of activity makes more effective use of class time than simply going around a whole class getting the learners to read one by one. This activity can also be useful for the teacher to know what problems a learner is having when reading. However, a single learner reading aloud to a class is often said to be one of the most stressful activities in the English classroom. This is because it has the potential to embarrass learners and show up their poor pronunciation or their reading ability for the whole class to see. Moreover, if a teacher asks the learners to read around the class one by one, the other learners are likely to be practicing for their turn rather than listening to the other learners, or if their turn has finished they may switch off and not pay attention. Therefore, this activity is best done in small groups or one to one with a teacher and be used as a vehicle to identify and fix reading problems.

Repeated reading: We have already looked at repeated reading. A strength of this technique is that it can be used with material that has some difficulties for the reader. By repeated reading, these difficulties are overcome and in the later repetitions the activity can thus meet the conditions needed for fluency development.

Paired reading: Paired reading is a form of assisted reading. In this activity, the learner is paired with a more proficient reader. They sit side by side and read the same text aloud together with the more proficient reader keeping at the same speed as the less proficient reader. The less proficient reader nudges the more proficient reader as a signal that she wants to read alone. If the less proficient reader strikes problems, the more proficient reader joins in reading again. Word recognition errors are corrected as soon as they happen, simply by the proficient reader saying the word without further explanation. The same activity can be used with a parent or a cross-age peer. A paired reading activity can last for about 15 to 30 minutes, and the learners should be trained in the use of the procedure. Research on this activity shows that learners make very substantial progress in accuracy and comprehension. The tutors also make progress in their reading (Rasinski & Hoffman, 2003; Topping, 1989). There are variations of this activity where the better reader models the reading first, or where the same text is read several times.

4/3/2 reading: This is an adaptation of the 4/3/2 speaking activity (Nation, 1989) for reading aloud. Each learner has a text to read. All the learners could have the same text but it is more interesting for the listeners and more suitable

Developing Reading Fluency   129

for a class with a wide range of proficiency if they all have different texts. The learners form pairs. One member of each pair is the listener and the other is the reader. When the teacher says "Go!", each reader reads their text to their listener. After four minutes the teacher says "Stop!", and the readers stop reading. They change partners and the readers then read the same text for three minutes to their new listener. They change partners again and the readers now read the same text to the new listener for two minutes. The learners are told that they should try to speed up each reading so that each listener hears about the same amount of text even though the time is less. As a variation, after each reading the reader can mark in pencil the place in the text they reached.

Extensive reading aloud: A part of the class time can be set aside for learners to read to each other or for one learner to read a continuing story to a small group. The story should be easy to read and the reader can concentrate on making it interesting. A variation could be learners making a tape-recording of a story for others to listen to.

Read-and-look-up: This activity does not meet many of the conditions for a fluency activity but it is one that encourages learners to work with a basic unit beyond a single word. Michael West (1960, pp. 12–13) devised this technique as a way of helping learners to learn from written dialogues and to help them put expression into the dialogues. West regarded the physical aspects of Read-and-look-up as being very important for using the technique properly. The learners work in pairs facing each other. One is the reader, the other is the listener. The reader holds the piece of paper or the book containing the dialogue at about chest level and slightly to the left. This enables the reader to look at the piece of paper and then to look at the listener, moving only her eyes and not having to move her head at all. The reader looks at the piece of paper and tries to remember as long a phrase as possible. The reader can look at the paper for as long as is necessary. Then, when ready, she looks at the listener and says the phrase. While she looks at the paper, she does not speak and can only read silently. While she speaks, she does not look at the paper. These rules force the reader to rely on memory. At first, the technique is a little difficult to use because the reader has to discover what length of phrase is most comfortable and has to master the rules of the technique. It can also be practiced at home in front of a mirror. West saw value in the technique because the learner:

> has to carry the words of a whole phrase, or perhaps a whole sentence, in his mind. The connection is not from book to mouth, but from book to brain, and then from brain to mouth. That interval of memory constitutes half the learning process.... Of all methods of learning a language, Read-and-Look-up is, in our opinion, the most valuable.
>
> (West, 1960, p. 12)

Good spoken reading speeds range from 100 to 200 wpm. These are necessarily slower speeds than silent reading speeds.

130 *Developing Reading Fluency*

Reading aloud is a useful activity to practice accurate decoding and it is a useful activity in its own right – people gain pleasure from listening to stories and talks and from reading stories to others. The activities in this section provide a useful preparation for the silent reading activities described in the next section.

Increasing Careful Silent Reading Speed

The classic way of increasing reading speed is to follow a speed reading course consisting of timed readings followed by comprehension measures. For learners of English as a second or foreign language, such courses need to be within a controlled vocabulary so that the learners are not held up by unknown words. The first published course for foreign learners of English was *Reading Faster* by Edward Fry (1967) which had an accompanying teachers' book called *Teaching Faster Reading* (Fry, 1965). The course consisted of texts around 500 words long, each followed by ten multiple-choice questions. The texts were taken from a graded reader and were written at the 2,000 word level. The course worked well but it was not suitable for learners with vocabularies of less than 2,000 words and it also contained the names of diseases like *bilharzia, kwashiorkor,* and *yaws* which tended to slow the reading. Quinn and Nation (1974) developed a course written well within the first 1,000 words of English consisting of 25 texts each exactly 550 words long and followed by ten comprehension questions. Sonia Millett has developed a wide range of free speed reading courses within a carefully controlled vocabulary from the 500 level up (available from Paul Nation's web site).

There have been mechanical reading pacers where the text is revealed at a pre-set speed and there have been films which reveal text at a certain rate. Such aids are fun but are not necessary for increasing reading speed. The essential requirements are suitable texts and questions. Some digital systems present words in sequential order one at a time but in exactly the same place on a screen and is called 'rapid serial visual presentation' (RSVP). The notion is that by seeing all the words in the same position, the reader can avoid making saccadic movements and process more words quickly with claims of speeds up to 500 wpm being made. One problem with this is that it requires the learner to focus more on word recognition than comprehension and ignores the time and cognitive effort required to combine words in a text for comprehension which is often facilitated by regressions. Boo and Conklin (2015) found that comprehension slowed dramatically after 500 wpm possibly as a result of suppressed parafoveal processing (Benedetto, Carbone, Pedrotti, Le Fevre, and Amel Yahia Bey, 2015).

Easy extensive reading: Another very effective way of increasing reading speed is to get learners to read graded readers at a level which is much easier than the level they would normally read to gain meaning-focused input. This is a widely adopted strategy used in many Japanese extensive reading programs and is called *Start with Simple Stories* (SSS). When reading easy

Developing Reading Fluency   131

books, learners should be encouraged to do large quantities of such reading and to re-read books that they really enjoyed. It is important to remember that there needs to be two types of extensive reading involving reading graded readers at two different speeds. One type, reading for meaning-focused input, involves learners reading at a level where about one word in 50 is unknown. These words can be guessed from context and add to the readers' vocabulary knowledge. The second type of extensive reading, reading for fluency development, should involve texts where there are virtually no unknown words. Such texts should be read quickly for enjoyment, and large numbers of them should be read. In an extensive reading program, about one-third of the time should be spent on very easy extensive reading for fluency development.

Silent repeated reading: In this activity the learners silently re-read texts that they have read before. In order to encourage faster reading, they can note the time each reading took so that they have the goal of reading it faster each time.

Issue logs: At the beginning of a language course the learners each decide on a topic that they will research each week. Each learner should have a different topic. The topics can include pollution, global warming, oil, traffic accidents, the stock market, etc. Each week the learners find newspaper reports, magazine articles, academic texts, information from the internet, television reports, etc. on their topic and write a brief summary. Because they are reading lots of material on the same topic, they will soon be in control of the relevant vocabulary in their topic area and will bring a lot of background knowledge to what they read (Watson, 2004). This is a kind of narrow reading (Kang, 2015; Krashen, 1996; Schmitt & Carter, 2000).

Careful silent reading is the most common kind of reading. Learners need to be able to read with good comprehension near the upper speed limits of such reading.

Increasing Silent Expeditious Reading Speed

Sometimes we only have time to read a text to get the general gist of it, or maybe to look over the text to find a specific piece of information such as looking for the time a bus departs on a bus timetable, or the price of a product on a webpage. These types of reading are expeditious because they serve particular purposes or aims and focus the learner only on that which is essential for the particular task in hand (Khalifa & Weir, 2009). There are two major kinds of expeditious reading: *skimming* and *scanning*. The major goal of speeded expeditious reading would be to increase skimming speed.

Skimming: In skimming, the reader goes through a text quickly, not noting every word but trying to get the main idea of what the text is about. This is sometimes called getting the gist of the text. After such reading, the reader is unlikely to have noticed details, but should be able to say in a general way what the text is about. The more background knowledge that a reader brings to

132 *Developing Reading Fluency*

skimming, the faster the skimming speed is likely to be. Reading speeds higher than 300–400 wpm are the result of skimming, not careful reading.

Being able to skim text is a useful skill, because skimming can be used to help decide if a text or section of a text deserves careful reading. Skimming activities should involve texts which are at least 2,000 words long and which are on topics that the learners are familiar with. Comprehension should be measured by questions which ask "What was the text about?" Multiple-choice or true/false questions which focus on the gist of the text could also be used.

Scanning: Scanning involves searching for a particular piece of information in a text, such as looking for a particular name from a list, or a particular number such as finding the specific time a TV show starts from a TV schedule. It is probably better to spend time increasing skimming speed than to devise scanning activities. This is because effective scanning depends on good careful reading and skimming skills, and training in scanning is unlikely to result in more fluent access to items.

Typical scanning tasks include searching a text for a particular quotation, someone's name, a particular date or number, or a particular word; or searching a list for a telephone number, someone's name, or a particular word or phrase.

However, these two tasks are so common in daily life, they probably do not need much attention in class. For example, when the learners enter a classroom, they scan the room for an empty seat or to look for which friends have arrived already, then they skim through their textbook to find the right page so they can start the lesson. Our learners are probably very proficient at these skills, so instruction should focus the learners on where to skim or scan for information, how texts are structured, and so on.

Frequently Asked Questions About Reading Speed

What About Comprehension?

Comprehension is very important when developing fluency in reading. There is no point in reading faster if only a little of the passage is understood. For careful silent reading, readers should score seven or eight out of ten on a comprehension test. Higher scores than this indicate that the reader is going too slowly and is trying to get too much from the text. Readers should be trying to stretch their speed without losing too much comprehension. If readers are scoring too highly, it would be easy for them to increase their speed at the expense of a little less detailed comprehension. Scores of six or less out of ten are too low, suggesting the readers are reading too quickly, or do not know enough of the text and the readers should read more of the same type of texts at the same speed until comprehension improves. Speed reading courses use both wpm graphs and comprehension score graphs. Lower comprehension scores are acceptable for skimming tasks because while skimming, readers do not give attention to every part of the text. Questions on skimming texts should look for the main ideas.

Developing Reading Fluency 133

How Can Reading Fluency Be Measured?

Reading fluency is typically measured by timing the reading of a text to find reading speed. The reading should be accompanied by an untimed comprehension check to make sure that fluency includes understanding. The speed of reading should be measured in standard words per minute rather than just words per minute (Kramer & McLean, 2019).

How Much Time Should Be Spent on Fluency Development?

The principle of the four strands (Nation, 2007, 2013b) says that one-quarter of the course time should be spent on fluency development. This time needs to be divided across the four skills of listening, speaking, reading, and writing, suggesting that about one-16th of the time in a language course needs to be spent on developing reading fluency. This degree of precision in the amount of time should not be taken too seriously, as it will depend on learner needs, but it is a useful guide. In a language course involving four hours of class time a week plus a roughly similar amount of time for homework, this would mean that around about half an hour a week would be spent doing a speed reading course, reading very easy graded readers, doing narrow reading, and doing occasional skimming and scanning practice. Fluency development should be a focus at all levels of proficiency, because fluency is not only skill-based but also relates to knowledge of particular words, phrases, and grammatical constructions. As we learn more language, we also need to become fluent in its use.

How Can Progress in Reading Fluency Be Monitored?

One-minute reading: An interesting activity for regularly checking on reading speed is One-minute reading (Iwano, 2004). The learners read a text with the time being recorded by a stopwatch. After exactly one minute the teacher says "Stop!", and the learners mark where they reached in the text. They then count how many words there are up to that point. Doing this on the same text before and after a speed reading program can be a good way of showing learners how their speed has increased. They can also re-read the same text and try to get beyond that mark. However, because it is only a single measure and involves only a small amount of text, it is not a very reliable measure.

Reading logs: A log is a regular record of what happened at particular times. Learners can keep a log of their regular extensive reading, noting the name of the book, the time they started reading, and how much they read. If this is accurately done, it may provide a rough indicator of reading speed and increases in speed. Many extensive reading programs use MReader which records which books were read, and records the number of words read (for books whose test was passed). Researchers need to be cautious when interpreting speeds over time. Sometimes speed increases are not seen

134 *Developing Reading Fluency*

over a course because the learner finished one level and then their speed slowed down as they read the next level and they finished the course before gains were seen at the same level. So logging speed must be noted for each different reading series level.

Speed reading graphs: When learners do a speed reading course with short texts and questions, they score their speed and comprehension on graphs (see Quinn & Nation, 1974, p. 51). Teachers should regularly look at learners' graphs and give them advice and encouragement. Where progress is not being made, the teacher can suggest remedial procedures like repeated reading, skimming before reading, and discussion of the content with a friend before reading.

Online tracking: Online reading sites like ER-Central.com allow learners to select material to practice speed reading. The system tracks their speed and comprehension and allows the students to measure their progress.

What Are Good Reading Speeds?

A good oral reading speed is around 150 wpm. A good careful silent reading speed is around 250 wpm. A good skimming speed could be around 500 wpm. These are reasonable goals for foreign and second language learners who are reading material that contains no unknown vocabulary and grammar. However, many second language learners don't get near this speed. Tran (2011), for example, found that her Vietnamese learners averaged 150 wpm.

It is not easy to measure skimming speed because skimming is an activity we might do for a maximum of 30 seconds and the number of words will depend on the text type, for example whether we are skimming a webpage with lots of sections or a business report or a novel.

What Are the Advantages and Disadvantages of Reading Faster?

There are disadvantages of reading faster. The pressure to go faster can be a source of stress. Such pressure can reduce the enjoyment that learners get from reading. It is best to see the skill of reading faster as providing a wider range of choices for a reader. Sometimes it is good to read fast. At other times it is not. Being able to make the choice is an advantage. Research, however, suggests that native-speaking readers have a fairly standard reading speed for material that is within their capability (Carver, 1976) and they tend to stick to that.

Research on reading faster has shown that increasing reading speed in one language can result in increases in another known language. This has been tested from the first language to English (Bismoko & Nation, 1974) and from English to the first language (Cramer, 1975; West, 1941). It is likely that the transfer of training here is the transfer of confidence, that is, the confidence that you can read faster and still comprehend.

It has been suggested that reading too slowly at speeds of much less than 100 wpm can have negative effects on comprehension. Anyone who has

Developing Reading Fluency   135

learned to read another script knows the phenomenon of slowly sounding out the script and then having to go back and read the sentence again more fluently to see what it means. They do this because the basic unit they are working with might be a few letters or a whole word, but there are too many of them in working memory and by the time they get to the end of the sentence they have forgotten the beginning. When learners read faster, they work with larger chunks of texts. These chunks more closely correspond to 'meaning units' or 'idea units' raising the possibility that the readers will remember the context of a passage more than if they were working at the word-by-word level. In normal life we rarely remember the exact words people say, but we remember the content.

In this chapter we have looked at the nature of reading fluency and a wide range of activities that can support reading fluency development. Basically, however, learners should do a speed reading course at the right level for them, and should maintain the fluency gains from this course by doing plenty of extensive reading and plenty of easy extensive reading.

Fluency development is an essential strand in a language course. Learners need to be able to make the best use of what they already know at every stage of their learning. Giving attention to reading fluency is one part of this strand. As with the development of listening fluency, speaking fluency, and writing fluency, the development of reading fluency can have clear practical and motivational benefits for a language learner.

11 Designing Research Into Extensive Reading

Over the last 40 or more years a considerable amount of experimental extensive reading research has been conducted. The ERF's bibliography of extensive reading research (http://erfoundation.org/wordpress/bibliography/) has curated over 600 individual papers, many of which report research into extensive reading. There are studies that ask whether subjects can learn from extensive reading (including many involving incidental learning from reading experiments), other studies that compare extensive reading approaches with other treatments (such as with 'normal' approaches or 'translation' approaches), and yet others that have looked at the effect of extensive reading on other aspects of language learning (such as on writing, confidence, motivation, and so on) among many other topics.

Research in extensive reading has been undertaken to demonstrate that language gains of many types occur from exposure to simplified second language texts. Research by Elley (1991), Hafiz and Tudor (1990), Lituanas, Jacobs, and Renandya (2001), Waring and Takaki (2003), Brown, Waring, and Donkaewbua (2008), among others, report linguistic gains as a result of extensive reading. Writing ability is said to improve as a result of extensive reading (Elley & Mangubhai, 1981; Hafiz & Tudor, 1990; Robb & Susser, 1989; Tsang, 1996) as is spelling (Krashen, 1989; Polak & Krashen, 1988). Reading extensively has also been reported to increase motivation to read and the development of a positive attitude to reading in the second language (Burrows, 2013; Constantino, 1994; Hayashi, 1999; Lipp, 2017; Liu, 2016; Yamashita, 2004). Oral proficiency was (anecdotally) said to have improved after reading large amounts of text (Cho & Krashen, 1994; Lado, 2009). There are a considerable number of vocabulary studies that report gains in vocabulary from extensive reading (Chun, Choi, & Kim, 2012; Day, Omura, & Hiramatsu, 1991; Dupuy & Krashen, 1993; Grabe & Stoller, 1997; Vidal, 2011; Webb, 2015; Yamashita, 2007, 2008 are just a few examples). There is also research into the nature and quality of graded readers (e.g. Claridge, 2005) and attitudes to them (e.g. Cheetham, Harper, Elliott, & Ito, 2016).

Almost all of this research has been done by researchers who wish to show extensive reading in a positive light and there is considerable cross-citation

Designing Research Into Extensive Reading 137

within this literature which is used as evidence to support the claims made in the research. However, rarely does one find in these citations any critique of this literature and most often it is accepted as fact and cited without comment. The extensive reading research literature (as a body of research) has been severely criticized by many researchers. For example, Coady (1997, p. 226), referring to some oft-cited extensive reading research, says, "there appears to be a serious methodological problem with these studies". Horst, Cobb, and Meara (1998) also point out that some of the incidental learning from exposure experiments that are often cited as supporting an extensive reading approach are "methodologically flawed" (p. 210). Unfortunately, a detailed examination of these 'flaws' is not made apparent in the papers and researchers need to be made aware of what problems exist (Nakanishi, 2015).

As the popularity of extensive reading, both as an approach to learning and as a research topic, has boomed in recent years, it seems timely and pertinent to look carefully and in detail at a broad range of extensive reading studies to determine what we do know about ER, what problems these researchers have had while undertaking this research, and how that can inform future research so that we can learn from past mistakes. Unless we have a solid foundation of research upon which to form our ideas about what extensive reading can do effectively and what it cannot do, it will be that much more difficult to promote the need for extensive reading within foreign language learning contexts. Thus, our concern should be with the quality, reliability, and accountability of much, but not all, of the research surveyed in the following sections (and the claims emanating from them) as a canonical base upon which the house of extensive reading rests.

A Critique of Some Specific Extensive Reading Studies

It needs to be stated plainly that we know very little about reading and about the assessment of reading. Alderson (2000) makes the point that in order for us to be able to say something about reading we have to know what reading is. He goes on to say that:

> in order to devise a test or assessment procedure for reading, we must surely appeal, if only intuitively, to some concept of what it means to read texts and understand them. How can we possibly test whether somebody has understood a text if we do not know what we mean by 'understand'? How can we possibly diagnose somebody's 'reading problems' if we have no idea what might constitute a problem and what the possible 'causes' might be? How can we possibly decide what 'level' a reader is 'at' if we have no idea what 'levels of reading' might exist, and what it means to be 'reading at a particular level'? In short those who need to test reading clearly need to develop some idea of what reading is, and yet that is an enormous task.
>
> (pp. 6–7)

138   *Designing Research Into Extensive Reading*

This should not stop us trying to find out about reading in second languages, but research into second language extensive reading will always be fraught with problems. First, the volume of reading that subjects have to undertake in order that the research can be labeled 'extensive reading' means that it will take a lot of time. This necessitates that the reading be done over many sessions and often out of class and in non-controlled environments, which naturally brings up cries of contamination due to outside influence during the period of the experiment. Second, some research in extensive reading has to be done in real classrooms under real conditions or it loses its face validity, which *necessarily* means that conditions for investigating the nature of extensive reading will be less than ideal and it will not always be possible to control all variables. It is just not practical in most circumstances to cleanly control all variables other than the ones we are looking at when researching ER, so we must learn to be happy with doing our best. However, sometimes the researchers did not do their best to control variables and it is worth reviewing some of the areas of concern that have become apparent when reading extensive reading research so we can better understand the pitfalls.

The Range of Questions That Have Been Investigated

Research into language gains and gains in affect (e.g. confidence and motivation) from extensive reading in second languages is still in its infancy, is quite fragmented, and is rather difficult to interpret when looking for concrete 'evidence'. However, a number of points are clear.

First, this research has mostly been conducted with the learning of English and on Asian and Oceanic learners. In comparison, there is very little widely known research into the second language learning of Mandarin, French, Spanish, Arabic, and other major world languages. While there are hundreds of studies on English, the ERF bibliography shows there are only about 20 in French (e.g. Dupuy & Krashen, 1993; Dupuy & McQuillan, 1997; Pigada & Schmitt, 2006), 16 in Spanish (Alessi & Dwyer, 2008; Brantmeier, 2005; Rodrigo, Krashen, & Gribbons, 2004), ten in German (e.g. Mason, Vanata, Jander, Borsch, & Krashen, 2008; Maxim, 1999, 2002) and few in Japanese (e.g. Tabata-Sandom, 2013, 2016) and Chinese (e.g. Sin, 2007). Second, quite a number of these studies seem to have used convenience populations (i.e. those available in the researcher's own classes) and/or are conducted on highly educated individuals (those at college) rather than a more 'normal' profile of the population in general. Third, there is also a tendency to use populations of individuals of a specific demographic (e.g. English majors at universities). Fourth, there is also a very narrow ability range of subjects who have been investigated, most of whom might be considered 'intermediate' level and there is a tendency to use the upper streamed students rather than lower-streamed ones (see Evans, 1999 for one example). Fifth, most research has been conducted with adults rather than children and in foreign language environments rather than second language environments. This narrow range

Designing Research Into Extensive Reading 139

is rather troubling. We cannot hope to have much to say about extensive reading in general until we have extensive amounts of research into language learning from extensive reading in a whole range of languages, ages, educational backgrounds, and so on.

When we look at the *methodology* of the research that has been done, quite a different picture appears, and almost the full range of experimental variables have been explored. There are experiments that have been conducted on individuals as cases studies (Cho & Krashen, 1994; Grabe & Stoller, 1997; Nishino, 2007; Rausch, 2004; Ro, 2013) and on very large populations (e.g. Elley & Mangubhai, 1983; Lai, 1993; Mason, 2018). There are experiments that have investigated learning from short texts (e.g. only 1,032 words in Day, Omura, & Hiramatsu, 1991) to very large amounts of text (e.g. a graded reader a day in Lai, 1993; 18 graded readers in nine weeks in Yamazaki, 1996; and 161,000 words by the Korean student Jin-hee in Cho & Krashen, 1994). There are experiments that have lasted up to two years (e.g. Elley's (1991) Book Flood experiments) or six years (Nishizawa, Yoshioka, & Ichikawa, 2017). Some research into extensive reading has investigated language development in children and others in adults. Some studies were with monolingual groups while others were with subjects of varied backgrounds.

There is also a wide range of testing instruments that have been used. Some studies (e.g. Laufer-Dvorkin, 1981) used a battery of in-house general proficiency tests while others used standardized commercially available tests (Evans, 1999 used KET; Hafiz & Tudor, 1989 used the NFER tests; Hayashi, 1999 used TOEFL; and Lituanas, Jacobs, & Renandya, 2001 used the Informal Reading Inventory and the Gray Standardized Oral Reading Test) and the Edinburgh Project on Extensive Reading (EPER) test (e.g. Takase, 2007). Sometimes essays are written pre- and post- a treatment and assessed for gains in writing ability (e.g. Hafiz & Tudor, 1990; Mason, 2018) and sometimes in-house research-specific tests have been used (e.g. Day, Omura, & Hiramatsu, 1991; Pitts, White, & Krashen, 1989).

From this, several *types* of study are apparent. There are studies which compare extensive reading with other treatments, and others which seek to show how extensive reading benefits other language skills (e.g. the effect of extensive reading on writing or on vocabulary building). Others only wish to determine whether extensive reading can lead to gains in language development from exposure to text. These categories are by no means clearly defined and some studies can fit the profile of two or more.

The following section will look at some of the main issues with some of the extensive reading research.

Poorly Defining the Extensive Reading Construct

There are hundreds of studies which have used the label 'extensive reading' in their title. A casual reader might assume that having this label in the title would qualify it as an extensive reading study, however the definition and

140 *Designing Research Into Extensive Reading*

conceptualization of extensive reading is quite fragmented. Unfortunately, the label 'extensive reading' has been applied to a very wide range of variables, each with their own variability, and without much care. For example, many extensive reading studies are done with graded readers but without establishing that the learners were reading extensively. Using graded readers does not mean the subjects were reading extensively, even though it might imply it. In order to claim the label 'extensive reading' for the study, researchers have to establish that the students were in fact reading a lot of material, and were reading fluently and with minimal interruptions to comprehension but this is often not the case (e.g. Kirchhoff, 2013; Yamashita, 2013). It may be the learners were using the dictionary too much, or were struggling. Therefore, at a minimum, we encourage researchers to state average reading speeds to help clarify the *speed* at which students were reading. Similarly, there is variability in the *amount* of reading to qualify for the extensive reading label. The amount read can be as little as nine books or 140 pages over the duration of the study, or five books over a year (e.g. Robb & Kano, 2013; Sheu, 2003), or as long as six years (e.g. Nishizawa, Yoshioka, & Fukada, 2010). Along the dimension of *how* learners read, there are studies which require the learners to read fluently and without follow-up, all the way to operationalizing extensive reading as the intensive reading of difficult material (e.g. Kweon & Kim, 2008). We need a common framework to understand what extensive reading is, so we can evaluate studies and compare them and talk a common language.

Another issue concerns whether the study was done in an EFL or ESL (English as a second language) environment. In ESL extensive reading studies, often the subjects are asked to read books written for natives (e.g. Cho & Krashen, 1994) with the benefit of the target language in the community to support the reading. In EFL extensive reading studies, often the reading makes up a substantial part of the total input a learner gets, whereas in ESL the reading is only part of the input received in an English-speaking community. This difference in setting can drastically affect learning outcomes and may overstate gains that can be expected in a different setting, because extensive reading in an L1 setting is most likely to have contamination from the additional target language met in the environment. It is therefore important to clearly state what additional input is being received in extensive reading studies.

Issues in Studies Comparing Extensive Reading to Other Treatments

The focus of these studies is to compare extensive reading to other treatments or approaches. This type of study (with the 'gains from exposure' literature) makes up the majority of studies in L2 extensive reading research or others such as comparing extensive reading with paired-associate learning (e.g. Chun, Choi, & Kim, 2012). There are two sub-groups. There are studies comparing extensive reading with another treatment (such as a

Designing Research Into Extensive Reading 141

'normal' class, eclectic teaching, TOEFL classes), and those that compare extensive reading under different conditions, such as extensive reading research with extensive reading and book reports in the L2, compared to extensive reading with book reports written in English that were corrected and book reports written in English that were not corrected.

The basic premise behind the research design of these studies is to find a 'winner'. This is often conceptualized as a zero-sum game that suggests that if either of these 'wins', then the other 'loses'. What's missing from this design is that it suggests that somehow both A and B are equal in some way except for one variable and thus can be compared. This is rarely the case. McQuillan (2019) and Krashen (2004), for example, make the case that the incidental learning of vocabulary is better than intentional for the same time on task. McQuillan (2019) says:

> simply comparing the absolute number of words gained in a given period of instruction, without calculating the rate of acquisition, has led researchers to conclude that direct instruction of vocabulary 'works' better than incidental acquisition. Once we correct for the time spent on each condition, however, it becomes clear that the opposite is true, as found in the studies reviewed here.
>
> (p. 34)

McQuillan and Krashen are both trying to show that incidental learning is better and suggest, therefore, that time spent on intentional learning is wasted to a large degree. Moreover, reading involves spending much more time with words you already know than words you do not, so the opportunity for learning is less. Intentional learning, by contrast, allows the learner to focus only on the unknown words. In addition, intentional learning involves seeing the meaning of the word and its form at the time of learning, but incidental learning involves guessing the meaning with the possibility of error. Thus putting the two in opposition is a false equivalency because intentional word learning and incidental word learning have different goals, and are designed for different aspects of word acquisition. Intentional learning is good for initial form-meaning level acquisition of word knowledge, and can be done very quickly with word cards and spaced repetition learning because it is focused directly on making that connection. Although form-meaning relationships *can* be learnt incidentally, to do so one has to read several thousand *other* words, many of which will already be known, only to pick up a few words in a given time. By contrast, extensive reading as an incidental vocabulary learning exercise focuses not so much on initial form-meaning knowledge, but on providing opportunities to acquire the deeper aspects of vocabulary such as its word partners, collocation, mastering a sense of knowledge, learning its use in context, and so forth. If learners only learn vocabulary intentionally, then they will not master the deeper aspects of word relationships as the learning is out of context.

142   *Designing Research Into Extensive Reading*

If they only learn incidentally, they will need to wait a very long time until the target words have met the 10–12 meetings required even to get to the form-meaning level.

The point here is that designing studies with variables in opposition to each other creates false dichotomies or equivalences and hides the more fruitful ground between. This same principle applies for research comparing, say, extensive reading and grammar study, a 'general English class', or TOEIC test preparation, and so on, and we should be careful to avoid designing over-simplistic experiments especially to prove an existing pre-conceived notion and accept that other treatments and approaches exist for a reason. This does not mean this research should not be done, but it should be done without expecting a 'winner'. A more valid paradigm would be to determine how much of each component of reading ability is needed in order to enable extensive reading for learners of differing backgrounds and abilities to answer questions like, "How much intentional vocabulary learning needs to take place for a learner to start extensive reading?" or "Does making certain words salient in the reading foster greater vocabulary retention?" or "What is a good balance of time spent on building reading skills versus extensive reading and at what proficiency levels?"

Apart from the concerns with the premise underlying the research design, there are several experimental concerns with much of this research, too. First, in several studies (e.g. Evans, 1999; Mason & Krashen, 1997, all three experiments; Robb & Susser, 1989; and Yamazaki, 1996) extra time for contact with English was given to the experimental extensive reading group. For example, in Robb and Susser (1989), the experimental group had to read 500 pages out of class during the year, whilst the control group only had a short extra assigned reading per week. In Evans (1999) the extensive reading group had extra reading while the controls did not. This means that with this design we will not be able to see the comparative benefit of extensive reading over other methods as more exposure in one group will bias the results to that group, thus we should be cautious in interpreting the effectiveness of this research over other methods.

Second, the data for a considerable number of these studies were probably affected by outside influences (this also applies to the 'gains from exposure' literature) where the tuition variable was not controlled, some of this contamination was reported in the studies and some was not. The most common factor influencing the study was the presence of concurrent classes or tuition that were not part of the study (Evans, 1999; Hayashi, 1999; Lai, 1993; all three experiments in Mason & Krashen, 1997; Milliner, 2017; Park, 2016; Renandya, Rajan, & Jacobs, 1999; Robb & Susser, 1989; Sakurai, 2017; Tsang, 1996; and Yamazaki, 1996 are a few examples). In one study (Hafiz & Tudor, 1989), which is probably the most cited extensive reading study, the data were collected in the UK despite the subjects living in a Punjabi community. The effect of outside exposure in the community at large and from their other classes at school was hardly mentioned as influential in the study. This makes it extremely unlikely that gains were directly affected by extensive reading, and makes it difficult to determine how much of the gains were due to only extensive

Designing Research Into Extensive Reading   143

reading or to the other tuition. Similar problems exist with all ESL extensive reading research due to contamination from the English-speaking community (Cho & Krashen, 1994; Martinez, 2017; Petrimoulx, 1988). As was mentioned earlier, the nature of assessing extensive reading is that it will take time, and practicalities demand that it be done with real classes. It is therefore vital to try to minimize the effect of the external influence, and to report as fully as possible how the external influence may have affected the results so that a more nuanced interpretation is possible.

Third, extensive reading is typically compared with instructional approaches which do not have the benefit of the 'rich' environment of the extensive reading approach (Coady, 1997). Comparisons are made with conscious word learning (Chun, Choi, & Kim, 2012), 'audiolingual approaches' (Elley, 1991), or 'translation' (Yamazaki, 1996), or 'regular classes' (Mason & Krashen, 1997, experiment 2), or classes which were 'taught in the conventional way' (Lituanas, Jacobs, & Renandya, 2001). The question of how extensive reading is comparable to other rich environments has yet to be resolved and will not be until the right data are collected after having asked the right questions.

Fourth, often the extensive reading component involved much more time-on-task (e.g. Chun, Choi, & Kim (2012) compared nine weeks of extensive reading with the learning of 80 paired-associates) which will favor the study with more input.

'Gains in Writing' Experiments

This research asks whether writing ability can be affected by extensive reading (Elley & Mangubhai, 1983; Hafiz & Tudor, 1990; Hedgcock & Atkinson, 1993; Janopoulos, 1986; Park, 2016; Park & Ro, 2015; Robb & Susser, 1989; Sakurai, 2017; Tsang, 1996 are but a few). A typical design is as follows: Students are given an essay test, they read something, and they are given another essay test (most often the same title, but not always). Then the essays are scored on a variety of measures to check for differences pre- and post- extensive reading. Some studies used only statistical data such as the number of words used, the number of clauses, the number of error-free clauses, and so on. Other studies had a holistic evaluation (e.g. Mason & Krashen, 1997, experiment 2) and yet others had an evaluation of factors such as coherence, cohesion, organization, logical progression, impression, and so on (Tsang, 1996). It is important to clearly note when citing this research that different procedures were used in the 'effects of extensive reading on writing' research because the analyses are looking at different things. The advantage of statistical data are that they are statistical and can be easily analyzed using a computer, but the disadvantage is that they do not indicate levels of the *quality* of writing. Thus in these types of analysis it may be best to combine all of these factors in the analysis as Tsang (1996) did.

144 *Designing Research Into Extensive Reading*

'Gains in Affect' Experiments

This research looked at whether an extensive reading approach has a positive effect on motivation, confidence, and general perception of the usefulness of extensive reading. The term 'pleasure' that is attached to this type of reading research is used in two ways. The first investigates reading that is not done as part of school work as it is done voluntarily. The second meaning occurs in research that asks about the reader's subjective reaction to extensive reading.

The positive effect of extensive reading on motivation and attitude to reading is very commonly reported and probably the strongest finding in all the papers reviewed here (e.g. Constantino, 1994; Elley, 1991; Evans, 1999; Hayashi, 1999; Mason & Krashen, 1997; Mikami, 2017; Sánchez & Gavilánez, 2017; Waring & Husna, forthcoming; Yamazaki, 1996). Some of these data come from formal post-reading interviews but much of this evidence is anecdotal. While there are measures of motivation (e.g. Smith, 1973) and ways to reading confidence, none of these as yet have been used to provide quantitative data.

Quite a number of studies have asked what readers feel about their reading and whether it was 'pleasurable' (e.g. Beglar & Hunt, 2014; Beglar, Hunt, & Kite, 2012; Ro & Chen, 2014). McQuillan (1994) and Dupuy (1997) found that extensive reading is preferred to grammar instruction and practice and to assigned readings. However, it should be noted that the preferences for other types of 'pleasurable' language instruction such as listening to music, watching videos, free conversation, surfing the internet, and so on were not asked which leaves open the question of a preference for extensive reading over these other 'pleasurable' language pursuits.

'Gains From Exposure' Experiments

Experiments that have assessed gains from exposure to extensive reading texts (most often they are called 'incidental learning' experiments) seek to demonstrate how much (usually vocabulary) has been learned. A few problems with some of the studies will be made in the following sections.

Lack of Quality Control in Test Construction and Conceptualization

It is very common in this research for the vocabulary tests or cloze tests to be written by the authors (e.g. Day, Omura, & Hiramatsu, 1991; Pitts, White, & Krashen, 1989; Mason & Krashen, 1997; Yamazaki, 1996). Others have taken part of an established test battery such as the Vocabulary Levels Test or the Vocabulary Size test, or parts thereof. Some of these in-house tests were subjected to extensive piloting and review (e.g. Yamazaki, 1996) while most were not (or at least were not reported to have been piloted and trialed, nor assessed for their quality). Some tests appear to be either of poor quality or insufficient care seems to have been taken in their construction. For example, in Dupuy and Krashen (1993) some items were easy to guess and several spelling mistakes

Designing Research Into Extensive Reading 145

were evident. In Cho and Krashen (1994) the subject was tested on the words learned by another student. The apparent lack of quality control (and even a lack of a mention of quality control procedures) in some of these tests is a matter of grave concern as it is upon the quality of these tests that the data were gathered. In addition, only two of the 12 experiments that used their own test instrument published the test with the report.

Problems With the Most Commonly Used Test Format For Assessing Gains From ER

The most common vocabulary test used for extensive reading 'gains from exposure' research is the multiple-choice test (e.g. Day, Omura, & Hiramatsu, 1991; Dupuy & Krashen, 1993; Pitts, White, & Krashen, 1989). There are numerous reasons why this test may not be the most appropriate for assessing gains from exposure to extensive reading texts. First, the multiple-choice test is very limited in its ability to assess gains from reading as it ignores many of the other potential gains or benefits from the reading of an extended text. This test is attempting to assess prompted recognition but other potential linguistic benefits that are largely ignored by multiple-choice tests include lexical access speed gains; the noticing of collocations, colligations, or patterns within text; the learning of new word forms and the meaning of new words; the recognition of new word forms yet to be learned; an increase in the ability to guess from context; a (dis)confirmation that a previously guessed word's meaning is probably correct; recognition of new word associations; the raising of the ability to recognize discourse and text structure; an increase in the ability to 'chunk' text; the development of saccadic eye movements and so on and so on. Thus many 'gains' from extensive reading are ignored by the multiple-choice test and many potential benefits of extensive reading are under-estimated.

Second, in addition to the inability of the multiple-choice test to capture many aspects of reading, the design of the test compounds the problem because of the nature of the test's criteria for successful completion. The multiple-choice tests are designed to assess receptive understanding and are either correctly answered or not and as such have the problem of both ignoring and under-estimating language gains at the same time. First, we need a little background. It is widely stated that all words are not equal as some are more frequent than others and some are 'easier' to learn (e.g. Laufer, 1997). The threshold for success on multiple-choice vocabulary tests is little understood, but these tests (and other tests that have the right/wrong criteria for success) are severely limited in their ability to only reflect the knowledge of the words that have met the 'success threshold' as a result of the reading. For example, if a learner has met the word *abominable* two times before the reading and meets it once more during the reading, then although the learner has gained a little piece of knowledge about the word (such as a greater awareness of its general meaning or its spelling) he would not have enough knowledge to tip it over

146   *Designing Research Into Extensive Reading*

the 10 to 20 meetings threshold into success. Thus, the learner's incremental knowledge gain from reading *abominable* once is ignored by the strict criteria for success of the multiple-choice test and he gets zero on the test. Conversely, if a learner knew enough about *abominable* to meet the criteria for success *before* reading the text, and by reading the text her knowledge of *abominable* increased, this increase in knowledge also cannot be measured by the multiple-choice test and thus it will under-estimate her gains.

Third, this threshold is not a uniform one for all multiple-choice tests. A test with distractors with similar meanings (*anger, irritate, annoy*, and *frustrate*) would be more difficult than one in which the distractors are dissimilar (*boat, tree, cat*, and *hospital*). It is likely that a learner will have more troubles in determining the correct answer from a set of similar words as more knowledge is required to separate them. This means that results from different tests and with multiple-choice tests that have distractors with different words will vary considerably. Thus interpretation of the results of an experiment can only be done properly when the test is published with the research. In addition, there is no common agreement on the number of choices to be used in multiple-choice tests in extensive reading research. Dupuy and Krashen (1993) used three; Pitts, White, and Krashen (1989) and Day, Omura, and Hiramatsu (1991) used four. All three used a 'don't know' option to reduce guessing.

It is therefore clear that the full nature of vocabulary learning from the reading is not captured by the use of a multiple-choice test and more sensitive measures (Nation & Webb, 2011) than multiple-choice tests are necessary to capture the full nature of learning from exposure.

Lack of Control For Guessing

Some studies that used multiple-choice tests did not correct for guessing (e.g. Dupuy & Krashen, 1993) while others did (e.g. Day, Omura, & Hiramatsu, 1991; and Pitts, White, & Krashen, 1989). The guessing factor is important because raw scores will only inflate true knowledge and leave misleading data. If a 40-item test has four choices (three distractors and a correct item) and the test taker knows none of the words then wild guessing will mean a score of 40/4=10. If the test taker knows 20 items and guessed at a further 16 then her uncorrected score is likely to be 20 + (16 items/4 choices) = 24. Although the guessing factor reduces with ability level as there are fewer items to guess at, it is a major factor for lower ability learners or for learners who have a tendency to guess. Thus it is crucial that guessing be controlled for in multiple-choice tests and correcting scores for guessing is most often better than not adjusting the scores at all (Choppin, 1988).

Sample Sizes

These matters become especially relevant when the tests contain very few items. For example, Day, Omura, and Hiramatsu (1991) tested only 17 items,

Designing Research Into Extensive Reading 147

Dupuy and Krashen (1993) tested 30. At the other end of the spectrum we have Cho and Krashen (1994) who assessed each of their case studies on several hundred words that they underlined from their reading. Nation (1993) points out that the sample size is a crucial factor in determining if the test is reliable. If the sample size is too small there is a high chance of statistical error. He says that statisticians have determined the confidence interval within which an observed score should be seen. He points out that:

> if a learner's observed score on the test was 50 out of 100 (50%) we could be 90% sure that the true value of his or her score lay between 42 (42%) and 58 (58%) out of 100 (i.e. a range of plus or minus 8).
>
> (pp. 35–36)

In other words, a 50% score on a test means that we can only be 90% sure that the subject's true score is between 42 and 58, and not that it is exactly 50%. Nation points out that if a test of 100 items has a 16% confidence window (42 to 58) then a test with a much smaller sample size will have a much greater confidence window, which makes the test less reliable. A test with only 17 items would most probably be quite unreliable from this point of view.

There are other equally serious factors that are impacted by item sample size. It is a common finding in the L2 extensive reading experiments surveyed here that the gains from the learning from reading are low. Horst, Cobb, and Meara (1998) report an average of 10 to 20% gains on short experiments, and much lower figures for longer texts (but no retention data are given). One possible reason for this apparently low intake on these experiments with multiple-choice tests is to do with the relationship between the opportunity for success and the number of chances to demonstrate the learner's knowledge. We have seen that each word takes time to pass the 'success threshold', and we know that it takes between 10–20 meetings for this threshold to be met. Thus, if a test has 60 items and each word is only met once, we can expect only 1/10 or 1/20 of these 60 words to pass the 'success threshold', or a maximum of six (60/10) or three (60/20) words to be gained. If the test item sample is only 20, then we can only expect one word to pass the threshold and that is not enough to provide reliable data.

Few Data on Retention

Another very common element in the early 'gains from exposure' research is the lack of concern for the retention of what was learned. Only one of the studies under investigation attempted to systematically gather retention data (Yamazaki, 1996). Retention data from the reading are important because they give us an idea of the quality, not only the quantity, of learning that occurs from exposure to the reading texts. Further, as most of

148   *Designing Research Into Extensive Reading*

the tests were given immediately after treatment, there is a very high probability that the subjects will score higher on the test than if the test was given even a few hours or even days later due to the nature of short-term memory loss (Baddeley, 1997). Thus the 'real' and lasting gains demonstrated in the research would probably have been over-estimated. This result was found in Yamazaki (1996) and is common throughout the second language vocabulary learning literature (see Weltens & Grendel, 1993 for a discussion). This therefore means that we should be cautious when accepting as fact that the gains that were reported in this kind of research were natural as we can expect a certain level of over-estimation due to the nature of language loss. In more recent years we see many more studies now taking decay into account (Brown, Waring, & Donkaewbua, 2008; Chun, Choi, & Kim, 2012; Min, 2008; Waring & Takaki, 2003, among others) but delayed tests should become standard when investigating vocabulary gains.

Controls Not Exposed to the Target Vocabulary

In some of the research that looked at how much can be learned from exposing subjects to a text, the controls were not exposed to the tested vocabulary. The assumption is that the controls should not need to see the vocabulary so that true learning could be measured. This design was used in the Pitts, White, and Krashen (1989) replication of the Saragi, Nation, and Meister (1978) *Clockwork Orange* study in which the subjects met 30 *nadsat* words (special vocabulary from Russian that only occurs in that book). Other studies that did not expose their controls to the tested vocabulary include Day, Omura, and Hiramatsu (1991), and Hafiz and Tudor (1990). In Evans (1999) and Lai (1993), comparison groups were mentioned and tested but confusingly were not compared with the experimental groups.

'Gains from exposure' designs where the controls were not exposed to the tested vocabulary can tell us how many words were learned from exposure to an extensive reading text. However, it is important to note that these studies cannot tell us anything important about whether extensive reading 'works better' than any other treatment for language gains for things such as vocabulary. This is because the same amount of language gains that are found in these studies may have been gained more effectively from another treatment (say, direct vocabulary learning or by working on improving dictionary skills). Thus these studies basically are saying that 'we gave the subjects something to read and they learned something' or 'subjects can learn X amount from reading' and nothing more. This crucial point seems to have been missed by many researchers because it is very common for these studies to be cited as examples of how *effective* extensive reading is, when in fact no such conclusion could or should be drawn as no comparisons were made in the studies and, by definition, things can only be considered effective when they are compared to something else.

Contamination

Quite a number of these studies were probably influenced by contaminating factors and some examples have already been mentioned. Sometimes the contamination was faithfully reported (e.g. Elley, 1991, experiment 1; Evans, 1999; Robb & Susser, 1989; Yamazaki, 1996) and in other studies it was unreported (e.g. Horst, Cobb, & Meara, 1998; Mason & Krashen, 1997).

Several types of contamination were evident. First, the subjects did not finish all their reading (Pitts, White, & Krashen, 1989), or the same children were used as both the experimental and control group (Elley, 1991, experiment 1). Second, contamination was in evidence when the instruction was very similar in both control groups and treatment groups. For example, in Robb and Susser (1989) both the treatment group and the control group received reading strategy instruction and in Lituanas, Jacobs, and Renandya (2001) 45% of the experimental class instruction was the same as the control group. Third, in Dupuy and Krashen (1993), for example, the subjects were told to expect a test at the end of the reading and viewing, which in their academic settings it is to be expected that students who are told they will be tested would try extra hard to do well and this may have compromised the results above a 'natural' acquisition level. Fourth, in other studies Hawthorne contamination effects were in evidence. These effects occur when a new element is introduced to the study. For example, in the REAP study in Elley (1991) some of the teachers taught both control and experimental groups, and new materials were introduced.

Controls for Ability Levels

Another factor that needs to be discussed is pre-treatment ability level and the importance of controlling for ability levels. In some studies the pre-treatment ability levels were controlled or matched with similarly performing pairs in other groups (e.g. Elley & Mangubhai, 1983; Lituanas, Jacobs, & Renandya, 2001; Robb & Susser, 1989) or were randomly assigned to groups (Day, Omura, & Hiramatsu, 1991) while in other studies ability levels were not controlled (Dupuy & Krashen, 1993; Lai, 1993) or there was no randomization of individuals as intact classes were used (e.g. Dupuy & Krashen, 1993).

The lack of control for ability level can have adverse effects on the experiment because there is a definite advantage to the lower ability learner whom in normal circumstances we can expect to learn more in a given time than advanced learners because they meet more unknown language in a given period of time. From a vocabulary perspective, Nation (1997) has demonstrated that as the beginner meets many more unknown words when reading than an advanced learner, she has more opportunities to pick up new language than an advanced learner who has to read much more to meet the same number of unknown words. Thus in experiments where the pre-treatment ability levels of the subjects is not controlled for, we can

150 *Designing Research Into Extensive Reading*

expect more gains to be shown for beginners than for intermediate or advanced subjects provided both groups have to read the same amount of graded readers. Similarly, in experiments where beginners and advanced learners read the same text, we can expect beginners to have more chances to pick up language than more advanced learners. This implies that controlling the pre-treatment ability level is crucial in getting reliable results.

There are two qualifications to this position. First, if motivation is not there then the weaker students might not make many gains despite the presence of much unknown language. In Lai (1993) one of the three groups, who all were given a book a day as summer reading, had far larger gains (S2 an initially stronger group) than the other two groups on the reading test. Lai suggests that motivation may have played a factor in explaining why the weaker learners did not gain as much as the more advanced learners. Second, a learner's reading level might not be at the same level as their general ability which could be higher or lower for a given individual, so 'level' must be determined by their reading ability not their general language ability.

Insufficient Reporting

In some studies there was excellent reporting and in others there was very little detail. For example, we know very little about the effect of the subjects' background in learning French in the Dupuy and Krashen (1993) study. In other studies, the amount of reading that was done was left unreported (e.g. Constantino, 1994; Elley, 1991, experiment 2; Elley & Mangubhai, 1983), or there is insufficient reporting on how much was read. Not knowing how much was read makes interpretation almost impossible, but a lack of detail can also affect interpretation. A common problem is for the researcher to report how many books were read rather than how many pages or how many words. If both advanced and beginning learners read the same number of books, a beginner would read an easier, more illustrated book which is usually shorter than those an advanced learner would read, thus the page count is different for each. Reporting page numbers is a better method than just counting the number of books, but it is more preferable to report the number of words that have been read (but as publishers do not indicate the length of their books, this will be too troublesome for researchers to calculate).

Full reporting is also needed so that studies can be replicated (Waring, 1997). The nature of extensive reading research means that replication will be difficult. However, this is not to say that procedures should not be put in place to ensure that replication can be done. Unfortunately, much of the L2 extensive reading cannot be replicated because the research was specific to a particular group and group specific tests were used and there was insufficient reporting to allow for careful re-construction.

Another concern centers around the applicability of the L1 tests to L2 subjects. Hafiz and Tudor (1990) and Lituanas, Jacobs, and Renandya (2001) both

Designing Research Into Extensive Reading 151

used assessment instruments that were designed for L1 rather than L2 subjects and their applicability to L2 subjects has not yet been explored.

Longer Term to Internalize

Laufer–Dvorkin (1981) concluded that the nature of the treatment meant that it was unlikely that there had been sufficient exposure to the target vocabulary to make a difference. Lai (1993) also hinted at this as an explanation for why the weaker group did not progress as well as the others. Tsang also suggested that the "lack of gains … may be caused by insufficient input" (Tsang, 1996, p. 227). This raises the question of what we mean by 'extensive' reading. Susser and Robb (1990), when reviewing various applications of 'extensive', observed that they ranged from a page per day to at least two books a week. If we are to label a piece of research as relevant to extensive reading then we need to have a common understanding for what we mean by 'extensive'. Further work in defining 'extensive reading' and standardization of this definition is necessary if we are to compare like with like. Nation and Wang (1999) suggest that a book a week at the student's ability level is sufficient for enough vocabulary recycling to take place where learning is possible. This amount of reading seems an adequate benchmark for it to be called 'extensive' reading. Nishizawa, Yoshioka, and Ichikawa's (2017) research showed that even reading one hour a week over seven years was not enough to gain high TOEIC scores. This is not surprising as the materials their subjects read were mostly narrative texts that would not contain many of the mid-frequency words needed for TOEIC tests. Nevertheless, these data seem to show that very large amounts of comprehended input are needed to meet high language goals and we need many more very long-term studies to ascertain how much.

Citing the Work of Others

It is common practice within research to cite the work of others to defend or add weight or evidence to one's argument. This is also very much in evidence in this literature. Some of the citations have been very clear about the research and have mentioned shortcomings and qualifications where necessary (e.g. Tsang). However, there are also papers which cite the extensive reading research literature as fact with little regard for the problematic nature of much of the research. More worrying are the odd occasions when results are cited that bear little relation to what the research actually said. Indeed, on occasions a piece of research is so mis-cited that it is almost unrecognizable from the original. Ellis (1995, p. 424), for example, cites the Dupay (sic) and Krashen (1993) study as testing 42 (15) L2 learners of French learning from '*Trois hommes et un coffin*' (sic) (*couffin*) after 80 (40) minutes of exposure to reading. It is hoped that there is a thoroughness and accuracy in the reporting of this literature and in particular for research for which it is difficult to locate copies.

152 *Designing Research Into Extensive Reading*

Sometimes the conclusions in papers reflect false equivalences or cognitive bias made to show extensive reading in a good or poor light despite other explanations being possible. Overlooking alternative explanations is very common by authors with a particular ax to grind in order to provide evidence for their case. For example, McQuillan (2019), who is an advocate for extensive reading to be voluntary, suggests when reviewing Milliner (2017) that the reason the amount of words read did not correlate with TOEIC scores (despite significant gains pre- and post-) was that the reading was required, rather than voluntary. There is no question that voluntary free-reading without pressure is desirable in ideal circumstances. However, despite the author even saying there was no evidence for his claim that a lack of voluntary reading was the culprit, he nevertheless uses this notion as the thrust of the review to build a case against forced extensive reading and titled the paper as such. An alternative explanation could be that the online reading in the Milliner study was mostly fiction, whereas TOEIC is non-fiction. The significant difference in the vocabulary profiles and genres found in fiction and non-fiction (especially test texts) should lead us to not assume that reading fiction can lead to gains on non-fiction vocabulary tests especially as the TOEIC test is of more than just reading. Moreover, conditions under which the reading is done vary dramatically and there is no direct reason that learning under one condition *necessarily* will have an impact in others, as is assumed in McQuillan's review. Reading a dozen or so short texts of varying difficulties with a focus on getting correct answers, and under time-pressure, is not the same as the circumstances facing the free reader. The gains on the TOEIC test could also have come from contamination, as both the author and reviewer acknowledge, and therefore we should read the Milliner paper as informative, but with unfortunate flaws. It would be disingenuous to jump to a conclusion from limited but flawed evidence in order to press one's case. Krashen (2004), when reviewing the vocabulary gains found in Waring and Takaki (2003), is another example of this.

Analytical Errors?

Finally, it needs to be mentioned that in some of the most widely cited studies rather odd statistical data are reported. While the source of these errors may be typographical, either on the part of the author or the publisher, or a more serious problem with incorrect statistical procedures, it does raise concerns about the thoroughness of the research or the level of care taken in presenting the work. In Dupuy and Krashen (1993), a t-test was used to compare 15 experimental subjects with two control groups of nine and 13 (i.e. a comparison of 15+9 =24 and 15+13=28 subjects in both analyses). The degrees of freedom were reported as 14 and 14 (the dfs for a *matched* t-test) when the standard way of calculating degrees of freedom in a normal t-test involving two independent groups is n-2 thus the dfs should be 22 and 26. If inappropriate procedures were applied to the data, this may have compromised the findings and the claims based upon these findings. Similar confusing data are found in all

Designing Research Into Extensive Reading 153

three of the Mason and Krashen (1997) experiments and elsewhere in the L2 extensive reading literature.

Another common issue is when standard correction for errors is used without specifying which equations are used even though the choice of equation can affect the corrected scores.

Discussion

The review has raised more questions about L2 extensive reading research than it answered. Despite the problems mentioned in this chapter, it is almost certain that measurable gains for learners reading extensively can be found. However, the extent and type of these gains is unknown for various input conditions and we do not know which conditions 'make a difference'.

It is important to make a distinction between studies looking at gains from extensive reading and those looking at incidental learning from reading. When assessing gains from exposure to *extensive reading* we should expect low gains and several reasons for this have already been presented. Commonly, it is recommended that the students read at a level where 95% to 98% of the words on the page are understood (Nation, 2013a) or where there are two or three unknown words on a page. It is *precisely because* extensive reading is done at levels where few new items are introduced that little vocabulary will be 'learned' (Waring & Takaki, 2003). Thus to make a difference to vocabulary gains, massive amounts of reading will be needed to provide enough input to make a difference and many of the shorter studies reported here may not have been able to reflect natural gains from extensive reading. This is not to say that gains in new language are the only important reason second language learners should read extensively. Other excellent reasons include building reading fluency and reading speed, developing lexical access speed, building reading confidence and motivation, and so on. However, if research is looking at *incidental gains from reading* and for the purposes of the research the researcher does not consider it important that the text is long and graded to the student level, then we can expect results to vary depending on the ability level of the learner, and on the amount of grading and the amount of reading done. Thus when citing this research, it is important to understand that the one type of study can expect different gains from the other and to cite them together without mentioning the difference may be misleading.

Horst, Cobb, and Meara (1998), looking from an 'incidental' learning perspective, suggest that "one way of improving the methodology of this kind of study would be to test much larger numbers of potentially learnable words in order to ensure that the subjects have ample opportunity to demonstrate incidental gains" (p. 219). The assumption is that we need to understand incidental vocabulary learning from ER, so if we create conditions where more of it occurs, then we will be better able to understand both process and the product. This could be done either by testing more words that are likely to be tipped over the 'success threshold' (i.e. those words which the students are expected to partially know already), or by having words repeated many times in the text, thus raising the chance of success. Several researchers have already tried to test only words that the learners are likely to know (Horst, 2005), or modified the input to make the words more available to the subjects and this also needs to be considered when interpreting 'gains' (e.g. Day, Omura, & Hiramatsu, 1991).

We are not wholly convinced by this avenue of research for extensive reading because if researchers only test items which are likely to be learned, then greater gains will be shown than those that would have occurred naturally from exposure and these results will only cloud rather than clear the picture for natural gains from exposure. This means one needs to be cautious when comparing studies and looking at language gains from this kind of research design as this design may greatly over-estimate natural gains (dependent on how much manipulation occurred). It is therefore important in experiments that seek to ask how much is naturally learned from exposure to extensive reading that the words selected for assessing gains be randomly and naturally selected, and that the tests be published with the research.

This has other implications for the comparison of extensive reading studies that look at vocabulary gains. Some studies (as part of the research design) have looked at the effect of frequency on the acquisition of vocabulary from reading and have controlled the frequency of the test words in order to ascertain what the effect of repetition is (e.g. Brown, Waring, & Donkaewbua, 2008; Horst, Cobb, & Meara, 1998; Waring & Takaki, 2003; Yamazaki, 1996). The assumption is that the more repetitions there are in a text, the more likely it is that there are more gains. Thus, caution must be exercised when comparing studies which have carefully controlled frequency (larger gains can be expected) with studies that have not purposely controlled input frequency (smaller gains can be expected). Extra special care should be made when citing the 'gains from exposure' research to identify which studies modified the input to increase the potential for gains and which did not. Care should also be taken when citing research with small populations or case studies (e.g. Cho & Krashen, 1994; Grabe & Stoller, 1997) because these gains made in these studies are much more likely to reflect what these individuals did rather than provide us with a picture of the larger population which they represent.

In this review, numerous problems have been found with this research and some of these are quite serious (e.g. contamination, poor quality tests and/or test method, and poor research design). Many of the studies investigated showed some evidence of contamination either by the presence of outside tuition or exposure, or the controls were not exposed to the tested vocabulary or the extensive reading group had longer exposure to English. Some of these studies suffered from all these forms of contamination. This lack of experimental control, mostly as a result of the use of convenience populations, means that while *circumstantial* evidence supporting extensive reading abounds, the presence of contamination factors undermines the

Designing Research Into Extensive Reading 155

research, as it cannot provide *unequivocal* evidence of the effectiveness of extensive reading, and is one reason some researchers are not convinced by the effect of extensive reading, namely that it cannot be *proven*.

However, as was mentioned before, it is extremely difficult to find or create experimental conditions when the nature of extensive reading means that we can only measure the effectiveness of it over time, but stringent efforts must be made to find and create these conditions. In the meantime, we have to accept that most extensive reading research only has real meaning if situated in real circumstances, otherwise it suffers from face validity. Extensive reading, therefore, is, and forever will be, caught between a rock and a hard place.

12 What Makes a Good Graded Reading Scheme?

Why Graded Readers At All?

Graded readers are written in a series with several to dozens of books at each of several levels of difficulty. The aim from the readers' perspective is to read enough books at one level until they can read them effortlessly and with high comprehension. They then move up to the next level and read those until they feel comfortable, and so on up the levels in a systematically programed scheme which builds on previous learning. One might reasonably ask, however, why we should make graded readers at all given that there are already millions and millions of English language books, webpages, and so on for learners to read already. Bookstores are awash with English language books for all ages, from books for children with no words in them, picture books for your readers, 500-page novels, and academic materials on every topic on earth. So as one of the aims of learning a foreign language is to interact with native materials, why not just use them? It turns out that often these materials are unsuitable for foreign language learners and there are several very good reasons why we should write graded readers and require learners to read them.

A casual look in any bookstore will reveal that there are many reading series, originally written for native-speaking L1 children, which are being marketed as materials suitable for EFL. Typically, these books are written with the knowledge that the native-speaking child would already possess a several-thousand-word vocabulary, and fairly good oral skills before they even pick up a book, or hear a story at ages 4 or 5. These children also meet the language all day, every day, getting over a hundred or more hours of input each week. Because of this, the first language child reader only has to match a written form to the words, grammar, and structures they probably already know. This is not the case for non-native speakers starting to learn English who may only meet English for an hour or two a week, and are starting from nothing. A second major difference is that most native reading series have no syllabus that EFL teachers will recognize in terms of levels and grammatical syllabus because each book is independent of all the other books, and the vocabulary and structures are not being carefully recycled for the learners. This often means foreign language learners reading native materials will be getting largely random input rather than purposefully

What Makes a Good Graded Reading Scheme? 157

structured and scaffolded input from materials designed to build on previous reading. The task facing the foreign language learner, therefore, is massively different from that of the native child, and means that the EFL learners need a different philosophy, starting point, and learning path. For graded readers used in EFL, the *starting point* is a sensible word list and grammar syllabus and a clear learning path mapped out *before* the writing of the materials starts.

For these reasons alone, any publisher trying to sell readers written for first language children into the EFL market should put the books into some kind of levels of difficulty into a structured and organized system that the EFL learners and teachers understand. One way to do this is by analyzing the text and grammatical structures in each title of a native series, and across the series as a whole, and then assigning levels to each title *post-hoc*. While this is not completely satisfactory, it is better than no leveling at all. However, in our experience, we have yet to see any L1 publisher do this in any meaningful way that is recognizable in EFL.

In L1 reading, the books and series published in North America are often leveled with *lexiles* or ATOS scores which use a mathematical formula based on word frequency and sentence length to calculate a book's level. There have been some attempts, most notably in South Korea, China, and elsewhere, to use lexiles to level the native materials so as to repackage them and market them as EFL materials. It is important to note that the word frequency lists used by Metametrics, the company behind lexiles, are based on native speaker norms, and not on a corpus of language foreign language learners would meet, and thus the lexile levels may not be suitable for EFL. Moreover, it is not obvious that books should be leveled only by a mathematical formula ignoring grammar structures, the number of characters, the complexity of the plot, the age of the reader, visual support, and so on, or that an L1 measure naturally crosses over to foreign language reading. To ensure the foreign language learner is getting structured rather than random input especially at the early stages of learning foreign language, the reading books must be put into a structured system. They should be written as a series and to pre-determined guidelines, and designed so as to not overburden a learner and to recycle the language input in structured but interesting and engaging ways especially for lower level learners. This is what graded readers do.

What Makes a Graded Reader Series?

There are several common and distinct stages when creating a graded reader series. These include formulation, development, production, manufacturing, and finally marketing and sales.

158   *What Makes a Good Graded Reading Scheme?*

Formulation

The formulation stage is when the series editor and publishing house design the series and set out its parameters. The first step is to survey the current graded reader series on the market and to identify a target readership and product whether it is for children, teens, or adults, or if it is fiction or non-fiction or if it is to be targeted at a particular audience such as for business, or to develop cultural awareness. This might mean having to consider regional needs and feedback from the market before a product is commissioned. The series editor will flesh out the details of the number of titles at each level, what titles will be published, the word lists, and the grammatical syllabus.

Creating the Language Framework For the Series

The primary aim of extensive reading is for learners to read a large volume of books for enjoyment and at a good pace where they focus more on the story and content than the language itself by reading at 120–150 words per minute (wpm) or more. In order to achieve this, the learners should not be troubled by an unnecessary burden of unknown words and phrases which will slow their reading. If readers need to stop and think about or look up words and phrases, their reading speed will slow to 10–20 wpm, making the reading more of a study task than a fluent reading one. Graded readers are written within a controlled language framework to make sure that learners reading at a given ability are not meeting too much language that will slow them down so they can keep their speed up. All graded reader series, therefore, have some kind of scaffolded linguistic framework within which the titles will be published.

Levels

Almost all graded reader series are written at various levels going from easy to hard, with sometimes only three or four levels, and others up to ten or more. These titles might be assigned levels such as *Starter, Beginner, Elementary, Intermediate,* and so on, or the CEFR scale (pre-A1, A1, A2, B1, B2, C1, and C2), or the Cambridge test levels (*Starters, Movers, Flyers, KET, PET, FCE,* etc.), and so on. Another common practice is to have levels determined by using the most frequent words in English at the earliest levels and less frequent words at higher levels on the assumption that the learner needs to master the most highly frequent words before the rarer ones. Alongside the vocabulary syllabus often is a grammatical syllabus and sometimes a plot difficulty syllabus. A combination of these features will determine a book's level.

Word Lists

Making a word list for a graded reader series is not a trivial process. A typical starting point is the use of a frequency list of words ranked from the most to

What Makes a Good Graded Reading Scheme? 159

least frequent words as well as words often used in a variety of language situations. Under this scheme, Level 1 titles would be written using only the most frequent and useful, say, 200 word families. Level 2 titles would use the Level 1 word families and would have an additional, say, 100 word families and so on up the levels. (A 'word family' includes the root word and its inflections). In this way, the levels build systematically one upon another with each level building on the previous one in progressively difficult steps. From a vocabulary perspective, the best graded reading scheme would cover all of the high frequency words of both spoken and written English, and would use a series of steps that allows learners to move to the next level without meeting too many unknown words. Table 12.1 shows a scheme that fits roughly with Nation and Wang's (1999) guidelines and is reasonably representative of existing graded reader schemes.

Authors are supposed to stay within these lists as much as possible and remove words outside the level they are working on. They might be able to use them if they add extra context to make the meaning clear – a process called adding redundancy. But there will always be some words which authors will inevitably need to use for which no substitute is possible. We should not, for example, write *He ate the hard red or green fruit that grows on trees and is sometimes used in pies* instead of *He ate the apple*. So, in practice, some items outside these are allowable if they can be dealt with in the text, or can be illustrated, or will be put in the glossary at the back, or in a *Before you read* vocabulary study list at the front of the book. A major aim at the development stage is to edit out as many of these out-of-level words and ensure the grammatical syllabus is being followed as much as possible.

However, there is no standard policy adopted by all graded reader publishers about what constitutes a word family with huge differences about which words belong in a family, even within a publishing house. In the same way that no car will ever be perfect for everyone, each publisher of graded readers has their own word lists depending on the nature of a particular series. That said, the first one to 1,000–1,500 words from any well-made high-frequency word list would tend to be very similar given the nature of the

Table 12.1 A Proposed Graded Reader Scheme

Level	New words	Cumulative words
1	200	200 word families
2	100	300 word families
3	200	500 word families
4	200	700 word families
5	300	1,000 word families
6	500	1,500 word families
7	800	2,300 word families

160 *What Makes a Good Graded Reading Scheme?*

frequency profile of English vocabulary, and it is possible to design the steps of a series that have a sensible rationale behind them, namely that the unknown words introduced at each successive level of the series account for a very small and roughly similar proportion of the running words (Nation & Wang, 1999). The words in the word lists and the size of steps between the levels in a series are usually not selling points, and yet many publishers treat their word lists as something to be kept secret and do not make them available to teachers, learners, or researchers. This is a change from the 1970s when Longman and Collins actually published their word lists for all to see and use. However, there are some exceptions such as those for several National Geographic Learning series which are available for download.

Each series of graded readers will not only have its own cut off points in the frequency list, it will also assign different words at each level. For example, the 500 words selected at, say, Level 1 in a teenage fiction series would most likely be different from the 500 words selected at Level 1 for books from an academic or business focus set of graded readers. This makes comparison between series difficult from a vocabulary perspective and hard for teachers to level books into a common scheme. To compound the problem even further, our imaginary teenage series might define a word family differently than a business readers series. The teenage series might only count the root word and its inflections (*use, used, using, uses*) as 'legal', whereas the business series might also accept some derived forms as well (*use, uses, using, used, useful, useless*, etc.). Some word list makers also include the same form with a different part of speech *a use* vs *to use* or *a walk* and *to walk* (making it a *flemma*), while others do not. And others might include phrases (*I'm sorry, pleased to meet you, how do you do?*) and yet others might include secondary meaning senses as in *bank* (financial), vs *bank* (a row), *to bank on someone*, and when a *plane banks*. These issues make it difficult for the series editor to decide which derived forms would be known, and therefore allowed to be used at a certain level. For example, when would a learner be likely to know adverbs derived from adjectives ending in –*ly* (*quickly, happily*) and how about derivatives with prefixes like *re-, dis-*, and *un-*? These could be easily understood if the student knows some basic morphology, but there are at least 100 other affixes and thousands of derived forms to consider, some of them exceedingly rare. The series editor needs to have a policy to allow certain affixes such as *uselessness, disuse, misused, usability*, or even *utility*, and do this rationally and consistently. The simplest solution is to include them all together on the assumption that if the root's meaning sense is retained in all the words in the family, then the reader will be able to work out its meaning from context. In practice, and especially at lower levels, this isn't straightforward because many learners still haven't automated the process of noticing the inflections (especially if they are irregular) and may not see the root form embedded in the derived form either. We could not expect a beginner to guess what *inexcusably* means even if they know the term *excuse me* without having put some serious time into morphology, roots, and derivations. Therefore, word list makers could put the root or 'easier derivatives' at one level and their

What Makes a Good Graded Reading Scheme? 161

lower frequency siblings at higher levels in the series. For example, *excuse* could be Level 3, whereas *inexcusably* might come at Level 8.

Alternatively, the word list maker may make all derived forms their own headword. So, for example, we may count the lemma *assign* (*assigns, assigning,* and *assigned*) as one item in at, say, Level 6, but put *assignment* (and its inflected form *assignments*) at, say, Level 8 whereas *reassign* and *reassignment* might go elsewhere. Doing this for thousands of word forms can be very time-consuming and often leads to some arbitrary allocations. To make matters even more complicated, some derived forms are often more frequent than their heads. For example, *excitement* is five times more frequent than *excited* which is three times more frequent than *excite*. Which should be the root? Similar decisions need to be made about compound words (*handbag, bookcase*); two part words (*pencil case, traffic jam*); words that appear in phrases, idioms, and figurative speech (*piece of cake, do your best*); sayings (*time is money*); expressions (*Happy birthday, how are you*); phrasal verbs (*set up, get along with*), and so on.

Typically, the words in word lists are ranked by some scheme often by using several criteria including *frequency* (words ranked by the number of occurrences in a very large corpus), or *range* (how often a word appears in a variety of texts — the more texts it appears in, the higher the range), or a combination of the two. These can be quickly calculated from any corpus of text using software applications such as *AntWordProfiler* on Laurence Anthony's website (www.laurence anthony.net/software/antwordprofiler/). However, using only frequency, range, and even dispersion can be a problem. For example, the very well-known words *pencil, cat, seventeen,* and *Tuesday* would all be taught in the first few weeks of any typical course, but in fact they are mid-frequency words and according to the frequency principle should not be included till, say, Levels 8 or 9, despite almost every learner knowing them. This then leaves the word list maker with a dilemma — whether to put them in the highest levels (and thus move out other words), or leave them where they are. And what do we do with internationally well-known words or cognates such as *bye, pizza, taxi, phone, okay, hello,* etc.? One solution for words in bound lexical sets such as the days of the week, numbers, seasons, and so on is to count them as inflections of a single word representing the set and put them all in a single family at a certain level on the expectation that these are often taught and learnt together. But what do we do with other unbound sets that are often taught and learnt together such as colors, foods, names of buildings, classroom objects, etc.? Some answers to some of these issues can be found in the guidelines for making word lists in Nation (2016).

Grammar

Many graded reader series have a grammatical syllabus with certain forms appearing in line with their typical presentation order in course books. These grammar syllabuses are very rarely based on any serious linguistic analysis and tend to be pedagogical in nature, often following the conventions of how grammar items are sequenced in coursebooks. For example, in

162 *What Makes a Good Graded Reading Scheme?*

terms of tenses, at Level 1 maybe only the *be* verb and simple present tense are allowed; at Level 2 there could be present continuous and present simple questions forms; Level 3 might have some simple modals such as *will, can*, and regular past tenses. Authors must also try to stay within these lists, but in practice they will often be ignored.

Concurrent Concerns

Another factor that may need to be considered is how the graded reader syllabus fits other, or existing, products. A series may be written in tandem with a coursebook, or may be written as preparation for a test (say *Cambridge Flyers*, or *PET*), to gain a certain score (TOEIC 500, CEFR B1), or even to match a country's curriculum as set out by a Ministry of Education.

Assigning Levels

In practice, most EFL publishers publish their series somewhat vaguely along recognizable levels such as beginner, elementary, and so on, that teachers and learners understand. Many of the major series on the market have been on the market for decades either in their current or re-packaged forms and were developed long before the CEFR levels came to dominate EFL, so their CEFR ratings were allocated post publication.

Practitioners do, though, have to be careful about assuming that an 'intermediate' level graded reader is in fact at the right level for a learner in an 'intermediate' class. Very often learners are labeled 'intermediate' based on either the coursebook they are using (e.g. *Headway Intermediate*) or by the label of the class they are in (*English II − Elementary*). However, we need to remember this is the level at which they are being *instructed*, i.e. taught intensively, and that is not necessarily the same as their level of fluency. For example, a learner might be assigned to the Intermediate class, but this assessment is often based on her performance on a multiple-choice comprehension test score on an intensively read text, not her fluent reading ability. Similarly, our learner might be tested as knowing 2,000 words which might place her in the Intermediate class. Importantly, this does not mean she can read 2,000 words smoothly and fluently, because some of the items making up her test score would have been guessed, others might have been 'worked out' using test taking strategies and so a large proportion of this 2,000 words could be called slow access vocabulary. The actual size of her fast fluently accessed vocabulary (her level for reading extensively) might be the 600–800 word level so our 'intermediate' level learner can only actually read elementary level graded readers with fluent high comprehension. It is deeply regrettable that the EFL publishers do not recognize this when assigning names for the levels to their headword counts as it means, unwittingly, too many learners are being assigned reading books at 'their level' which are being read at an instructional level (i.e. intensively) rather than extensively.

The Development Stage

Once the series parameters have been set, the development stage will begin. A series editor will create a series specification document which outlines the parameters identified at the formulation stage. The series editor and the commissioning editor at the publishing house will also identify authors, write an author's guide, and commission titles. After this, the process of writing can begin. The series might be 'closed' in that the storylines or topics are decided in advance and given to selected authors to write, or it could be 'open' whereby any author can submit stories for possible publication within the set guidelines, or a combination of both. This will depend on the series and the publisher's needs.

Graded readers are not published like novels. Publishers do not commission graded readers as one-off titles as they do novels, they publish them in a series. This is necessarily so because graded readers and their authors have to work together as a team because they are writing to a series with a predetermined plan decided by a publisher, or a series editor. It is essential when constructing an overall plan that books appear as a series in terms of linguistic need, tone, voice, art work, and in other ways. The publisher must ensure that each title at a certain level is roughly equivalent to others linguistically and so after the first drafts from the authors are in, they may need to be adjusted to meet the level's linguistic specifications. To do this often there is a linguistic analysis of the language used across all the books at a certain level to make sure the words assigned to be used at that level are being used somewhere in the level, and to make sure words are being recycled soon enough before the memory of them is forgotten, and that there are not too many out-of-level words being used. This often leads to significant editing and re-editing by the author.

From the author's perspective, there are two ways to approach the writing of graded readers. The first is to attempt to 'get the story right' without being too concerned about grading for a particular level in the belief that the grading can come later. The other is to find experienced people who understand what can be comprehended at various ability levels and ask them to write to that audience using their EFL grading knowledge with the story being created at the same time. This is often the case when a story is being adapted from a previous published 'classic', for example. In general, it is best to get the storyline right first. While a person good at manipulating text to a level does not always make for a good storyteller, a good story can be ruined by poor editing.

Therefore, it is important for aspiring authors to be familiar with the types of graded readers currently being published by the publishing houses and understand their guidelines and the series parameters. Several reviews of various series are regularly published and make for an excellent overview although they are a bit dated (see Hill, 1997; Hill 2001; Thomas & Hill, 1993). The downloadable *Extensive Reading Journal* magazine

164   *What Makes a Good Graded Reading Scheme?*

published by the Japan Association of Language Teachers (JALT) Extensive Reading Special Interest Group (http://hosted.jalt.org/er/) regularly publishes reviews of graded reader series. The series editor will therefore be looking for titles of a certain type and even if a particular work is excellent, if it does not fit the publisher's series parameters, then it will be rejected. This decision is usually made very early in the process when the author submits a brief summary of the story for consideration before it is accepted. However, occasionally finished books will get rejected often for reasons of compliance.

Compliance and Fact Checking

Authors should also be aware of the degree to which certain topics and themes are permitted by various publishers because their policy may affect whether an author gets a story commissioned, or not, or even if it gets published after having been commissioned. This stage of checking the marketability and suitability of a story is often called *compliance*. Some publishers do not wish to alienate readers or decision makers from certain backgrounds and request their authors to refrain from certain topics such as drugs, sex, and violence or even discussions of alcohol, bars, and smoking. Other publishers do not have a firm policy on this and criteria can vary, even within a publishing house, as decisions are often market based. The treatment of delicate areas (including politics and religion) might need to be treated sensitively in some markets, but this does not prevent all authors from ever bringing up controversial issues. The publisher will undoubtedly have guidelines for what is acceptable or unacceptable content. These guidelines will most likely frown on couching opinion as fact, and where explicit criticism of any practice could cause problems for teachers or break a state's laws.

Not all publishers follow the same compliance guidelines which can lead to frustrations on all sides. Some will be very strict, especially if a series is to be sold in a particularly sensitive market, whereas others will be more flexible. At the simplest level, meeting compliance requirements might involve ensuring that anyone driving a car is illustrated with a seatbelt on, or cyclists are wearing helmets. On occasions, some series are banned from certain markets because one or more of the titles has something that might be considered insensitive by officials in that region (often a country) such as printing a picture of Mohammed, or even portraying females in dominant powerful roles. A title which brings up a country's sordid past, even if the event is well-documented and factual, might not pass regulators in some sensitive markets. For example, a story mentioning an event such as a mass murder by an emperor or tyrant hundreds of years ago might be considered 'insensitive' in some markets even today. Another challenge of writing to compliance can occur when the line about what is and what is not acceptable does not meet common-sense. For example, while we can accept that it might not be acceptable in some

What Makes a Good Graded Reading Scheme? 165

cultures to have an illustration of a bare-chested man canoeing down a river, requiring that man to wear a life-jacket in a story about Pocahontas would be ridiculous. Similarly, while one could argue that children should not take the law into their own hands and should call the police in times of violence or robbery, we should not expect teenagers to idly stand by when a man is beating up their friend in front of them. When writing non-fiction materials, editors need to check facts and look for biases in writing. Confirmation bias is often hard to spot and series editors must be aware of different interpretations of 'facts'. For example, claiming that a particular plant can cure a disease, or that ghosts and aliens are real might also be explained by other factors and editors have to guard against some singular explanations. These are the daily headaches of a series editor.

The Storyline

By far the most important consideration when conceptualizing a series of graded readers is the storyline. The characterization, plot (or information content), its development and treatment are paramount to the success of a series both in marketing terms, and whether the book is actually going to be a hit after it enters the library. If it is not interesting and engaging, then the learner will put the book down half-finished and will be reluctant to pick up another one. A positive reading experience is particularly relevant for both teachers and learners who are reading a graded reader for the first time, because their first experience should be achievable and motivate them to want to read more. However, the importance of having a good storyline does not imply that linguistic considerations should take a backseat to the plot, as it would be a grave mistake to assume that 'anything goes' when writing a graded reader.

At all times, the author should be focused on writing a 'good read' and one they can engage in rather than just have the story told to them. The main theme of the story should emerge from the plot, the decisions, and characterization, rather than by creating scenes to fit the plot because this can result in heavy-handed writing. Telling us that Jack is brave is not as powerful as showing him running into a burning building to save a cat. Writing that Jack watched and grinned as the cat died in the fire tells us something very different about him. An important principle of story writing is that a person's character emerges from their actions and decisions, not from being told what they are. Developing the ideas can be difficult at times, so imagining the person or setting in the mind's eye can help flesh out reasons why characters are in certain situations, sitting in certain ways, and doing certain things in relation to others. Asking 'what would Jack do now?' can help the character emerge into the story and will help build characterization and depth. If the reader cannot empathize with the characters in the books, they will not care about them. Similarly, we should create situations where the characters cannot escape from their decisions or environment. If a person is being chased in a story, they should eventually

166   *What Makes a Good Graded Reading Scheme?*

meet some kind of dead end where they have to face the attackers and make decisions. It would be unsatisfactory if the character could just escape by running into a police station, by summoning up a time portal, or suddenly the cavalry arrive from nowhere. Moreover, the quandaries the characters face should be real dilemmas and of vital importance to them. Losing a mobile phone is unlikely to evoke much empathy in the reader, but it might if the protagonist's phone is wanted by foreign spies because it contains the formula for a poison that could kill everyone on earth.

The plot, of course, should not be predictable and it does not necessarily have to be told in a linear fashion, but must include a series of dramatic moments each hinting at several plausible directions the story may lead. Keeping the reader guessing and keeping the endings unpredictable are always preferable. The story should be progressive too, ramping up the drama as the story progresses. The story should also have a logical progression that becomes apparent at some stage, and it should lead to a satisfying conclusion but this does not imply that every loose end needs to be tied up. On occasions, leaving things unresolved may suggest that the characters will live on after the story ends, suggesting a certain realism as well as leaving things open for sequels. Emotional resolution is often more difficult to achieve than plot resolution and considerable care should be taken over this.

Authors should also be careful about making the storyline too complex for beginning readers who may soon get lost in a maze of subplots and a bewildering array of characters. The plots need not be complex but can be simple and plain provided they have passion and richness in their development and the importance of what is at stake for the characters should show through. It is therefore important to think through the logic of the positioning of parallel plots, sub-plots, and flashbacks in relation to the main story as it is all too easy to go off topic. Similar considerations should be made for pacing with careful attention being paid to the ratio of new to old ideas and language so as not to overload the reader.

Fiction authors are often advised to write from experience, but this should not mean that everything should be from one's own past experience because library research and second-hand experiences can help deepen and thicken the plot and setting and so forth. Reading the work of other authors within the same genre is therefore essential when getting a feel for the genre. It will also be important for authors to see the structure in other authors' writing to see how they construct their fiction by paying special attention to their use of transitions, verbs, and the balance between summary and scene and so forth. When doing this it is useful to ask oneself how the scenes are constructed, how they link together, and what affect these have on the writing style and development of the story. Crucial in this is good linkage between exchanges, scenes, chapters, and so forth.

The old saying that "the first paragraph should hook the reader, and the first chapter should make them hungry for the rest of the book" applies as much to the writing of graded readers as to any fiction. An essential part, therefore, of the writing process is extensive revision and may at times

What Makes a Good Graded Reading Scheme? 167

involve fearless pruning of scenes, a whole character, a chapter, or even a whole ending. One should also not be afraid of cutting out some excellent, carefully honed but ill-fitting paragraphs simply because they are excellent. It will not be time wasted, because the end product would not have been made if it were not for the original writing.

Characterization and Setting

The characters should be believable but not wooden and predictable. Neither should they be larger than life. The best remembered characters are usually flawed in some way and need their own personality, pasts, motivations, and so on and should appear human – likeable, scary, or vulnerable, for example. Their personalities need pushing and developing and may involve some change in character by the end of a story (e.g. they may have learned love and family are more important than ambition). However, there is no need to over-elaborately describe minor characters unnecessarily and the various dimensions of the personality of the main characters should emerge as the story progresses rather as one long description near the beginning of the book.

The authors may care about their characters, but the reader will not until they get to know them. Therefore, the characters should be kept separate and easy to remember, even to the point of giving each character differently pronounced names. A story with a Mike, Mitchel, and Miguel is likely to get quite confusing quite quickly. The aim should be to reduce confusion and ambiguity for the reader and insist on clarity. So as part of the writing process there may emerge a need to merge several characters into one or split a complex character into two. The setting too must be believable and it is often better to use a known setting rather than an imaginary one, or to draw it out on a piece of paper so that characters don't turn left at the end of their street and end up in two different places in different chapters!

Voice

Voice is an important consideration because it involves not only the point-of-view (whether first-person narration, a third-person view limited to what the character knows and sees, an all knowing omniscient view, and so forth) but also involves style, word choice, atmosphere, tone, and subject matter. It is common not to change the point-of-view in graded readers as this can lead to confusions especially at early levels. Whether a story should be light and airy, or reflective and profound, or dark and mysterious will be determined to some extent by the subject matter, setting, characterization, and plot.

One's own writing style (that is retained from book to book) is an important consideration for many authors and it is instructive to experiment with various styles before settling on a particular one. Some authors prefer a dense descriptive style, while others prefer to leave things unsaid but imagined. One way to

168   *What Makes a Good Graded Reading Scheme?*

explore this is by writing the same scene several times each with a different tone, one comic, one emotional, and another spookily ominous, for example until one gets it 'right'. At lower levels it is more important to 'spell things out' and 'tell' the reader what is happening rather than forcing the reader to imagine what is happening in a scene from a few clues. The reason for this is because lower ability learners are still working at the decoding (word-by-word) level of reading and may not have space in working memory to work at higher cognitive levels of inference, evaluation, or synthesis.

The Importance of Background Knowledge

Authors have to consider what content knowledge the learner will need in order to understand the cultural or informational assumptions and ideas in the text. Clearly themes and scenes that contain highly culturally specific information will be more difficult to grasp than those shared by many cultures or languages. For example, a European audience would probably find European folk tales easier to comprehend than African or Arab folk tales whose discourse structure, characterization, and cultural assumptions differ from those generally used in Europe. Thus care must be taken when writing the graded reader to ensure that this background knowledge is made explicit in the text in ways that highlight the differences. This is especially relevant if the graded reader is to be read internationally.

It is sensible to know one's subject especially when writing non-fiction materials. For example, writing about Arab life will be difficult unless one has had experience with Arabs, their ways and so forth. Researching one's subject is vital if the plot and characterization are to be believable. It is wise, therefore, to consult others about any elements which may cause problems, particularly those that may offend or mislead, and fact checking is essential.

Language Control

It goes without saying that graded reader authors need to be aware of what EFL readers can do with English at certain ability levels and be familiar with where they might probably be heading next. This is why many graded reader authors are EFL teachers who have an intuitive feel for what an appropriate level might be. Too much new language slows the learner down as does too many facts or pieces of information. Careful attention to anaphora (backward reference using pronouns e.g. *she, this*) prevents overload, avoids ambiguity, and facilitates reading forward, so that readers do not have to look back to see who or what is referred to. Similar care should be taken with the overuse of cataphora (forward referencing) and references to things not in the text (exophora) such as knowing who *The Beatles* were. Authors should also try to avoid too many nominalizations, passive forms, and embedded sentences, and should prefer to use constructions that are simple and clear rather than complex. Similarly, the writing should avoid unnecessary padding, and keep sentences short and clear using appropriate vocabulary. At all times it will be important to disambiguate for the learner.

The comprehension of a text is enhanced by the careful conceptualization of new words. This can be achieved by making sure that they are met in an unambiguous context or explained by the surrounding text, by the use of illustration at lower levels, and by the repetition of new words. The over-use of simile, idiom, and metaphor is likely to provide an unnecessary burden to many EFL readers as are an overabundance of adjectives and adverbs. Verbs are usually the key to a good sentence and it will be useful to look at how other authors have chosen their verbs by studying their use in a graded reader of the same genre. It is not easy to write an engaging, motivating story with only ten verbs! In a similar way, clichés such as "a dark and stormy night" should be avoided so as not to make the book feel dry and lifeless.

Successful reading comprehension is dependent on vocabulary, text type, context, and semantic load rather than grammatical grading. Moreover, grammatical difficulties may well occur at the text rather than sentence level through lack of cohesion, or poor reference, for example. A further cause of difficulty may be 'grammatical lexis' such as phrasal verbs. Just as the lexical levels can be overridden by the requirements of an individual title, so most publishers are flexible about these grammatical levels which can be overridden with occasional use of forms from the level immediately above when the context is clear and the needs demand it.

Gillis-Furutaka (2015) studied aspects of the writing of graded readers which can cause readability issues for learners. She found that onomatopoeia (*bang, whoosh, oink*), idiomatic and figurative language, literary devices, the illustrations, unexpected plot changes, and cultural assumptions are major factors leading to a potential break down in reading and considerable care needs to be taken to ensure readability by the target audience.

The Use of Dialogue

Many graded readers contain dialogue and the choice of dialogue should reflect the characterization of each speaker. Some characters will be laconic, while others may be chatty or secretive and suspicious. Dialogue should be unforced and without unnecessary exchanges (such as "Hello, how are you?" "I'm fine") and should be moving the plot forward or develop characterization and resolving or creating conflict as well as adding emotional energy. Authors should not try to encapsulate too much natural conversation with all its false starts, *umms* and *errs*, stammerings, and so forth, because written dialogue is for reading not speaking. Authors are encouraged to read their own dialogue aloud to ascertain if it has the rhythm of natural conversation, and does not sound forced and dry.

170   *What Makes a Good Graded Reading Scheme?*

Illustrations, Charts, Tables, etc.

It is very common when writing graded readers to use illustrations to provide comprehension support to the story. Typically, the publisher will pay for and commission these, and the author does not need to be concerned about this. If asked to provide or select illustrations, you should stay within budget and be aware of the additional workload it may put on the publisher to get copyright permissions. Publishers do, however, require authors to supply a numbered list of illustrations as a separate artwork brief which describes the illustration in as much detail as possible. Some publishers use stock photo websites for non-fiction titles but fiction usually needs specially drawn illustrations. It should be impressed on illustrators that the illustrations in a story flow together as a book, and should not be drawn as individual stand-alone images. Care should also be taken to ensure that the key objects that are needed for the story (e.g. a specific animal or object) are illustrated well, and the characters are doing what is said in the text and so on. On occasions, illustrations may need to be sent back several times until the artwork matches the original intention of the author. At lower levels, the illustrations could account for a very high percentage of the comprehension of a story, and getting the images to work well with the story will affect readability, which can affect market acceptance of a whole series. Care must also be taken to ensure that illustrations that depict characters using specific or local gestures in their natural context may not add comprehension support to the story, or worse be completely misunderstood by the readers or generate stereotypes.

The Process of Simplification

Some graded readers are adaptations or abridged versions of previously published work. Most typically this would be a story now out of copyright. Many publishers publish a 'classics' series using these out-of-copyright stories, not necessarily to save money (they still need to pay the author), but because the stories such as *Jane Eyre* or *Frankenstein* are easily recognizable by teachers and learners as well as being good stories. The previously published text will be modified (either abridged or adapted) into a graded reader. An adaptation of a previously published text involves shortening it from the original length, which could be several hundred pages, to graded reader length of maybe 80–90 pages. This means the whole story needs to be re-written from the ground up which is often achieved by removing or simplifying events, and in extreme cases eliminating characters or even whole chapters or sections of the original book may be necessary. Necessarily, this is going to make the adaptation unlike the original work and it will take on the particular authorial (and editorial) style of the adaptor.

We have already discussed ways in which an original text can be simplified by shortening it, omitting characters, and by providing a simpler account of the story. However, there are other forms of simplification that operate at the sentence or multi-sentence level and authors of both adaptations and original works will need to decide how to grade the reader to the appropriate level. *Lexical substitution* involves the use of easier or already known words instead of more difficult and less useful ones. This can take place not only at the individual word level but also at the phrase level and will probably involve a change in the collocational and colligational relationships. Modifications based on a cognitive processing perspective include paraphrasing, clarifying, elaborating, explaining, and providing motivation for important information and making connections explicit (Beck, McKeown, Sinatra, & Loxterman, 1991). Authors can also write *adding redundancy* and explicitness to help the reader deal with unfamiliar items. Such modifications might involve ensuring clarity of referents, the removal of potentially confusing pronouns, the deletion of irrelevant details, the use of context clues, highlighting important sections, and adding extra information to make things clearer, for example. The degree of simplification will crucially depend on the level of the book. Beginning and intermediate learners will need to have their material modified in some ways, but this may not be as relevant for more advanced readers. The specifics of simplification are quite technical matters and are beyond the scope of this book (see Honeyfield, 1977; Tickoo, 1993; and Young, 1999, for more detail).

Production, Manufacture, and Marketing Stages

At the end of the Development stage of a particular title, the publisher has accepted the final story and this now needs to be turned into an actual book. The publisher will copyedit the book, do the page layout, and add illustrations and end matter such as exercises, glossary, and any front matter such as the title page or maybe a character list. The author may or may not see their title mocked up in book form before it is printed. After the final proofs have been made, they go to a printer who then prints the books and sends them to the distributor and the marketing team.

This chapter has highlighted the stages in producing a graded reader series and an individual graded reader and provided some input for aspiring authors who wish to write graded readers. The process is complex and involves balancing a lot of factors to make the series a success.

13 A Way Forward

This book has looked at extensive reading in many different ways, theoretical, practical, and from a research perspective. In this final chapter we will make some predictions about how extensive reading will develop in the future and set out a research agenda for the extensive reading research community.

Being Clear About the Extensive Reading Message

Extensive reading is both very simple but very complex at the same time. On the one hand, it just asks teachers to make books available to learners at the right reading level, and give them time to read them and share their experiences. But to make this happen teachers need to balance numerous factors to make them suit their particular learners. Teachers need to make decisions about what to do in the extensive reading class, how much should be read, if and how the reading will be evaluated, and by when, among many more decisions. Because of all the various factors, many teachers are still unclear about what extensive reading is and how to do it effectively.

In 1998, Richard Day and Julian Bamford released their book *Extensive Reading in the Second Language Classroom* which was a watershed moment in promoting extensive reading. It introduced many to the world of extensive reading in not only theoretical ways, but also it helped teachers understand the practice of extensive reading. One of the most well-known parts of this book is a list of ten items that show a successful extensive reading program. In 2002, this became the top ten principles for teaching extensive reading (Day & Bamford, 2002). The list is as follows:

1 The reading material is easy.
2 A variety of reading material on a wide range of topics must be available.
3 Learners choose what they want to read.
4 Learners read as much as possible.
5 The purpose of reading is usually related to pleasure, information, and general understanding.
6 Reading is its own reward.

7 Reading speed is usually faster rather than slower.
8 Reading is individual and silent.
9 Teachers orient and guide their students.
10 The teacher is a role model of a reader.

This list has been useful because it indicates some of the major factors involved in extensive reading. It proposed that learners read a lot of easy reading materials with a focus on comprehension, pleasure, and enjoyment. However, an unfortunate and unintended consequence is that this list gave the impression that there was only one way to do extensive reading (e.g. Waring & McLean, 2015) and that anything less is not really 'true' extensive reading. This has led some people to not do extensive reading because they feel it could not be done 'properly'.

There are two different dimensions of a definition of extensive reading. The *cognitive* dimension concerns what is happening in a learner's head as they read – whether the text is read quickly, comprehended, and enjoyable, etc. If they are processing words quickly and fluently we could say they are reading extensively. The second dimension concerns the *pedagogy* of extensive reading which determines how much is read, of what materials, with what follow-up, whether the reading is assessed or not, who selects the materials, and so forth. Day and Bamford's list doesn't clearly distinguish between these and their list can appear to a naïve eye as being prescriptive about what should be done in an extensive reading class.

Extensive reading needs a 'big tent' where all different flavors of extensive reading pedagogy are acceptable provided the reading is fast, fluent, and highly comprehended. For example, the list does not take into account many other factors such as a learner's desire to be assessed, or to read something difficult, or to read the same book as a friend. Similarly, there are good reasons a teacher might want all the learners to read the same book, or do follow-up activities. The ten principles seem to be grounded too heavily in the 'read what you enjoy' aspect of extensive reading rather than the linguistic arguments for controlled, scaffolded, interesting input. Moreover, some of the ten principles might not meet expectations and demands in other areas of the world. For example, in some areas of the world, a teacher sitting silently reading in class as the learners read (item 10), might be considered shirking their duty as a teacher and could face losing their job.

Given these arguments, we propose our own list, but not one of 'principles' of extensive reading, but one of activities and tasks that are likely to lead to a successful extensive reading program if time and resources allow. This list is not meant to be definitive and considerable variation is expected. It acknowledges that not all schools have the time and resources to devote to a full extensive reading program. Some extensive reading programs might not have the luxury of time for follow-up activities, or there are inappropriate or insufficient books in the library, or the school requires some form of assessment. Doing these things does not disqualify the program

174 *A Way Forward*

from its extensive reading label, but reading one–two books a semester might not qualify as an extensive reading class.

An extensive reading program is likely to be successful if:

- the primary focus of the extensive reading class is to get students to read something silently and fluently that they can understand without needing a dictionary;
- the learners typically choose their own books at their own fluent reading level, but teachers can help them choose as well;
- it requires learners to silently read large amounts of text to build and recycle vocabulary so they can create an internal sense of how the grammar, words, and phrases go together;
- the reading is integrated into the curriculum by using follow-up activities to practice other skills and deepen knowledge;
- there is a large variety of materials from various genres, levels, and topics, both fiction and non-fiction, which should be purposeful, interesting, and motivating, and should challenge the students cognitively;
- the extensive reading program is set up so it is valued by the learners, teachers, and administrators (and even parents);
- learners spend some of the extensive reading time reading in class to show it is valued and to allow the teacher to monitor the reading and provide guidance;
- teachers and learners should know their library well so they will select the right books;
- the reading should be monitored in some way so the student and teacher can observe progress;
- goals are set for the amount of reading, and the program itself.

Why Is Extensive Reading Not Well Accepted Yet?

Only recently has extensive reading started to gain much attention within English Language Teaching (ELT). Despite graded readers being around for several decades, even as far back as Michael West's *New Method Supplementary Readers* from the 1930s, extensive reading still hasn't been fully accepted into the ELT family. The reason is most certainly not because extensive reading is ineffective, because numerous studies have shown many benefits as we saw in earlier chapters. Why would this be so? Why is extensive reading often not done?

If you asked the 'man in the street' about how he learnt his first language, he would most likely say he learned it by communicating, listening, reading, writing, and doing things in that language. If you then ask him how to learn a foreign language, you most likely will hear the words *test, study, memorize, word lists, course, lessons, level*, and *course book*. This perception of how foreign languages are learnt not only pervades society as a whole, but extends into the classrooms and is ingrained in the discourse about foreign language learning and beyond. Rarely will you hear the words *massive input, reading fluency, a balance between form and use,* etc. A casual search for 'Learn English' in a search engine will bring up form-focused materials and advertisements for language courses. A simple trip to a bookshop that sells English language learning materials in say, Japan, China, Vietnam, or Spain also illustrates this default position about learning a language. Front and center on the stands are course books, test preparation materials, intensive reading materials, and books promising huge vocabulary gains in a short period. If there are any reading books on display, they are most likely the latest native-speaker novels or books written for native-speaking children, not literature for learning a foreign language. We never see graded readers at airport or train station bookshops. Why? Why not? Similarly, at EFL or ESL teacher conferences, the publishers are much more likely to fill their stands with the latest four skills course book than a new series of graded readers. This is no surprise because they are trying to sell dozens of the same copy of a $20 book. This is a far easier 'sell' than one copy each of a set of readers at $4 each.

The graded readers, if at all present, are not center stage when we enter bookstores in non-English-speaking communities. If anywhere, they are put in the corners or lower shelves and put spine forward. We see this also when schools make their curriculums. Very often they select a course book to be the main focus and the 'finish the book' mentality in EFL is strong. This is not a criticism of focus on form, but an unwitting outcome of this perception that *study* matters. In this light, it is not surprising that graded readers are therefore seen as supplementary, additional, or expendable even in these days when we are supposed to be focusing on 'communication'. Schools are far more likely to offer speaking classes than free-reading classes and when stand-alone reading classes are offered, reading is most often seen as something one learns through a course book and intensively by building language knowledge and reading skills. It is against this default mindset that extensive reading must compete for time, resources, and eyeballs.

But in the past 20 years or so the message is being heard more and more. The ERF has been at the forefront of this effort alongside its affiliate extensive reading associations in Japan, Taiwan, Korea, China, Indonesia, the Middle East, and elsewhere. The ERF holds a World Congress on extensive reading every two years which attracts hundreds of people to discuss extensive reading from all parts of the globe. The ERF bibliography now contains hundreds of articles, books, and other resources. So, the voices are being heard.

176   *A Way Forward*

The Future of Extensive Reading

In the coming decades it seems sure that the extensive reading message will become more accepted. Indeed in some areas of the world there is a growing hunger for extensive reading with the only constraint being that teachers do not 'know how' to do it or what their learners should be reading. More and more administrators, teachers, and learners will come to realize what extensive reading is and why all learners should be doing it. But apart from more extensive reading practitioners and learners, what will the future look like?

It is likely we will see more niche graded reader series targeting specific audiences, and less reliance on blockbuster series from the major ELT publishers. Currently there are about 3,000–4,000 generic graded readers available in all genres from romance, human drama, mystery, detective, thrillers, and so on. Many of these titles are written to be digestible to even the most demanding of sensitive markets, and some markets will be less than satisfied with the overly sanitized stories. We predict that new series or titles will emerge that are more like the range of topics and themes currently in the thousands of new no-holds barred novels we see each year. And in contrast, we will probably see more series that are specifically written for particularly sensitive cultures under the banner of protecting their citizens from outside influences or to promote a particular ideology. In the coming years, and as technology develops, we are likely to see more multi-media materials such as movies written with a graded syllabus, anime and comics, or even some extensive reading game environments.

Part of the future will be a response to the changing nature of learners. Most learners in school even today up to university age are considered to be 'digital natives' who live in digital playgrounds and tend to multi-task more. It is reported that they have shorter attention spans, and are in constant communication with others, so extensive reading needs to be relevant to these learners. It is often hard enough now to get learners to sit and concentrate on a book for half an hour, in the future ten minutes might be a struggle and extensive reading practice would have to adapt by having more but shorts bursts of extensive reading in the curriculum.

The past few years have seen several digital extensive reading platforms emerge. Most graded reader publishers offer their wares online but often in hard to access ways and so this is unlikely to be a long-term digital solution. Teachers do not want to set up accounts with four or five different publishers so their learners can read a variety of digital graded readers. Xreading.com has solved this problem by hosting graded readers from many publishers on one website, allowing them to track their learners' reading in one place. Other websites like www.er-central.com offer free extensive reading and extensive listening texts and allow the learning to be tracked. ER-central has responded to the shorter attention spans by hosting shorter 200–1,000 word articles rather than having the full, several-dozen-page graded readers found on Xreading. www.elllo.org also has almost 2,000 one–three-minute free audio and video texts serving hundreds of thousands of users every month. This move to digital bite-sized extensive reading in some markets will also lead many to see extensive reading differently. This move to accepting shorter digital texts as a valid form of extensive reading input will free us from the notion that extensive reading can only be done with graded readers and with 'literature'. While graded readers will remain a very valid form of extensive reading, the acceptance of the shorter digital graded articles will sprout many types of fleet-of-foot websites and apps able to adjust to the changing learner landscape. India, for example, has seen a massive growth in online platforms that allow readers to write for the platforms alongside their author heroes.

We are also likely to see different kinds of extensive reading research emerge as a result of these digital systems. A lot of current research into extensive reading is based on a snapshot of a class or groups of students in one location at a particular moment in time. The common current paradigm is to measure the learners' ability pre-extensive reading and then again after it, for example. But with the rise of digital extensive reading systems, data can be gathered from a far larger population of various backgrounds, first languages and levels, and over far greater learning intervals. The systems will be able to track the acquisition of an individual or of a community looking at what texts they read and like, and new texts can be written in response to this in minutes rather than the months or years a graded reader might take to get to a bookshelf. Moreover, the system could track which words, meanings, and grammar each learner had met, allowing us to get a clearer picture of how a language learner's ability develops as a result of this reading and listening allowing for much more targeted pedagogical interventions.

A Research Agenda

Although there are now hundreds of pieces of research in extensive reading, we suspect that we have only scratched the surface of what we need to know to optimize extensive reading instruction and practice. For example, the relationship between grammar, and the uptake of lexis and extensive reading is almost unexplored. There are very few studies that have directly researched the direct acquisition of lexical phrases, grammar, or syntax from being exposed to extensive reading, although some of the 'gains in writing' experiments provided some weak evidence from comparison studies pitting grammar or translation tests against extensive reading (e.g. Khansir & Dehghani, 2015; Lee, Schallert, & Kim, 2015). Or the results were inconclusive (Johansson, 2014) probably because the data were collected from only one Spanish-speaking subject.

Another very large body of research we still need is in extensive listening because it remains the little sister of extensive reading despite being equally important. There are only a handful of papers on extensive listening such as

178   *A Way Forward*

Alm (2013), Bozan (2015), Brown (2007), Brown, Waring, and Donkaew-bua (2008), Chang (2018), Chang and Millett, (2013), Chang, Millett, and Renandya (2019), Reinders & Cho (2010), Renandya (2011), Renandya and Farrell (2011), Rodgers (2018), Rodgers and Webb (2011), Stephens (2011), and Webb and Rodgers (2009a, 2009b) but many more are needed. Currently, many decisions in extensive listening are based on assumptions from extensive reading research, such as how much listening needs to be done, the expected uptake rates, how to determine levels, and what are the optimal materials; many other questions are largely unexplored. There are several careers of data that need to be gathered and we strongly encourage researchers to research this area.

The following is a list of *some* research questions we still need full, or fuller, answers to. The first set could be undertaken by teachers in their own classrooms using an action research paradigm to fine-tune the extensive reading program to those particular learners. The second set would need more formal experimental research designs. In almost all of these questions we could replace the word 'reading' with 'listening'.

Action Research Questions

These questions could be researched by any teacher casually or formally:

- Do learners read faster if they have easier books?
- Do they learn more words if they have difficult books?
- Do they remember more (does comprehension increase) if they read faster?
- What is the best reading speed for my students?
- Why do they go down difficulty levels as the semester goes on? Is it because they are moving up the levels? Did they become lazy?
- Does the way I introduce extensive reading influence their opinions about the readers?
- Does their writing get better if they only read, or if they write summaries as well as read?
- What types of summaries are best for improving their writing?
- Do the learners prefer to write or talk about their books?
- What are their favorite books and genres they read?
- Do positive reports from previous extensive reading classes lead to positive initial attitudes to extensive reading?
- Do they prefer 'native texts' or graded readers?
- How much of their reading do they understand?
- What is the best way to prepare learners for reading extensively?
- Which types of reading strategy training can have an effect on extensive reading ability?
- How much is the 'right amount' of reading for my learners?
- Which post-reading activities help their other skills?
- Which post-reading activities do they engage with most?

A Way Forward   179

- Has their reading helped them grow as a person?
- Do my learners like reading the paper or digital versions, or those on YouTube? Which helps their language learning more? Why?

Research questions needing more formal experimental approaches:

- What is an optimum relationship between intensive reading, extensive reading, and reading strategy instruction for my learners?
- What is the relationship between extensive reading motivation and confidence in reading?
- What are the minimum linguistic requirements for my students to read extensively?
- How much vocabulary do we learn from reading or listening to texts at various difficulty rates?
- At what vocabulary coverage rate can learners pick up new words from reading? How does this vary for part of speech?
- What is the optimum known/unknown word ratio to introduce new words without losing comprehension?
- What kind of words do learners pick up from their reading?
- How many repetitions of a word are needed to learn it receptively and to make it available for production in extensive reading follow-up activities?
- What non-textual features of graded readers help or hinder comprehension?
- How much do visual elements affect learning rates? Are they different for still images vs moving images, for example?
- How many words need to be known to read fluently at the intermediate level?
- How much reading and/or listening is needed to read at certain ability levels?
- What volume of text is necessary for gains to take place at different ability levels?
- What prevents/encourages comprehension in fluent reading?
- What are the essential features that allow reading to be called 'extensive reading'?
- What would a universal placement test for extensive reading look like?
- How do learners from different language groups/ability levels benefit from extensive reading?
- Can all learners benefit from extensive reading? (Are gains from extensive reading independent of learning style?)
- When is the optimum time to introduce extensive reading into the curriculum?
- What is the best way to prepare learners for reading extensively?
- How do gains in extensive reading compare with those from other 'rich' forms of input?

180 *A Way Forward*

- Which types of reading strategy training can have an effect on extensive reading ability?
- What is an optimum relationship between intensive reading, extensive reading, and reading strategy instruction for learners of different L1s and different abilities?
- How does extensive reading impact other language skills? Which skills? Why? Are there more effective methods than extensive reading in affecting these skills?
- At what stage in the acquisition process do learners benefit most from extensive reading?
- At what stage can learners move up to native texts?
- How does moving up a level affect reading speeds?
- What are the different effects on learners of reading extensive reading text at i-1, i, or i+1? How does this change with proficiency level? Is this consistent for all learners?
- Do different types of gains occur at i-1, i, or i+1?
- What is the optimum comprehension level for most gains to take place?
- What is the optimum reading speed for gains to take place?
- What is the optimum level of i for developing reading speed?
- Which features of an L2 are more readily picked up through extensive reading than other methods?
- Is there an acquisition order for the language that can be learned from extensive reading?
- At what level do learners from different L1s benefit most?
- How fragile is learning from extensive reading? What is the optimum recycle rate for structure and vocabulary within ER, and at what levels? What are the best ways to reinforce learning from extensive reading?
- What text types lead to the most gains?
- What is the optimum balance between simplification and elaboration of the text for comprehension and for language gains? How does this vary by reading level?
- Does simplification, elaboration, or the adding of redundancy lead to more language gains?
- How is pragmatic competence affected by extensive reading?
- Does general extensive reading prepare learners for technical/academic extensive reading? How?
- What is the best way for a teacher to assess language gains from extensive reading?
- How well can learners notice new words, collocations, idioms, etc., when reading?
- How much does reading slow down if a dictionary is used?
- How do pop-up definitions on websites affect comprehension and vocabulary development?

There are of course many more possible questions.

In a book called *What Should Every EFL Teacher Know?* when listing the most important improvements a teacher could make to an EFL course, Paul Nation wrote that the number one most important change would be to:

> Add an extensive reading program. Just under one quarter of the course time should be spent on the extensive reading of books which are at the right level for the learners. For elementary and intermediate learners with a vocabulary size of less than 3,000 words, these books should be graded readers of various levels written within a controlled vocabulary. This extensive reading program should include reading for meaning-focused input and reading for fluency development. Learners should read with enjoyment and read at least one book every two weeks and preferably one per week. Adding an extensive reading program to a language course is the most important improvement that a teacher can make, and if this was the only improvement made, the teacher could still feel very satisfied about that.
>
> (Nation, 2013b, p. 18)

When that paragraph was written, the main evidence considered was largely the Book Flood study, the research on vocabulary learning such as the Waring and Takaki, Pigada and Schmitt, and Horst studies, and the research on speed reading. Now that a much greater body of research on extensive reading has been reviewed, is there any reason to change that recommendation?

We consider that the recommendation would not be changed for the following reasons:

1   Meta-analyses of studies of extensive reading (Jeon & Day, 2016; Krashen, 2007; Nakanishi, 2015) consistently show small to medium effect sizes on language proficiency. Extensive reading works.
2   The most carefully conducted studies show positive effects on a range of learning outcomes including motivation to read, vocabulary learning, reading comprehension, reading fluency, writing and language proficiency. These effects are robust, and are well supported by a large number of less carefully conducted studies.
3   When extensive reading is compared with other uses of class time such as intensive reading, it equals their results or achieves better results.
4   Extensive reading is easy to include in a program. It requires minimal teacher training, minimal teacher effort once the program is running, and a moderate amount of financial cost.
5   Sustained extensive reading is feasible, even in a very limited language learning program. It requires a small amount of time each week which should increase as proficiency develops.
6   The positive effects of extensive reading soon become obvious to learners and teachers.

182   *A Way Forward*

7   Extensive reading provides an opportunity for learners to take control of their own language learning and to work as much as they wish to independently develop their own language proficiency.
8   When the activity of extensive reading is analyzed, it can be shown to set up conditions favoring language learning.

There are cautions that learners and teachers need to be aware of:

1   Extensive reading is not magic. Extensive reading provides learners with large quantities of input which provide opportunities for the learning conditions of repetition and quality meetings to occur. However, these large amounts of input need to be maintained over several years to ensure that learners reach proficiency levels high enough to read uncontrolled text. Learning another language is a lengthy process.
2   Extensive reading is only one part of a well-balanced language learning program. Such a program should also include deliberate study of the language, and attention to the other language skills of listening, speaking, and writing.
3   Learners of EFL need to read at the right level for extensive reading to be effective, and this requires the use of graded readers with learners at elementary and intermediate proficiency levels.
4   The positive effects of extensive reading are most noticeable when the alternatives to extensive reading involve poor teaching or misdirected learning. When teachers learn to make better use of learners' time, the effects of extensive reading will still be positive but will be more similar to the effects of other parts of the learning program.
5   Setting up an extensive reading program is relatively easy but it may meet opposition from others in the school system who have different views of the nature of learning and the role of the teacher. This opposition can be prepared for.

However, the best advice is still this: If you want to make the most positive change that you can to your language course, set up an extensive reading program.

References

Abraham, L. B. (2008). Computer-mediated glosses in second language reading comprehension and vocabulary learning: A meta-analysis. *Computer Assisted Language Learning*, 21(3), 199–226.

Alderson, C. (2000). *Assessing Reading*. Cambridge: Cambridge University Press.

Alessi, S., & Dwyer, A. (2008). Vocabulary assistance before and during reading. *Reading in a Foreign Language*, 20(2), 246–263.

Al-Homoud, F., & Schmitt, N. (2009). Extensive reading in a challenging environment: A comparison of extensive and intensive reading approaches in Saudi Arabia. *Language Teaching Research*, 13(4), 383–401.

Alm, A. (2013). Extensive listening 2.0 with foreign language podcasts. *Innovation in Language Teaching*, 7(23), 266–280.

Anderson, J. (1971). Selecting a suitable reader: Procedures for teachers to assess language difficulty. *RELC Journal*, 2(2), 35–42.

Baddeley, A. (1997). *Human Memory. Theory and Practice*. Hove: Psychology Press.

Bandura, A. (1977). Self-efficacy: Toward a unifying theory of behavioural change. *Psychological Review*, 84, 191–215.

Barcroft, J. (2015). *Lexical Input Processing and Vocabulary Learning*. Amsterdam: John Benjamins.

Barcroft, J. (2007). Effects of opportunities for word retrieval during second language vocabulary learning. *Language Learning*, 57(1), 35–56.

Barcroft, J. (2004). Effects of sentence writing in second language lexical acquisition. *Second Language Research*, 20(4), 303–334.

Beck, I. L., McKeown, M. G., Sinatra, G. M., & Loxterman, J. A. (1991). Revising social studies text from a text-processing perspective: Evidence of improved comprehensibility. *Reading Research Quarterly*, 26, 251–276.

Beglar, D., & Hunt, A. (2014). Pleasure reading and reading rate gains. *Reading in a Foreign Language*, 26(1), 29–48.

Beglar, D., Hunt, A., & Kite, Y. (2012). The effect of pleasure reading on Japanese university EFL learners' reading rates. *Language Learning*, 62(3), 665–703.

Bell, T. (2001). Extensive reading: Speed and comprehension. *The Reading Matrix*, 1(1), 1–13.

Benedetto, S., Carbone, A., Pedrotti, M., Le Fevre, K., & Amel Yahia Bey, L. (2015). Rapid serial visual presentation in reading: The case of Spritz. *Computers in Human Behavior*, 45, 352–358.

184   *References*

Bernhardt, E. (2005). Progress and procrastination in second language reading. *Annual Review of Applied Linguistics*, 25, 133–150.

Bismoko, J., & Nation, I. S. P. (1974). English reading speed and the mother-tongue or national language. *RELC Journal*, 5(1), 86–89.

Boo, Z., & Conklin, K. (2015). The impact of Rapid Serial Visual Presentation (RSVP) on reading by nonnative speakers. *Journal of Second Language Teaching and Research*, 4(1), 111–129.

Bozan, E. (2015). The effects of extensive listening for pleasure on the proficiency level of foreign language learners in an input-based setting. Masters Thesis presented to the University of Kansas. 2015. Accessed January 30, 2019 from https://kuscholarworks.ku.edu/bitstream/handle/1808/21594/BOZAN_ku_0099M_14230_DATA_1.pdf?sequence=1

Brantmeier, C. (2005). Nonlinguistic variables in advanced second language reading: Learners' self-assessment and enjoyment. *Foreign Language Annals*, 38(4), 494–504.

Brown, D. (2009). Why and how textbooks should encourage extensive reading. *ELT Journal*, 63(3), 238–245.

Brown, R. (2007). Extensive listening in English as a foreign language. *The Language Teacher*, 31(12), 15–19.

Brown, R., Waring, R., & Donkaewbua, S. (2008). Incidental vocabulary acquisition from reading, reading-while-listening, and listening to stories. *Reading in a Foreign Language*, 20(2), 136–163.

Burrows, L. (2013). The effects of extensive reading and reading strategies on reading self-efficacy. (Unpublished doctoral dissertation). Temple University, Tokyo, Japan.

Carney, N. (2016). Gauging extensive reading's relationship with TOEIC reading score growth. *Journal of Extensive Reading*, 4, 69–86.

Carver, R. (1976). Word length, prose difficulty, and reading rate. *Journal of Literacy Research*, 8(2), 193–203.

Chang, C-S. (2018). Extensive listening. *The TESOL Encyclopedia of English Language Teaching*. doi:10.1002/9781118784235.eelt0564.

Chang, A. C.-S., & Millett, S. (2017). Narrow reading: Effects on EFL learners' reading speed, comprehension, and perceptions. *Reading in a Foreign Language*, 29(1), 1–19.

Chang, A. C-S., & Millett, S. (2013). The effect of extensive listening on developing L2 listening fluency: some hard evidence. *ELT Journal*, 68(1), 31–40.

Chang, A., Millett, S., & Renandya, W. (2019). Developing listening fluency through supported extensive listening practice. *RELC Journal*, 50.

Cheetham, C., Harper, A., Elliott, M., & Ito, M. (2016). Assessing student attitudes toward graded readers, MReader and the MReader challenge. *The Reading Matrix*, 16(2), 1–19.

Cheng, Y. H., & Good, R. L. (2009). L1 glosses: Effects on the EFL learners' reading comprehension and vocabulary retention. *Reading in a Foreign Language*, 21(2), 119–142.

Chin, R., & Benne, K. (1970). General strategies for effecting changes in human systems. In W. Bennis, K. Benne, and R. Chin (Eds.) *The Planning of Change*. London: Holt, Rinehart and Winston.

Cho, K. S. (2014). The lasting impact of a short SSR experience on EFL teachers in Korea. *The International Journal of Foreign Language Teaching*, 10(1), 13–16.

Cho, K., & Krashen, S. (1994). Acquisition of vocabulary from the Sweet Valley Kids series: Adult ESL acquisition. *Journal of Reading*, 37, 662–667.

References 185

Cho, K., Ahn, K., & Krashen, S. (2005). The effects of narrow reading of authentic texts on interest and reading ability in English as a foreign language. *Reading Improvement*, 42(1), 58–63.

Choppin, B. (1988). Correction for guessing. In J. Keeves (Ed.) *Educational Research, Methodology and Measurement*. Oxford: Pergamon Press.

Chun, E., Choi, S., & Kim, J. (2012). The effect of extensive reading and paired-associate learning on long-term vocabulary retention: An event-related potential study. *Neuroscience Letters*, 521(2), 125–129.

Chung, T. M., & Nation, P. (2003). Technical vocabulary in specialised texts. *Reading in a Foreign Language*, 15(2), 103–116.

Chung, M., & Nation, I. S. P. (2006). The effect of a speed reading course. *English Teaching*, 61(4), 181–204.

Claridge, G. (2012). Graded readers: How publishers make the grade. *Reading in a Foreign Language*, 24(1), 106–119.

Claridge, G. (2005). Simplification in graded readers: Measuring the authenticity of graded texts. *Reading in a Foreign Language*, 17(2), 144–158.

Coady, J. (1997). Extensive reading. In J. Coady and T. Huckin (Eds.) *Second Language Vocabulary Acquisition: A Rationale for Pedagogy*. Cambridge: Cambridge University Press.

Cobb, T. (2016). Numbers or numerology? A response to Nation (2014) and McQuillan (2016). *Reading in a Foreign Language*, 28(2), 299–304.

Cobb, T. (2008). Commentary: Response to McQuillan and Krashen. *Language Learning & Technology*, 12(1), 109–114.

Cobb, T. (2007). Computing the vocabulary demands of L2 reading. *Language Learning & Technology*, 11(3), 38–63.

Constantino, R. (1994). Pleasure reading helps, even if readers don't believe it. *Journal of Reading*, 37(6), 504–505.

Coxhead, A., Nation, P., & Sim, D. (2014). Creating and trialling six versions of the Vocabulary Size Test. *The TESOLANZ Journal*, 22, 13–27.

Cramer, S. (1975). Increasing reading speed in English or in the national language. *RELC Journal*, 6(2), 19–23.

Csikszentmihalyi, M., & Nakamura, J. (1989). The dynamics of intrinsic motivation: A study of adolescents. In C. Ames and R. E. Ames (Eds.) *Research on Motivation Education: Vol. 3. Goals and Cognitions* (pp. 45–71). London: Academic Press.

D'Agostino, P. R., O'Neill, B. J., & Paivio, A. (1977). Memory for pictures and words as a function of level of processing: depth or dual coding? *Memory and Cognition*, 5, 252–256.

Day, R. R., & Bamford, J. (2004). *Extensive Reading Activities for Teaching Language*. Cambridge: Cambridge University Press.

Day, R. R., & Bamford, J. (2002). Top ten principles for teaching extensive reading. *Reading in a Foreign Language*, 14(2), 136–141.

Day, R. R., & Bamford, J. (1998). *Extensive Reading in the Second Language Classroom*. Cambridge: Cambridge University Press.

Day, R., Omura, C., & Hiramatsu, M. (1991). Incidental EFL vocabulary learning and reading. *Reading in a Foreign Language*, 7(2), 541–551.

de Burgh-Hirabe, R., & Feryok, A. (2013). A model of motivation for extensive reading in Japanese as a foreign language. *Reading in a Foreign Language*, 25(1), 72–93.

de Morgado, N. F. (2009). Extensive reading: Students' performance and perception. *The Reading Matrix*, 9(1), 31–43.

186   *References*

De'Ath, P. (2001). The Niue literacy experiment. *International Journal of Educational Research*, 35(2), 137–146.

Deconinck, J., Boers, F., & Eyckmans, J. (2017). 'Does the form of this word fit its meaning?' The effect of learner-generated mapping elaborations on L2 word recall. *Language Teaching Research*, 21(1), 31–53.

Dowhower, S. L. (1989). Repeated reading: Research into practice. *The Reading Teacher*, 42(7), 502–507.

Dupuy, B. (1997). Voices from the classroom: Students favor extensive reading over grammar instruction and practice, and give their reasons. *Applied Language Learning*, 8(2), 253–261.

Dupuy, B., & Krashen, S. (1993). Incidental vocabulary acquisition in French as a foreign language. *Applied Language Learning*, 4(1), 55–64.

Dupuy, B., & McQuillan, J. (1997). Handcrafted books: Two for the price of one. In G. M. Jacobs, C. Davis, and W. A. Renandya (Eds.) *Successful Strategies For Extensive Reading* (pp. 171–180). Singapore: SEAMEO Regional Language Centre.

Elley, W. B. (2001). Editorial. *International Journal of Educational Research*, 35(2), 127–135.

Elley, W. B. (2000). The potential of Book Floods for raising literacy levels. *International Review of Education*, 46(3), 233–255.

Elley, W. B. (1991). Acquiring literacy in a second language: The effect of book-based programs. *Language Learning*, 41(3), 375–411.

Elley, W. B., & Mangubhai, F. (1983). The impact of reading on second language learning. *Reading Research Quarterly*, 19(1), 53–67.

Elley, W. B., & Mangubhai, F. (1981). *The Impact of a Book Flood in Fiji Primary Schools*. Wellington: New Zealand Council for Educational Research.

Ellis, R. (1995). Modified oral input and the acquisition of word meanings. *Applied Linguistics*, 16(4), 409–441.

Evans, S. (1999). Extensive reading: A preliminary investigation in a Japanese Senior High School. MA Thesis: Columbia University (Tokyo).

Fillmore, C. J. (1979). On fluency. In C. J. Fillmore, D. Kempler, and W. S-J. Wang (Eds.) *Individual Differences in Language Ability and Language Behavior*. New York: Academic Press.

Fry, E. (1967). *Reading Faster: A Drill Book*. Cambridge: Cambridge University Press.

Fry, E. (1965). *Teaching Faster Reading: A Manual*. Cambridge: Cambridge University Press.

Gardner, D. (2008). Vocabulary recycling in children's authentic reading materials: A corpus-based investigation of narrow reading. *Reading in a Foreign Language*, 20(1), 92–122.

Gardner, R. C. (2001). Integrative motivation and second language acquisition. In Z. Dörnyei & R. Schmidt (Eds.) *Motivation and Second Language Acquisition* (pp. 1–19). Honolulu: University of Hawai'i, Second Language Teaching & Curriculum Center.

Gary, J. D., & Gary, N. G. (1981). Caution: Talking may be dangerous for your linguistic health. *IRAL*, 19(1), 1–13.

Ghadirian, S. (2002). Providing controlled exposure to target vocabulary through the screening and arranging of texts. *Language Learning & Technology*, 6(1), 147–164.

Gillis-Furutaka, A. (2015). Graded reader readability: Some overlooked aspects. *Journal of Extensive Reading*, 3(1), 1–19.

Grabe, W., & Stoller, F. (1997). Reading and vocabulary development in a second language: A case study. In J. Coady and T. Huckin (Eds.) *Second Language Vocabulary Acquisition: A Rationale for Pedagogy* (pp. 98–122). Cambridge: Cambridge University Press.

References   187

Hafiz, F. M., & Tudor, I. (1990). Graded readers as an input medium in L2 learning. *System*, 18(1), 31–42.

Hafiz, F. M., & Tudor, I. (1989). Extensive reading and the development of language skills. *ELT Journal*, 43(1), 4–13.

Hardy, J. (2016). The effects of a short-term extensive reading course in Spanish. *Journal of Extensive Reading, 4*, 47–68.

Hatami, S. (2017). The differential impact of reading and listening on L2 incidental acquisition of different dimensions of word knowledge. *Reading in a Foreign Language*, 29(1), 61–85.

Hawker, V., & McPherson, K. (1990). Narrow reading – A self-directed approach to vocabulary extension. *EA Journal*, 8(1), 43–45.

Hayashi, K. (1999). Reading strategies and extensive reading in EFL classes. *RELC Journal*, 30(2), 114–132.

Hedgcock, J., & Atkinson, D. (1993). Differing reading writing relationships in L1 and L2 literacy development? *TESOL Quarterly*, 27(2), 329–333.

Hill, D. (2001). Survey review: Graded readers. *ELT Journal*, 55(3), 300–324.

Hill, D. R. (1997). Graded readers. *ELT Journal*, 51, 57–79.

Hitosugi, C., & Day, R. R. (2004). Extensive reading in Japanese. *Reading in a Foreign Language*, 16(1), 20–39.

Honeyfield, J. (1977). Simplification. *TESOL Quarterly*, 11(4), 431–440.

Horst, M. (2005). Learning L2 vocabulary through extensive reading: A measurement study. *Canadian Modern Language Review*, 61(3), 355–382.

Horst, M., Cobb, T., & Meara, P. (1998). Beyond a Clockwork Orange: Acquiring second language vocabulary through reading. *Reading in a Foreign Language*, 11(2), 207–223.

Huang, H. T., & Liou, H. C. (2007). Vocabulary learning in an automated graded reading program. *Language Learning & Technology*, 11(3), 64–82.

Huang, Y. C. (2015). Why don't they do it? A study on the implementation of extensive reading in Taiwan. *Cogent Education*, 2(1), 1–13.

Huffman, J. (2016). Response to the critique of the Huffman (2014) article, 'Reading rate gains during a one-semester extensive reading course'. *Reading in a Foreign Language*, 28(1), 148–150.

Huffman, J. (2014). Reading rate gains during a one-semester extensive reading course. *Reading in a Foreign Language*, 26(2), 17–33.

Hulstijn, J., Hollander, M., & Greidanus, T. (1996). Incidental vocabulary learning by advanced foreign language students: The influence of marginal glosses, dictionary use, and reoccurrence of unknown words. *Modern Language Journal*, 80(3), 327–339.

Hwang, K., & Nation, P. (1989). Reducing the vocabulary load and encouraging vocabulary learning through reading newspapers. *Reading in a Foreign Language*, 6(1), 323–335.

Iwahori, Y. (2008). Developing reading fluency: A study of extensive reading in EFL. *Reading in a Foreign Language*, 20(1), 70–91.

Iwano, M. (2004). One-minute reading. In R. R. Day and J. Bamford (Eds.) *Extensive Reading Activities for Teaching Language* (pp. 86–87). Cambridge: Cambridge University Press.

Jacobs, H. L., Zingraf, S. A., Wormuth, D. R., Hartfiel, V. F., & Hughey, J. B. (1981). *Testing ESL Composition: A Practical Approach*. Rowley, MA: Newbury House.

Janopoulos, M. (1986). The relationship of pleasure reading and second language writing proficiency. *TESOL Quarterly*, 20(4), 763–768.

188   *References*

Jeon, E. Y., & Day, R. R. (2016). The effectiveness of ER on reading proficiency: A meta-analysis. *Reading in a Foreign Language*, 28(2), 246–265.

Joe, A. (1998). What effects do text-based tasks promoting generation have on incidental vocabulary acquisition? *Applied Linguistics*, 19(3), 357–377.

Johansson, E. (2014). *Extensive reading and grammatical development: A case study within SLA*. Paper presented at University of Halmstad. Accessed January 30, 2019 from www.diva-portal.org/smash/get/diva2:693782/FULLTEXT01.pdf

Judge, P. (2011). Driven to read: Enthusiastic readers in a Japanese high school's extensive reading program. *Reading in a Foreign Language*, 23(2), 161–186.

Kang, E. Y. (2015). Promoting L2 vocabulary learning through narrow reading. *RELC Journal*, 46(2), 165–179.

Karlin, O., & Romanko, R. (2010). Examining multiple variables within a single ER setting. *The Reading Matrix*, 10(2), 181–204.

Khalifa, H., & Weir, C. J. (2009). *Examining Reading: Research and Practice in Assessing Second Language Reading*. Cambridge: Cambridge University Press.

Khansir, A., & Dehghani, N. (2015). The impact of extensive reading on grammatical mastery of Iranian EFL learners. *Theory and Practice in Language Studies*, 5(7), 1501–1507.

Kirchhoff, C. (2013). L2 extensive reading and flow: Clarifying the relationship. *Reading in a Foreign Language*, 25(2), 192–212.

Klein-Braley, C. (1997). C-tests in the context of reduced redundancy testing: An appraisal. *Language Testing*, 14, 47–84.

Knight, S. (1994). Dictionary use while reading: The effects on comprehension and vocabulary acquisition for students of different verbal abilities. *Modern Language Journal*, 78(3), 285–299.

Ko, M. H. (2005). Glosses, comprehension, and strategy use. *Reading in a Foreign Language*, 17(2), 125–143.

Kramer, B., & McLean, S. (2019). L2 reading rate and word length: The necessity of character-based measurement. *Reading in a Foreign Language*, 31(2), 201–225.

Kramer, B., & McLean, S. (2013). Improved reading measurement utilizing the standard word unit. *Paper in the Proceedings of the Second World Conference in Extensive Reading*, 2, 117–125 (www.researchgate.net/publication/266389351).

Krashen, S. (2007). Extensive reading in English as foreign language by adolescents and young adults: A meta-analysis. *The International Journal of Foreign Language Teaching*, 7(2), 23–29.

Krashen, S. (2004). *The Power of Reading* (2nd ed.). Portsmouth, NH: Heinemann.

Krashen, S. (1996). The case for narrow listening. *System*, 24(1), 97–100.

Krashen, S. (1989). We acquire vocabulary and spelling by reading: Additional evidence for the input hypothesis. *Modern Language Journal*, 73, 440–462.

Krashen, S. (1985). *The Input Hypothesis: Issues and Implications*. London: Longman.

Krashen, S., & Mason, B. (2015). Can second language acquirers reach high levels of proficiency through self-selected reading? An attempt to confirm Nation's (2014) results. *International Journal of Foreign Language Teaching*, 10(2), 10–19.

Kweon, S. O., & Kim, H. R. (2008). Beyond raw frequency: Incidental vocabulary acquisition in extensive reading. *Reading in a Foreign Language*, 20(2), 191–215.

Lado, A. (2009). Motivating beginners to read by conducting oral activities with picture books. In A. Cirocki (Ed.) *Extensive Reading in English Language Teaching* (pp. 439–450). Munich, Germany: Lincom.

Lai, F. (1993). The effect of a summer reading course on reading and writing skills. *System*, 21(1), 87–100.

References 189

Lao, C. Y., & Krashen, S. (2000). The impact of popular literature study on literacy development in EFL: More evidence for the power of reading. *System*, 28, 261–270.

Laufer, B. (2009). Second language vocabulary acquisition from language input and from form-focused activities. *Language Teaching*, 42(3), 341–354.

Laufer, B. (2003). Vocabulary acquisition in a second language: Do learners really acquire most vocabulary by reading? Some empirical evidence. *Canadian Modern Language Review*, 59(4), 567–587.

Laufer, B. (1997). What's in a word that makes it hard or easy: some intralexical factors that affect the learning of words. In N. Schmitt and M. McCarthy (Eds.) *Vocabulary: Description, Acquisition and Pedagogy* (pp. 140–155). Cambridge: Cambridge University Press.

Laufer, B., Elder, C., Hill, K., & Congdon, P. (2004). Size and strength: Do we need both to measure vocabulary knowledge? *Language Testing*, 21(2), 202–226.

Laufer, B., & Goldstein, Z. (2004). Testing vocabulary knowledge: Size, strength, and computer adaptiveness. *Language Learning*, 54(3), 399–436.

Laufer, B., & Hill, M. (2000). What lexical information do L2 learners select in a CALL dictionary and how does it affect word retention? *Language Learning &Technology*, 3(2), 58–76.

Laufer-Dvorkin, B. (1981). 'Intensive' versus 'extensive' reading for improving university students' comprehension in English as a foreign language. *Journal of Reading*, 25(1), 40–43.

Lee, J., Schallert, D. L., & Kim, E. (2015). Effects of extensive reading and translation activities on grammar knowledge and attitudes for EFL adolescents. *System*, 52, 38–50.

Lee, S. Y. (2007). Revelations from three consecutive studies on extensive reading. *RELC Journal*, 38(2), 150–170.

Lee, S. Y., & Hsu, Y. (2009). Determining the crucial characteristics of extensive reading programs: The impact of extensive reading of EFL writing. *The International Journal of Foreign Language Teaching*, 5(1), 12–20.

Lenders, O. (2008). Electronic glossing – is it worth the effort? *Computer Assisted Language Learning*, 21(5), 457–481.

Lightbown, P., Halter, R., White, J., & Horst, M. (2002). Comprehension-based learning: The limits of 'Do it yourself'. *Canadian Modern Language Review*, 58(3), 427–464.

Lipp, E. (2017). Building self-efficacy, strategy use, and motivation to support extensive reading in multilingual university students. *CATESOL Journal*, 29(2), 21–39.

Liss, D. (2009). *The Devil's Company*. New York: Random House.

Lituanas, P. M., Jacobs, G. M., & Renandya, W. A. (2001). An investigation of extensive reading with remedial students in a Philippines secondary school. *International Journal of Educational Research*, 35(2), 217–225.

Lituanas, P. M., Jacobs, G. M., & Renandya, W. A. (1999). A study of extensive reading with remedial reading students. In Y. M. Cheah and S. M. Ng (Eds.) *Language Instructional Issues in Asian Classrooms* (pp. 89–104). Newark, DE: International Development in Asia Committee, International Reading Association.

Liu, I. F. (2016). An exploration based on intrinsic, extrinsic, and interpersonal motivation that affect learners' intention to participate in an English reading contest: From extensive reading perspective. *Journal of Educational Computing Research*, 55(5), 699–723.

Macalister, J. (2010a). Investigating teacher attitudes to extensive reading practices in higher education: Why isn't everyone doing it? *RELC Journal*, 41(1), 59–75.

Macalister, J. (2010b). Speed reading courses and their effect on reading authentic texts: A preliminary investigation. *Reading in a Foreign Language, 22*(1), 104–116.

Macalister, J. (2008a). Implementing extensive reading in an EAP programme. *ELT Journal, 62*(3), 248–256.

Macalister, J. (2008b). The effect of a speed reading course in an English as a second language environment. *TESOLANZ Journal, 16*, 23–33.

Macalister, J. (1999). School Journals and TESOL: An evaluation of the reading difficulty of School Journals for second and foreign language learners. *New Zealand Studies in Applied Linguistics, 5*, 61–85.

Martinez, L. (2017). Adult Hispanic ESL students and graded readers. *The CATESOL Journal, 29*(2), 41–59.

Mason, B. (2018). A pure comprehension approach: More effective and efficient than eclectic second language teaching? *IBU Journal of Educational Research and Practice, 6*, 69–79.

Mason, B. (2011). Impressive gains on the TOEIC after one year of comprehensible input, with no output or grammar study. *The International Journal of Foreign Language Teaching, 7*(1), 1–5.

Mason, B., & Krashen, S. (1997). Extensive reading in English as a foreign language. *System, 25*(1), 91–102.

Mason, B., Vanata, M., Jander, K., Borsch, R., & Krashen, S. (2008). The effects and efficiency of hearing stories on vocabulary acquisition by students of German as a second foreign language in Japan. *Indonesian JELT, 5*(1), 1–14.

Maxim, H. (2002). A study into the feasibility and effects of reading extended authentic discourse in the beginning German language classroom. *The Modern Language Journal, 86*(1), 20–35.

Maxim, H. (1999). The Effects of Extensive Authentic Reading on First-Semester German Students' Reading Comprehension, Cultural Horizon, and Language Proficiency. Unpublished dissertation, University of Texas-Austin. UMI #99–47311.

McLean, S., & Kramer, B. (2015). The creation of a new Vocabulary Levels Test. *Shiken, 19*(2), 1–11.

McLean, S., & Poulshock, J. (2018). Increase reading self-efficacy and reading amount in EFL learners with word targets. *Reading in a Foreign Language, 30*(1), 76–91.

McLean, S., & Rouault, G. (2017). The effectiveness and efficiency of extensive reading at developing reading rates. *System, 70*(1), 92–106.

McQuillan, J. (2019). Forced pleasure reading may get you neither: Comment on Milliner (2017). *Language and Language Teaching, 8*(1), 18–20.

McQuillan, J. (2016). What can readers read after graded readers? *Reading in a Foreign Language, 28*(1), 63–78.

McQuillan, J. (2008). Commentary: Can free reading take you all the way? A response to Cobb (2007). *Language, Learning and Technology, 12*(1), 104–108.

McQuillan, J. (1994). Reading versus grammar: What students think is pleasurable and beneficial for language acquisition. *Applied Language Learning, 5*(2), 95–100.

McQuillan, J., & Krashen, S. (2008). Commentary: Can free reading take you all the way? A response to Cobb (2007). *Language Learning & Technology, 12*(1), 104–108.

Mermelstein, A. D. (2015). Improving EFL learners' writing through enhanced extensive reading. *Reading in a Foreign Language, 27*(2), 182–198.

Mikami, A. (2017). Students' attitudes toward extensive reading in the Japanese EFL context. *TESOL Journal, 8*(2), 471–488.

References 191

Mikulecky, B., & Jeffries, L. (1994). *Reading Power*. London: Longman.

Milliner, B. (2017). One year of extensive reading on smartphones: A report. *JALT Call Journal*, 13(1), 49–58.

Min, H. (2008). EFL vocabulary acquisition and retention: Reading plus vocabulary enhancement activities and narrow reading. *Language Learning*, 58(1), 73–115.

Mondria, J. A. (2003). The effects of inferring, verifying and memorising on the retention of L2 word meanings. *Studies in Second Language Acquisition*, 25(4), 473–499.

Mori, S. (2002). Redefining motivation to read in a foreign language. *Reading in a Foreign Language*, 14(2), 91–110.

Nagy, W. E., Herman, P., & Anderson, R. C. (1985). Learning words from context. *Reading Research Quarterly*, 20(2), 233–253.

Nakanishi, T. (2015). A meta-analysis of extensive reading research. *TESOL Quarterly*, 49(1), 6–37.

Nakata, T. (2017). Does repeated practice make perfect? The effects of within-session repeated retrieval on second language vocabulary learning. *SSLA*, 39(4), 653–679.

Nakata, T. (2015). Effects of expanding and equal spacing on second language vocabulary learning: Does gradually increasing spacing increase vocabulary learning? *SSLA*, 37, 677–711.

Nakata, T. (2011). Computer-assisted second language vocabulary learning in a paired-associate paradigm: A critical investigation of flashcard software. *Computer Assisted Language Learning*, 24(1), 17–38.

Nation, I. S. P. (2019). How does simplification of text affect vocabulary? Researching mid-frequency readers.

Nation, I. S. P. (2018). Reading a whole book to learn vocabulary. *ITL International Journal of Applied Linguistics*, 169(1), 30–43.

Nation, I. S. P. (2016). *Making and Using Word lists for Language Learning and Testing*. Amsterdam: John Benjamins.

Nation, I. S. P. (2014). How much input do you need to learn the most frequent 9,000 words? *Reading in a Foreign Language*, 26(2), 1–16.

Nation, I. S. P. (2013a). *Learning Vocabulary in Another Language*. (2nd Ed). Cambridge: Cambridge University Press.

Nation, I. S. P. (2013b). *What Should Every EFL Teacher Know?* Seoul: Compass Publishing.

Nation, I. S. P. (2007). The four strands. *Innovation in Language Learning and Teaching*, 1(1), 1–12.

Nation, I. S. P. (2006). How large a vocabulary is needed for reading and listening? *Canadian Modern Language Review*, 63(1), 59–82.

Nation, I. S. P. (1997). The language learning benefits of extensive reading. *The Language Teacher*, 21(5), 13–16.

Nation, P. (1993). Using dictionaries to estimate vocabulary size: essential, but rarely followed procedures. *Language Testing*, 10(1), 27–40.

Nation, P. (1989). Improving speaking fluency. *System*, 17(3), 377–384.

Nation, I. S. P., & Anthony, L. (2013). Mid-frequency readers. *Journal of Extensive Reading*, 1(1), 5–16.

Nation, P., & Wang, K. (1999). Graded readers and vocabulary. *Reading in a Foreign Language*, 12(2), 355–380.

Nation, I. S. P., & Webb, S. (2011). *Researching and Analyzing Vocabulary*. Boston: Heinle Cengage Learning.

192 References

Ng, S. M. (2001). The Brunei reading and language acquisition project. *International Journal of Educational Research*, 35(2), 157–167.

Ng, S. M., & Sullivan, C. (2001). The Singapore reading and English acquisition program. *International Journal of Educational Research*, 35(2), 169–179.

Nishino, T. (2007). Beginning to read extensively: A case study with Mako and Fumi. *Reading in a Foreign Language*, 19(2), 76–105.

Nishizawa, H., Yoshioka, T., & Fukada, M. (2010). The impact of a 4-year extensive reading program. In A. M. Stoke (Ed.) *JALT 2009 Conference Proceedings*. Tokyo: JALT.

Nishizawa, H., Yoshioka, T., & Ichikawa, Y. (2017). Effect of a six-year long extensive reading program for reluctant learners of English. *Modern Journal of Language Teaching Methods*, 7(8), 116–123.

Nord, J. R. (1980). Developing listening fluency before speaking: An alternative paradigm. *System*, 81, 1–22.

Nozaki, A. (2007). Which is faster, learning new vocabulary from incidental reading, or from a word list? Unpublished thesis presented to Notre Dame Seishin University, Okayama, Japan.

O'Neill, B. (2012). Investigating the effects of extensive reading on TOEIC reading section scores. *Extensive Reading World Congress Proceedings*, 30–33.

Oller, J. W. (1979). *Language Tests at School*. London: Longman.

Orwell, G. (1945). *Animal Farm*. Longman Bridge Series. London: Longman.

Park, J. (2016). Integrating reading and writing through extensive reading. *ELT Journal*, 70(3), 287–295.

Park, J., & Ro, E. (2015). The core principles of extensive reading in an EAP writing context. *Reading in a Foreign Language*, 27(2), 308–313.

Pellicer-Sánchez, A. (2016). Incidental L2 vocabulary acquisition from and while reading. *Studies in Second Language Acquisition*, 38(1), 97–130.

Pellicer-Sánchez, A., & Schmitt, N. (2010). Incidental vocabulary acquisition from an authentic novel: Do things fall apart? *Reading in a Foreign Language*, 22(1), 31–55.

Peters, E. (2007). Manipulating L2 learners' online dictionary use and its effect on L2 word retention. *Language Learning &Technology*, 11(2), 36–58.

Petrimoulx, J. (1988). Sustained silent reading in an ESL class: A study. Paper presented at the Annual Meeting of the Teachers of English to Speakers of Other Languages (22nd, Chicago, IL, March 8–13, 1988).

Pigada, M., & Schmitt, N. (2006). Vocabulary acquisition from extensive reading: A case study. *Reading in a Foreign Language*, 18(1), 1–28.

Pitts, M., White, H., & Krashen, S. (1989). Acquiring second language vocabulary through reading: a replication of the Clockwork Orange study using second language acquirers. *Reading in a Foreign Language*, 5(2), 271–275.

Polak, J., & Krashen, S. (1988). Do we need to teach spelling? The relationship between spelling and vocabulary reading among community college ESL students. *TESOL Quarterly*, 22, 141–146.

Pressley, M. (1977). Children's use of the keyword method to learn simple Spanish vocabulary words. *Journal of Educational Psychology*, 69(5), 465–472.

Qian, D. (1996). ESL vocabulary acquisition: Contextualization and decontextualization. *Canadian Modern Language Review*, 53, 120–142.

Quero, B. (2015). Estimating the vocabulary size of L1 Spanish ESP learners and the vocabulary load of medical textbooks. (PhD), Victoria University of Wellington.

References   193

Quinn, E., & Nation, I. S. P. (1974). *Speed Reading*. Kuala Lumpur: Oxford University Press. (Out of print. Now available from Paul Nation's website.)

Rasinski, T. V. (1990). Effects of repeated reading and listening-while-reading on reading fluency. *Journal of Educational Research*, 83(3), 147–150.

Rasinski, T., & Hoffman, J. (2003). Oral reading in the school literacy curriculum. *Reading Research Quarterly*, 38(4), 510–522.

Rausch, A. S. (2004). Extensive reading: A case study in one junior high school. *ETJ Journal*, 5(1), 21–22.

Rayner, K. (1998). Eye movements in reading and information processing: 20 years of research. *Psychological Bulletin*, 124(3), 372–422.

Reinders, H., & Cho, M. Y. (2010). Extensive listening practice and input enhancement using mobile phones: Encouraging out of class learning with mobile phones. *The Electronic Journal for English as a Second Language*, 14(2), 1–7.

Renandya, W. (2011). Extensive listening in the language classroom. In H. Widodo and A. Cirocki (Eds.) *Innovation and Creativity in ELT Methodology* (pp. 24–41). New York: Nova Publishers.

Renandya, W. A., & Farrell, T. S. C. (2011). Teacher the tape is too fast: Extensive listening in ELT. *ELT Journal*, 65(1), 52–59.

Renandya, W., Rajan, B., & Jacobs, G. (1999). Extensive reading with adult learners of English as a second language. *RELC Journal*, 30(1), 39–61.

Ro, E. (2013). A case study of extensive reading with an unmotivated L2 reader. *Reading in a Foreign Language*, 25(2), 213–233.

Ro, E., & Chen, A. C. (2014). Pleasure reading behavior and attitude of non-academic ESL students: A replication study. *Reading in a Foreign Language*, 26(1), 49–72.

Robb, T. (2015). Quizzes – A sin against the sixth commandment? In defense of MReader. *Reading in a Foreign Language*, 27(1), 146–151.

Robb, T. (2013). The effect of grade weighting on student extensive reading performance. *TESL Reporter*, 46(1&2), 21–27.

Robb, T. (2002). Extensive reading in the Asian context – An alternative view. *Reading in a Foreign Language*, 14(2), 146–147.

Robb, T., & Kano, M. (2013). Effective extensive reading outside the classroom: A large scale experiment. *Reading in a Foreign Language*, 25(2), 234–247.

Robb, T., & Susser, B. (1989). Extensive reading vs. skills building in an EFL context. *Reading in a Foreign Language*, 5(2), 239–251.

Rodgers, M. P. H. (2018). The images in television programs and the potential for learning unknown words: The relationship between on-screen imagery and vocabulary. *ITL International Journal of Applied Linguistics*, 169(1), 191–211.

Rodgers, M. P. H., & Webb, S. (2011). Narrow viewing: The vocabulary in related television programs. *TESOL Quarterly*, 45(4), 689–717.

Rodrigo, V., Krashen, S., & Gribbons, B. (2004). The effectiveness of two comprehensible-input approaches to foreign language instruction at the intermediate level. *System*, 32(1), 53–60.

Sakurai, N. (2017). The relationship between the amount of extensive reading and the writing performance. *The Reading Matrix*, 17(2), 142–164.

Samuels, S. J. (1979). The method of repeated reading. *The Reading Teacher*, 32(4), 403–408.

Sánchez, X., & Gavilánez, L. (2017). Learners' attitudes toward extensive reading in EFL (English as a Foreign Language) contexts. *Revista Publicando*, 4 12(1), 259–268.

194   *References*

Saragi, T., Nation, P., & Meister, G. (1978). Vocabulary learning and reading. *System*, 6(2), 72–78.

Schmitt, N., & Carter, R. (2000). The lexical advantages of narrow reading for second language learners. *TESOL Journal*, 9(1), 4–9.

Schmitt, N., & Schmitt, D. (2014). A reassessment of frequency and vocabulary size in L2 vocabulary teaching. *Language Teaching*, 47(4), 484–503.

Schmitt, N., Schmitt, D., & Clapham, C. (2001). Developing and exploring the behaviour of two new versions of the Vocabulary Levels Test. *Language Testing*, 18(1), 55–88.

Schollar, E. (2001). A review of two evaluations of the READ primary schools program in the Eastern Cape Province of South Africa. *International Journal of Educational Research*, 35(2), 205–216.

Sheu, S. (2003). Extensive reading with EFL learners at beginning level. *TESL Reporter*, 36(2), 8–26.

Sin, M. (2007). An evaluation of the effectiveness of a school-based Chinese extensive reading curriculum for junior secondary students. Unpublished PhD thesis, The University of Hong Kong.

Sindelar, P., Monda, L., & O'Shea, L. (1990). Effects of repeated readings on instructional and mastery level readers. *Journal of Educational Research*, 83(4), 220–226.

Singh, G. (2001). Literacy impact studies in Solomon Islands and Vanuatu. *International Journal of Educational Research*, 35(2), 227–236.

Smith, J. (1973). A quick measure of achievement motivation. *British Journal of Social and Clinical Psychology*, 12(2), 137–143.

Sorell, C. J. (2012). Zipf's law and vocabulary. In C. A. Chapelle (Ed.) *Encyclopaedia of Applied Linguistics*. Oxford: Wiley-Blackwell.

Stephens, M. (2011). The primacy of extensive listening. *ELT Journal*, 65(3), 311–316.

Stoeckel, T., Reagan, N., & Hann, F. (2012). Extensive reading quizzes and reading attitudes. *TESOL Quarterly*, 46(1), 187–198.

Storey, C., Gibson, K., & Williamson, R. (2006). Can extensive reading boost TOEIC scores? In K. Bradford-Watts, C. Ikeguchi, & M. Swanson (Eds.) *JALT2005 Conference Proceedings*. Tokyo: JALT. Retrieved from http://jalt-publications.org/archive/proceedings/2005/E034.pdf.

Suk, N. (2017). The effects of extensive reading on reading comprehension, reading rate, and vocabulary acquisition. *Reading Research Quarterly*, 52(1), 73–89.

Susser, B., & Robb, T. (1990). EFL extensive reading instruction: Research and procedure. *JALT Journal*, 12(2), 161–185.

Sutarsyah, C., Nation, P., & Kennedy, G. (1994). How useful is EAP vocabulary for ESP? A corpus based study. *RELC Journal*, 25(2), 34–50.

Swaffar, J. K. (1985). Reading authentic texts in a foreign language: A cognitive model. *The Modern Language Journal*, 69(1), 15–34.

Tabata-Sandom, M. (2017). L2 Japanese learners' responses to translation, speed reading, and 'pleasure reading' as a form of extensive reading. *Reading in a Foreign Language*, 29(1), 112–132.

Tabata-Sandom, M. (2016). What types of texts and reading aids are good for Japanese graded readers? *Journal of Extensive Reading*, 4(2), 21–46.

Tabata-Sandom, M. (2013). The reader-text-writer interaction: L2 Japanese learners' response toward graded readers. *Reading in a Foreign Language*, 25(2), 264–282.

Taguchi, E., Takayasu-Maass, M., & Gorsuch, G. J. (2004). Developing reading fluency in EFL: How assisted repeated reading and extensive reading affect fluency development. *Reading in a Foreign Language*, 16(2).

Takase, A. (2007). Japanese high school students' motivation for extensive L2 reading. *Reading in a Foreign Language*, 19(1), 1–18.

Tanaka, H., & Stapleton, P. (2007). Increasing reading input in Japanese high school EFL classrooms: An empirical study exploring the efficacy of extensive reading. *The Reading Matrix*, 7(1), 115–131.

Tavakoli, P., & Hunter, A. (2018). Is fluency being 'neglected' in the classroom? Teacher understanding of fluency and related classroom practices. *Language Teaching Research*, 22(3), 330–349.

Taylor, W. L. (1953). Cloze procedure: A new tool for measuring readability. *Journalism Quarterly*, 9, 206–223.

Thomas, H., & Hill, D. (1993). Seventeen series of graded readers. *ELT Journal*, 47 (3), 250–267.

Tickoo, M. L. (Ed.) (1993). *Simplification: Theory and Application*. RELC anthology series no. 31. Singapore: SEAMEO-RELC.

Topping, K. (1989). Peer tutoring and paired reading: Combining two powerful techniques. *The Reading Teacher*, 42(7), 488–494.

Tran, Y. T. N. (2012). The effects of a speed reading course and speed transfer to other types of texts. *RELC Journal*, 43(1), 23–37.

Tran, Y. T. N. (2011). EFL reading fluency development and its effects. PhD thesis submitted to Victoria University of Wellington, New Zealand.

Tsang, W. (1996). Comparing the effects of reading and writing on writing performance. *Applied Linguistics*, 17(2), 210–233.

Tudor, I., & Hafiz, F. (1989). Extensive reading as a means of input to L2 learning. *Journal of Research in Reading*, 12(2), 164–178.

Uden, J., Schmitt, D., & Schmitt, N. (2014). Jumping from the highest graded readers to ungraded novels: Four case studies. *Reading in a Foreign Language*, 26(1), 1–28.

Urquhart, S., & Weir, C. (1998). *Reading in a Second Language: Process, Product and Practice*. Harlow: Addison Wesley Longman.

Vidal, K. (2011). A comparison of the effects of reading and listening on incidental vocabulary acquisition. *Language Learning*, 61, 219–258.

Wan-a-rom, U. (2010). Self-assessment of word knowledge with graded readers: A preliminary study. *Reading in a Foreign Language*, 22(2), 323–338.

Waring, R. (2013). An analysis of the vocabulary in coursebooks and graded readers. Lecture at the JALT Vocabulary SIG seminar, Kyushu Sangyo University, Fukuoka, June 29, 2013.

Waring, R. (2001). Research in extensive reading. *Studies in Foreign Language and Literature (Notre Dame Seishin University, Kiyo)*, 25(1), 1–25.

Waring, R. (1997). Guest editor. 'Special edition on Extensive Reading'. *The Language Teacher*, 21(5).

Waring, R., & Husna, N. (forthcoming). What are the expectations and experiences of Indonesian teachers who have, and have not, done extensive reading? A report from the IERA workshops. *TEFLIN Journal*.

Waring, R., & McLean, S. (2015). Exploration of the core and variable dimensions of extensive reading research and pedagogy. *Reading in a Foreign Language*, 27(1), 160–167.

Waring, R., & Takaki, M. (2003). At what rate do learners learn and retain new vocabulary from reading a graded reader? *Reading in a Foreign Language*, 15(2), 130–163.

Watson, J. (2004). Issue logs. In R. R. Day and J. Bamford (Eds.) *Extensive Reading Activities for Teaching Language* (pp. 37–39). Cambridge: Cambridge University Press.

196 References

Webb, S. (2015). Learning vocabulary through meaning-focused input: Replication of Elley (1989) and Liu & Nation (1985). *Language Teaching*, 49(1), 1–12.

Webb, S. (2009). The effects receptive and productive learning of word pairs on vocabulary knowledge. *RELC Journal*, 40, 360–376.

Webb, S., & Chang, A. C.-S. (2015). Second language vocabulary learning through extensive reading with audio support: How do frequency and distribution of occurrence affect learning? *Language Teaching Research*, 19(6), 667–686.

Webb, S., & Macalister, J. (2013). Is text written for children useful for L2 extensive reading? *TESOL Quarterly*, 47(2), 300–322.

Webb, S., & Nation, I. S. P. (2017). *How Vocabulary is Learned*. Oxford: Oxford University Press.

Webb, S., & Rodgers, M. P. H. (2009a). The lexical coverage of movies. *Applied Linguistics*, 30(3), 407–427.

Webb, S., & Rodgers, M. P. H. (2009b). The vocabulary demands of television programs. *Language Learning*, 59(2), 335–366.

Webb, S., Sasao, Y., & Ballance, O. (2017). The updated Vocabulary Levels Test. *ITL International Journal of Applied Linguistics*, 168(1), 33–69.

Wei, Z. (2015). Does teaching mnemonics for vocabulary learning make a difference? Putting the keyword method and the word part technique to the test. *Language Teaching Research*, 19(1), 43–69.

Weltens, B., & Grendel, M. (1993). Attrition of vocabulary knowledge. In R. Schreuder and B. Weltens (Eds.) *The Bilingual Lexicon*. Amsterdam: John Benjamins.

Wesche, M. B., & Paribakht, T. S. (2010). *Lexical Inferencing in a First and Second Language*. Bristol: Multilingual Matters.

West, M. P. (1960). *Teaching English in Difficult Circumstances*. London: Longmans.

West, M. P. (1953). *A General Service List of English Words*. London: Longman, Green & Co.

West, M. P. (1941). *Learning to Read a Foreign Language*. London: Longmans.

Widdowson, H. (1976). The authenticity of language data. In J. F. Fanselow and R. Crymes (Eds.) *On TESOL '76* (pp. 261–270). Washington, DC: TESOL.

Winitz, H. (Ed.) (1981). *The Comprehension Approach to Foreign Language Instruction*. Rowley, MA: Newbury House.

Yamamoto, Y. (2011). Bridging the gap between receptive and productive vocabulary size through extensive reading. *The Reading Matrix*, 11(3), 226–242.

Yamashita, J. (2013). Effects of extensive reading on reading attitudes in a foreign language. *Reading in a Foreign Language*, 25(2), 248–263.

Yamashita, J. (2008). Extensive reading and development of different aspects of L2 proficiency. *System*, 36(4), 661–672.

Yamashita, J. (2007). The relationship of reading attitudes between L1 and L2: An investigation of adult EFL learners in Japan. *TESOL Quarterly*, 41(1), 81–105.

Yamashita, J. (2004). Reading attitudes in L1 and L2, and their influence on L2 extensive reading. *Reading in a Foreign Language*, 16(1), 1–19.

Yamazaki, A. (1996). Vocabulary acquisition through extensive reading. Unpublished doctoral dissertation, Temple University Japan.

Yano, Y., Long, M. H., & Ross, S. (1994). The effects of simplified and elaborated texts on foreign language comprehension. *Language Learning*, 44(2), 189–219.

Young, D. (1999). Linguistic simplification of second language reading material: Effective instructional practice? *Modern Language Journal*, 83(3), 350–366.

Zahar, R., Cobb, T., & Spada, N. (2001). Acquiring vocabulary through reading: Effects of frequency and contextual richness. *Canadian Modern Language Review*, 57 (4), 541–572.

Zipf, G. (1949). *Human Behavior and the Principle of Least Effort: An Introduction to Human Ecology*. New York: Hafner.

Zipf, G. (1935). *The Psycho-Biology of Language*. Cambridge, MA.: M.I.T. Press.

Index

4/3/2 reading 128

Akio Furukawa 36–8, 42 50, 101
amount of reading 14, 16, 37, 46, 60,
 63–5, 79, 90, 92, 102–3, 109, 140,
 150, 154, 174, 178
AntWordProfiler 89, 161
audio 45, 55–6, 121, 177
authentic 25, 27–8
autonomy 51, 100

background knowledge 19, 21,
 33, 100, 125, 131, 168
bibliography 16, 136, 138, 175
bilingual glossaries 74
blown-up books 39
BNC/COCA lists 30, 78, 89
book flood 38–9, 71, 82–5. 110–1, 113,
 119, 139, 181
book reports 7–8, 14, 47–8, 59, 141
book reviews 14
Bridge series 2, 29–30

Cambridge English Readers 11, 20–1,
 24, 31–2, 79
CEFR 43, 158, 162
ceiling effect 111–2
change 103
chunks 135, 145
cloze tests 110–2, 118, 144
contamination 138, 140, 142–3, 149,
 152, 154
controlled vocabulary 14–5, 19, 21, 24,
 26–9, 35, 76, 92, 130, 181
criticisms of graded readers 18, 24–7

definition of extensive reading 3–5, 16,
 117, 139–40, 151, 173

deliberate learning 7, 33, 73, 75,
 81, 90, 114–5, 117, 121–2
density of unknown words 6, 19, 34,
 80, 119–20
depth of processing 122
dictionary use 4, 9, 26, 74, 100
dual coding 73

ecological validity 82, 95, 108
E-future 55
elaboration 73
elaboration of text 180
electronic library 56
EPER 40, 139
ER-Central.org 13, 16, 34, 52,
 60, 67, 75, 134, 176
ESL composition profile 112–3
expeditious reading 125, 127, 131
expository text 35
extensive reading foundation 10, 16, 22,
 25, 45, 50
Extensive Reading Foundation graded
 reading scale 21, 40
Extensive Reading Foundation
 guide to extensive reading 10,
 16, 48, 57, 59, 71

face validity 138, 155
fixations 124–5
Flesch-Kincaid 107
fluency development 123–135
Footprint Reading Library 11, 20–1,
 23, 46
Foundations Reading Library 11,
 23, 45
four strands 6–9, 68–9, 90, 92,
 109, 133
frequency counts 19

Index 199

General Service List 2, 19
glossary 11, 30, 72, 74–5, 159, 171
graph 77, 100, 123, 132, 134
Gray Standardized Oral Reading Test
   111,139
guessing from context 7, 9, 26, 28, 66,
   72–4, 86, 115, 120–2
guidelines 157, 159, 161, 163–4

Heinle Reading 11
hyperlink 75

illustrations 17, 19, 21, 33, 165,
   169–71
independent reading 3–6, 19, 35, 44, 56
Indonesia 51–3, 175
informal reading inventory 111, 139
information density 19
intentional learning 8, 74, 115, 141–2
issue logs 131

Kyoto Sangyo University 41–4
Kyoto scale 43

language learner literature awards 12,
   16, 25–6, 55
language proficiency 10–1, 16, 29, 50,
   80, 109–10, 112–3, 114, 181–2
language-focused learning 6–8, 14–5,
   62, 68–70, 109
lexiles 19, 43, 157
list 69
logo 24
Lord Jim 17–8, 25
low-proficiency learners 6, 12, 14, 20, 37

Macmillan Readers 11, 21, 55
Mandarin 11, 138
meaning-focused input 6–9, 29, 54,
   68–70, 74, 105, 109, 130
meaning-focused output 6–8, 62,
   68–70, 74
meta-analysis 112
mid-frequency readers 28–32, 55, 79, 90
mid-frequency words 78–9, 90, 151, 161
Moodlereader 42, 60
Mreader.org 15–6, 42–4, 46–8, 52, 55,
   59, 71, 93, 95, 102, 133
multiple measures 94, 115–6

narrative 13, 35, 110, 151
narrow reading 32–5, 131, 133
National Geographic 11, 21, 24, 55, 160
New Method Readers 17

New Method Supplementary Readers
   2, 17, 174
New Vocabulary Levels Test 12, 58, 67,
   92, 118
non-fiction 13, 30, 67, 115, 152, 158,
   165, 168
note-taking 7
noticing 73–4, 145, 160
Notre Dame Seishin University 44–47

one minute reading 108, 133
online graded text editor 16, 33–4
online tracking 134
oral reading 110–1, 127–8, 134, 139
Oxford Bookworms 11, 13–4, 17–8,
   20–1, 23–4, 45, 63

paired reading 128
Park Language Academy 40–1
Pearson Readers 11, 20–1, 24
principles 1, 172
publishing lists 11, 27

read-and-look-up 129
reading-while-listening 87, 116,
   118, 121
regressions 124–5, 130
repeated reading 127–8
re-reading 7, 58, 86, 126
research agenda 172, 177–180
rich and varied map 126

saccades 124, 1340, 145
sample size 147
Sanata Dharma University 51–3
SEG 36–8, 42, 50, 91, 101
sequencing unsimplified texts 34
shared reading 39, 85
silent reading 4, 39, 45, 57, 84–5, 102,
   127–32
skimming 15, 125, 127, 131–4
Sonia Millett 2, 56, 62, 130
spaced retrieval 73
speed reading 2–3, 7–8, 14–6, 56, 62–3,
   90, 92–3, 105–8, 110, 124–135
spelling 7, 69–70, 72, 88, 94, 116, 118,
   136, 145
standard words 92–3, 104, 106, 108,
   125, 133
storyline 163, 165–6

technical words 13
threshold 145–9, 153
TOEFL 38, 43–5, 109, 139, 141

200 *Index*

TOEIC 40, 43, 50–1, 109–10, 112, 115, 142, 151–2, 162
transfer of training 134

unmotivated learners 58
unnatural language 26–8
unsimplified text 5–6, 18, 24, 27, 29–32, 34, 78, 89, 91, 94, 116, 119

Updated Vocabulary Levels Test 12, 58, 67, 92, 118
varied retrieval 73
verbatim retrieval 73
vocabulary control 17, 19–20, 26–31, 79–80, 90–3, 105–7

vocabulary levels test 118, 144
vocabulary load 31, 34
Vocabulary Size Test 12, 32, 144
Voice of America 34

well-beaten path 126
world congress 175
World History Readers 24
writing 112–3

Xreading.com 12, 23, 43, 55–6, 59, 62, 99, 102, 176

Zipf's law 76–8, 80–1

Printed in the United States
by Baker & Taylor Publisher Services